THE IVORY KING

THE IVORY KING

A POPULAR HISTORY OF

THE ELEPHANT AND ITS ALLIES

CHARLES FREDERICK HOLDER

ILLUSTRATED

GYAN

Published by

Gyan Publishing House
5, Ansari Road
Daryaganj, New Delhi-110002
Phone: 011-47034999, 9811692060
E-mail: books@gyanbooks.com

Distribution Network
gyanbooks.com
India, USA, Canada, UK, Australia, France

ISBN : 978-81-212-9196-5 (PB)
First Published, 1902

2nd Impression 2023

Printed at: Gyan Press, Delhi.

THE IVORY KING
Author: CHARLES FREDERICK HOLDER

A TIGER'S ATTACK.

By permission Illustrated London News. *Frontispiece.*

MARVELS OF ANIMAL LIFE SERIES.

THE IVORY KING

A POPULAR HISTORY OF

THE ELEPHANT AND ITS ALLIES

BY

CHARLES FREDERICK HOLDER

FELLOW OF THE NEW YORK ACADEMY OF SCIENCES, ETC.; AUTHOR OF "ELEMENTS OF ZOÖLOGY," "MARVELS OF ANIMAL LIFE," ETC.

ILLUSTRATED

NEW YORK
CHARLES SCRIBNER'S SONS
1902

TO

MY MOTHER

This Volume

IS AFFECTIONATELY INSCRIBED.

PREFACE.

THE elephant is the true king of beasts, the largest and most powerful of existing land animals, and to young and old a never ceasing source of wonder and interest. In former geological ages, it roamed the continental areas of every zone; was found in nearly every section of North America, from the shores of the Arctic Ocean to the Gulf of Mexico, and from New England to California. Where the hum of great cities is now heard, in bygone days the trumpeting of the mastodon and elephant, and the cries of other strange animals, broke the stillness of the vast primeval forest. But they have all passed away, their extirpation undoubtedly hastened by the early man, the aboriginal hunter; and the mighty race of elephants, which now remains so isolated, is to-day represented by only two species, the African and the Asiatic, forms which are also doomed.

To produce the eight hundred tons of ivory used annually, nearly seventy-five thousand elephants are destroyed; and it does not require the gift of prophecy to foresee their extinction in the near future. The Asiatic elephant is said to be holding its own; but the rapid advance of the British in the East, the introduction of railroads and improvements which mark the progress of civilization in India, where heretofore the elephant has been employed, cannot fail to have a fatal effect, and their extermination is only a matter of time. Knowing these facts, and the close relationship which the elephant has ever held in the advancement of mankind in the East, it stands a picture of absorbing interest, the last of a powerful race, worthy of earnest efforts for its preservation. The question of its extinction rests with the rising generation. In America and England the ornithologists have made an appeal for our feathered friends, and ladies have been asked to put their veto upon the excessive use of feathers, which is surely tending to the extermination of our birds. The elephant can be protected in the same way. Every ivory tusk that is brought to the African coast from the interior is said to cost a human life; and that we may have ivory fans, billiard-balls, chessmen, knife-handles, inlaid furniture, grotesque Japanese statuary, etc., the elephant, who has been man's helpmate from 1200 B.C., and perhaps earlier, to the present day, is threatened with extermination. The prominence of the elephant in early times is, I think, not generally appreciated. There was hardly a great public movement entailing war, in the early days of the East, in which these animals did not constitute an all-important element. Defeat and success were, as a rule, determined by the number of elephants; and the fate of nations may be said to have depended upon the prowess of the proboscidians.

In the present volume, I have endeavored to present as much of the history of the elephant as is compatible with popular interest, treating the animal in all its relations to man, and the economic questions involved: in war, pageantry, sports and games, as a faithful laborer and servant, comrade and friend, its ancestral forms, structure and anatomy. As the work is in no sense a scientific one, the student may regret the absence of details relating to anatomy, etc. To compensate for such omission, I have appended a carefully selected bibliography of all the most important works, papers, and monographs, ancient and recent, relating to the subject.

I am indebted to Mr. George P. Sanderson, officer in charge of the elephant-catching establishment at Mysore, Bengal, whose valuable work embracing his experience with the Asiatic elephant has been frequently consulted; also to the works of Sir Emerson Tennent, and especially to the author of "Menageries," published by Messrs. Charles Knight & Co., London.

C. F. H.

NEW YORK, June 1, 1886.

CONTENTS.

LIST OF ILLUSTRATIONS.

MEXICAN HIEROGLYPHIC, WITH ELEPHANT FEATURES.

Chapter V.

THE IVORY KING.

THE IVORY KING.

CHAPTER I.

NATURAL HISTORY OF THE ELEPHANT.

THE elephant is the largest living land animal; and, though numerous forms existed in early geological times, it is represented to-day by two species only, — the African elephant, *Elephas Africanus*, and the Asiatic elephant, *Elephas Indicus*. The geographical range of the former originally included nearly all Africa, but now the animals are more closely confined to the central interior regions. The Asiatic elephant is found in the forests of India, Ceylon, Burmah, Siam, Cochin China, Sumatra, and the Malay peninsula; and, while the introduction of railroads into these countries in ensuing years will perhaps result in its extinction, at present its numbers are not growing less. The African elephant differs from its Asiatic cousin in several particulars. The apparent distinguishing features are the tusks, that attain a much greater development, and occur in both sexes, while in the Asiatic species the males alone possess them. The African elephant is at least a foot higher than the Asiatic, attaining a maximum height of eleven feet.

Its ears are extremely large, covering the shoulder, and in some instances measuring three and a half feet in length by two and a half feet in width, while those of its Indian relative are comparatively small.

When Jumbo — who was an African elephant — and one of the Asiatic elephants stood side by side, the difference was very marked. The summit of the head of the Indian species forms a pyramid, while the front, or forehead, is concave. In Jumbo the front of the head was somewhat convex, the eye larger; and when we compare the feet, we find that while the African elephant has, as a rule, four nails on each foot, the Asiatic has four on each hind-foot, and five on each fore-foot. The number of nails often varies with individuals. The Indian natives esteem those animals most which possess five on each fore-foot, and four on each hind-foot, or eighteen, odd numbers being considered unlucky. The author of "Oriental Field Sports" says that he has observed elephants with fifteen nails, which no native would purchase; and he heard of one with twenty, and saw one with eighteen. These differences are external, as all elephants possess five toes upon each foot internally. The two species also differ as to their teeth. The incisor teeth of elephants are greatly developed, forming the tusks, and only occur in the upper jaw of living forms. They often attain enormous size, weighing from one hundred and fifty to three hundred pounds. The tusks of the Asiatic elephants born in this country were visible at birth. Concerning them in general, Sanderson states that they are not renewed, but are permanent; his information being based upon the personal observations of many years. Corse, who made observations in the last century, and published them in the "Philosophical Transactions," 1799, states that the elephants observed by him had milk, or deciduous tusks as well as permament ones; that the milk-tusks appeared at about six months of age, and fell out between the first and second years. He found in the young skull the place of the capsule of the permanent tusks, which appear a couple of months after the loss of the milk-tusks. Huxley says, "In recent elephants, only the two incisors are preceded by milk-teeth;" and this may be the generally accepted belief. The tusks have no roots, like the teeth of some animals, but fit firmly into what are called premaxillary sockets: and if we should examine this buried, or hidden, portion, we should find that it was partly hollow, so to speak; the ivory at the root being very thin, and surrounding a pulp where the ivory is being secreted. The length of this soft pulp varies according to the age of the animal: thus, in young elephants, only a small portion of the tusk outside of the gum is solid ivory; all the rest being hollow, or containing the pulp. As the animal grows, this cavity decreases in length, until in extremely old elephants it disappears entirely, and the tusk is solid ivory.

In the left tusk of the elephant shot by Sir Victor Brooke (p. 115), the pulp-cavity was wholly obliterated, its place occupied by an exceedingly dense nodular dentine. This tusk was diseased. In the right tusk of the same animal the pulp-hollow extended from the base through half the imbedded portion, or thirteen and a half inches. In a pair of tusks owned by Col. Douglas Hamilton, of the British army, the pulp-cavity occupies ten inches and a half of the imbedded length. From this it is evident that the length of a tusk cannot be accurately determined from mere observation, as in a large elephant the sockets are from one foot six inches to one foot nine inches in length; so that an animal might have a tusk three feet and a half long, and show only one foot and a half of it, the gum alone concealing about four inches.

As the ivory is so soft at the base of the tusk, it is evident that it can be easily broken; and, if a bullet or spear strikes this spot, it becomes embedded, and eventually incorporated, in the tusk. Workers in ivory are often surprised to find a leaden bullet in the solid ivory. In a collection in London, there is a section of a tusk which was cut at a piano-forte manufactory in 1805, which has a wrought-iron musket-ball firmly embedded in it; and other instances can be seen in the museum of the London University.

In their growth, tusks often assume strange shapes, being liable to twist, just as the horns of a cow. Livingstone saw an elephant with three tusks, the third one growing out between the other two. The tusks frequently grow straight; some twist in a spiral, others form a complete circle; and many elephants have only one from birth, — like the fictitious unicorn. These animals are called *Gunésh* by the natives. The name is that of the Hindoo god of wisdom; and, if the single tusk of the *Gunésh* is the right one, the animal is reverenced. Some dimensions of tusks will be given in the chapter on Ivory. Perhaps the largest was one sold in Amsterdam some years ago. It weighed, according to Kolokner, three hundred and fifty pounds. Eden measured several nine feet in length, and one described by Hartenfels exceeded fourteen feet. There is one in the museum of Natural History, Paris, seven feet in length. The uses to which the large incisors are put, are often exaggerated. The African elephant employs its tusks to uproot small mimosa-trees, but

PLATE I.

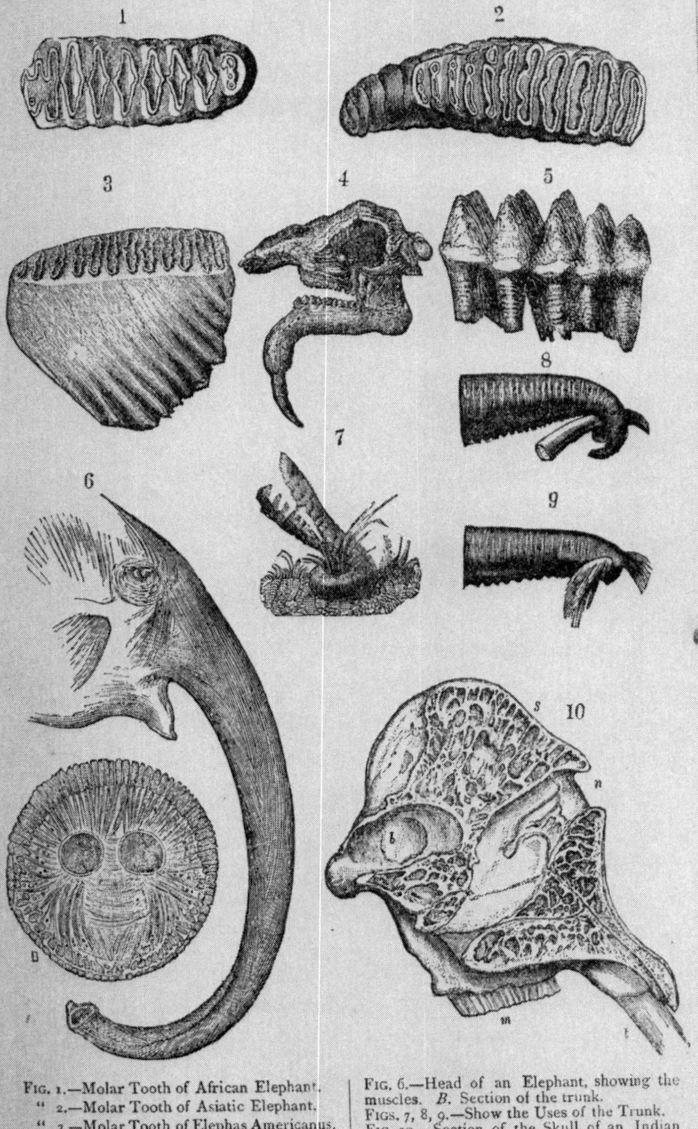

FIG. 1.—Molar Tooth of African Elephant.
" 2.—Molar Tooth of Asiatic Elephant.
" 3.—Molar Tooth of Elephas Americanus.
" 4.—Skull of Dinotherium.
" 5.—Molar Tooth of Mastodon giganteus.

FIG. 6.—Head of an Elephant, showing the muscles. *B.* Section of the trunk.
FIGS. 7, 8, 9.—Show the Uses of the Trunk.
FIG. 10.—Section of the Skull of an Indian Elephant. *s.* air sinuses. *n.* nostrils. *b.* brain. *m.* molar tooth. *t.* tusk.

they are never used to overthrow as large objects as is often stated. Sir Samuel Baker measured mimosa-trees four feet six inches in circumference, and thirty feet high, which elephants had pulled down; and the damage they cause in a mimosa-forest is almost incredible. These trees, however, have no tap-root, and are comparatively easy to overthrow. Cumming says, "I have repeatedly ridden through forests where the trees thus broken down lay so thick across one another that it was almost impossible to ride through the district." The female elephant uses her tusks to scrape the barks from trees; but the large tusks of the males are designed as a defence,—the elephant with the finest tusks ruling the herd,—and terrific wounds are made by them. The elephant Conqueror, in this country, was killed by being gored in this way; and in India, when it is necessary at the government corral to subdue a mad elephant, a reliable tusker is provided with steel tusks, or glavies, which fit over the stumps of the others, and with these they do terrible work.

If we examine the skull of the elephant, we find only two molar teeth on each side of each jaw,—eight in all; and no more, as a rule, are seen at one time, twenty-four in all appearing during the lifetime of an elephant.

The teeth appear in a curious way, moving gradually forward from behind in regular succession; each old front tooth as it is worn away being pushed out of place by its successor. This wonderful provision is necessary, as the front teeth are worn away by the sand and gritty substances taken in with the food. The molar, or grinding, teeth are extremely heavy and large, and are nearly buried in the socket, the upper portion only showing. They are made up of a number of transverse perpendicular plates composed of a mass of dentine incased in an outside layer of enamel, which is in turn covered by a layer of cement that fills the spaces between the plates, and seems to bind the whole together. Each of the enamel plates, though appearing separate at the surface, is connected with the others at the base. The difference between the teeth of the Indian and African species is shown in Plate 1. In the Indian elephant the ridges of enamel are narrower, more undulating, and appear in greater numbers than in the African species, in which the ridges are less parallel, and enclose lozenge-shaped spaces. There are certain other differences in the species, such as the number of bones in the vertebral column, or "backbone;" those of the African elephant numbering from twenty to twenty-one, and those of the Indian elephant nineteen to twenty. In examining the skull of an elephant, we are struck with its enormous size, and the comparatively small space taken up by the brain. The skull is not so heavy as it appears, the interior being divided off into partitions, or air-cells; so that, while there is a large surface for the attachment of the trunk-muscles, the head is massive, but not heavy. The neck of the elephant is so short, that, without some special provision, it could not feed from the ground; and this is seen in the trunk, or proboscis, that is a prolongation of the upper lip and nose, sometimes seven feet in length. It commences at the nasal opening of the face, contains a pair of tubes closed by a valvular arrangement, and at its end on the upper side is a small prolongation like a finger, opposite which is a prominence, or tubercle, that acts as a thumb. The trunk is made up of a vast number of muscles, estimated by Cuvier at about forty thousand. Upon the outside, the trunk appears to be ringed; and it is a most remarkable organ, combining the offices of a hand and nose, and exercising taste, touch, suction, expulsion, and prehension. With it the elephant lifts its driver, pulls over small trees, reaches for its food, takes in water which is in turn expelled into the mouth, squirts water or sand over its body; in fact, there is hardly any thing, from drawing a cork from a bottle, to hurling a tiger into the air, that this wonderful trunk cannot do for its owner. Without it the elephant would starve. One in India which had lost its trunk, had to be fed by having food placed in its mouth. Though the trunk is so useful, it is a very tender and delicate organ, and is not used in the rough manner generally supposed. In making an attack, it is raised high in air out of the way. When a great weight is lifted, it is not the trunk, but the tusks, which are employed, the former only holding the object upon the latter.

Once, when visiting the herd of elephants owned by Mr. Barnum, the trainer called my attention to a small hole, or opening of a gland, situated on each side of the head between the eye and the ear, that is scarcely perceptible. It is the opening of a duct, perhaps two inches in length, that extends toward the lachrymal organs, and leads to a secretory gland. From this orifice, there exudes at times a thick, gummy substance, which sometimes clogs up the opening, and undoubtedly affects the animal unpleasantly; as, when this is filled, the trainer told me that the elephant would take a small stick or straw in its trunk, and endeavor to remove the obstruction. This will be alluded to in the chapter on Rogue Elephants. This exudation is generally considered a warning in the East, that the elephant is going to be ugly, and is called *must*. In Asiatic wild elephants it occurs usually in cold weather, from November to February. This peculiarity has been noticed from the earliest times: it was remarked upon by Strabo, and is referred to in Hindoo mythology. "The Hindoo poets frequently allude to the fragrant juice which oozes, at certain seasons, from small ducts in the temples of the male elephant, and is useful in relieving him from the redundant moisture with which he is then oppressed; and they even describe the bees as allured by the scent, and mistaking it for that of the sweetest flowers. When Crishna visited Sanc'ha-dwip, and had destroyed the demon who infested that delightful country, he passed along the bank of a river, and was charmed with a delicious odor which its waters diffused in their course. He was eager to view the source of so fragrant a stream, but was informed by the natives that it flowed from the temples of an elephant, immensely large, milk-white, and beautifully formed; that he governed a numerous race of elephants, and the odoriferous fluid which exuded from his temples had formed the river."

It is evident that wild elephants probe this opening, which is a little larger than a pin-head, and that the sticks used often break off in the orifice, and by working in give the animals such agony that they go mad for the time. When Mr. Cowper Rose shot an elephant in Africa, the men immediately began to hunt for the "piece of wood in the head, to which they attached great value as a charm." Mr. Rose was evidently not familiar with the gland, or opening. He says, "I sat on one (a dead elephant) while they searched for the wood in his head. It lies about an inch beneath the skin, embedded in fat, just above the eye, and has the appearance of a thorn, or a small piece of twig broken off. Some are without it: and, on examining the spot minutely, we found that there was a small opening in the skin, — a large pore, it may be; and I conceive that this phenomenon is simply accounted for by the twig breaking in this hole when the animal is in the act of rubbing his head against the bushes."

The body of the elephant, weighing sometimes three tons, is supported by four ponderous, pillar-like legs, the movements of which, especially the posterior, or hinder pair attract immediate attention; and the first impression is, that the hind-legs of the elephant are entirely different from those of any other mammal. They seem to bend in the wrong direction. The difference consists merely in the greater length of the thigh-bone, or femur, which brings the knee much farther down than in other animals. The horse is equally remarkable for an opposite reason; as it walks and stands upon the toe-nail of its single toe, while its heel is as high up as the knee of the elephant is low. Covering this wonderful frame, or skeleton, is the loose, wrinkled skin an inch thick, so tough and heavy, — often weighing eight hundred pounds, — that the elephant and others were at one time included in a group called the thick-skinned animals (pachyderms). The skin is comparatively hairless; though some elephants have more than others, and young ones more than adults. The theory generally accepted, is that the elephants of southern countries have lost their hair by long-continued residence in regions where it was not necessary. Quite recently two young or dwarfed Asiatic elephants were exhibited in New York as mammoths, on account of their superabundance of hair; but it is needless to say that they were ordinary Asiatic elephants.

In the present work, it is not necessary to refer particularly to the internal organization of the elephant, but the subject is replete with interest. The enormous heart, a foot in diameter, in its contraction exerts tons of pressure; and the blood forced out by it must attain almost the force of water from the hose of a fire-engine. Hunters have often been astonished at seeing elephants, which they have been chasing for some time, insert their trunks into their mouths, and there obtain a supply of water that is blown over the dry and heated body. The explanation of this is, that the stomach of the elephant resembles that of the camel, in having a chamber that can be cut off or separated from the digestive cavity, in which about ten gallons of water is stored as a reserve supply, or to be used as occasion requires.

The female elephant is generally smaller than the male. The mammary glands are situated between the fore-legs, and the calf nurses with its mouth, instead of the trunk as was once supposed. The period of gestation is about five hundred and ninety-seven days. The weight of the elephant at birth differs in individuals. One observed by Owen weighed one hundred and seventy-five pounds, and stood two feet ten inches in height. The little elephant Bridgeport weighed two hundred and forty-five pounds at birth, and stood three feet in height. The baby elephant America, born in Philadelphia, weighed two hundred and thirteen and a half pounds, and measured thirty-four inches and a half at the shoulder. It grew so rapidly, that in eleven months it gained about seven hundred pounds, — not so very surprising, as it came of a very heavy family. Its mother weighed seven thousand and twenty pounds, and was only twenty-three years old; and the father, who was three years older, four tons. The baby's trunk, or proboscis, was at first twelve inches long, and nine inches in circumference at the root, or base.

The young Asiatic elephant grows about eleven inches in the first year, eight in the second, six inches in the third, five in the fourth, five in the fifth, in the sixth three and a half, and in the seventh, two and a half, the measurements having been made by Mr. Corse.

CHAPTER II.

HABITS AND WAYS OF ELEPHANTS.

THE most favorable locality to observe wild elephants in India is in Mysore, where the western ghats, the Billigarungun hills, and the Goondulpet and Kákankoté forests, afford fine opportunities to the naturalist and sportsman to observe the largest of living land animals in the haunts of its choice. It is here that the elephant-catcher of the British Government, Mr. George P. Sanderson, makes his headquarters, and has obtained such signal success for many years.

Wild Asiatic elephants usually travel in herds of from thirty to fifty, though sometimes the number is swelled to one hundred and over; but small herds are the rule, this division allowing them to obtain a much larger supply of food. The necessity of this can be better appreciated when it is known that a band of one hundred elephants require, or will consume, eighty thousand pounds of fodder in a day.

The favorite food of the wild Asiatic elephant in Ceylon is palms, especially the cabbage, the young trunks of palmyra and jaggery (*Caryota urens*). They are also very fond of figs, the sacred Bo-tree (*F. religiosa*) found near the temples, as well as the Negaha (*Messua fer rea*). The leaves of the jak-tree are considered a great luxury by the huge creatures;

while the bread-fruit, wood-apple, sugar-cane, palm, pineapple, watermelon, and the feathery part of the bamboo, are all to its taste. Among the grasses, the mauritius and Guinea grass are eaten; and all the grains. Cocoanuts they break by rolling them under foot.

The African elephant affects the succulent mimosa, and larger shoots and branches than its cousin, its teeth being fitted for a coarser diet. They are, according to Drummond, particularly fond of the fruit of the unganu-tree, which seems to intoxicate them; as they stagger about, performing the most remarkable antics for a clumsy beast; often trumpeting so loudly that they can be heard for miles, and sometimes engaging in terrific encounters.

When separated into small herds, the elephants all move in concert, as if there was a mutual understanding as to the general route to be taken. Elephants are extremely sure-footed, and will climb quite steep hills. A paper in the Journal of the Asiatic Society of Bengal describes the methods adopted by the elephant in going down-hill. The writer says, "An elephant descending a bank of too acute an angle to admit of his walking down it direct (which were he to attempt, his huge body, soon disarranging the centre of gravity, would certainly topple over), proceeds thus: his first manœuvre is to kneel down close to the edge of the declivity, placing his chest to the ground. One fore-leg is then cautiously passed a short way down the slope; and, if there is no natural protection to afford a firm footing, he speedily forms one by stamping into the soil if moist, or picking out a footing if dry. This point gained, the other fore-leg is brought down in the same way, and performs the same work, a little in advance of the first, which is thus at liberty to move lower still. Then the first one of the hind-legs is carefully drawn over the side, and then the second; and the hind-feet in turn occupy the resting-places previously used a ft by the first ones. The course, however, in such precipitous ground is not straight from top to bottom, but slopes along the face of the bank, descending till the animal gains the level below. This an elephant has done at an angle of forty-five degrees, carrying a howdah, its occupant, his attendant, and sporting apparatus, and in much less time than it takes to describe the operation. I have observed that an elephant in descending a declivity uses his knees on the side next the bank, and his feet on the lower side only." Elephants are often described as galloping, leaping, and gambolling about like a horse. Such movements are impossible; the only gait being a walk, that can be increased to a very rapid shuffle of fifteen miles an hour for a short distance. It appears to move the legs on the same side together, but this is not exactly so. Elephants cannot leap, and never have all four feet from the ground at the same time. Sanderson says, "I have seen an elephant go over quite high hurdles, but never take all four feet from the ground at once. Even the smallest spring is beyond its power; a small trench seven feet across being quite impossible by the largest elephant, although its stride may be six feet and a half long."

The sense of smell is so delicate that a tame elephant will recognize the presence of a wild one three miles away, and by its actions inform the mahout. Selous, the African hunter, watched a herd of elephants cross his trail from a place of security below them; and the moment the trunk of the leader crossed the spot where his foot had been, it stopped, waved its proboscis a few moments, then turned and ran, accompanied by the entire band. The herds of elephants, when divided, are family parties, generally all related, and on the march the mothers with young always take the lead; the old tuskers following along in the rear, taking the front, however, in case of alarm. This method of procedure might appear strange at first; but the mothers probably know how long a tramp the calves can endure, and so the responsibility is left to them.

All of my young readers who have visited the circus, must have heard the trumpeting of elephants. This is one of their methods of communication: in other words, elephants have a language that is expressed in different ways, — sometimes by the throat, and, again, by the trunk. When an elephant is pleased, it expresses it by a squeaking noise, — a most ear-grating sound made in the trunk. It also purrs gently, often so low that the keeper alone hears it. When fully enraged, and rushing upon an enemy, its war-cry is a shrill trumpeting that no one can mistake. Rage is also expressed by a low, hoarse rumbling in the throat. Fear or pain is manifested by a shrill squeak, and sometimes by a loud, reverberating roar. The expression of misapprehension or suspicion is entirely different from that of fear, being shown by rapping the trunk upon the ground sharply, at the same time emitting a volume of air from the trunk, that is said to sound like a sheet of tin being rapidly doubled. Desire or want is expressed by the throat, especially in young elephants; and any one who watched the famous baby elephant Bridgeport, must have heard the curious sounds it uttered.

In the open country the elephant seems to have regular trails, or drives, that are followed season after season with some regularity. During the dry time, that in India is from

January to April, they follow the beds of streams, and seek the deep forests, there finding protection from the intense heat; but when the rain commences, in June, they roam into the open country, grazing upon the new and fresh grass produced by the warm showers. With the latter also come innumerable flies, that also drive them out into the low jungles; one, a huge insect as large as a bee, with a long proboscis, being especially irritating. At this time they frequent the salt-licks, and have been seen to eat earth impregnated with soda. This is the elephant's medicine, certain kinds of earth being eaten for the same reason that dogs eat grass.

When the dry season comes, and the grass is withered and bitter, the herds leave the lowlands, remaining in the hills until the next season. Almost the entire time is spent in grazing; though they are often seen after a rain warming their great bodies in the sun, or standing upon the open rocks that form a characteristic of the hills of the Mysore country. When the fodder is exhausted in a locality, the march is taken up, and invariably in Indian file; so that it is often difficult to tell whether ten or one hundred elephants are ahead. Upon reaching a good locality, they disperse, and remain in the vicinity for two days or so. Their rest is taken, as a rule, in the middle of the night; particular friends lying down together, or often a family party. They are early risers, and by three o'clock in the morning are either feeding, or on the march. At ten o'clock they will perhaps collect for a rest, then from four in the afternoon until eleven at night they feed or march. There are, of course, exceptions to this. In very cool or wet weather they march all day, and often for various reasons do not lie down for several days at a time. Elephants sleep like horses, either standing or lying down.

The latter is the natural way, though the process of assuming a reclining position is a somewhat difficult one. When first captured, they often do not lie down for weeks. It is stated that an elephant owned by Louis XIV. did not lie down for the last five years of its life. It wore two holes in the stone buttress with its tusks, and seemed to support itself to some extent in this way while it slept. Wild African elephants have been observed leaning against a tree in the forests. The enormous ears of the African elephant are used as fans; and when a herd is seen upon a hot day, these huge members are continually moving, either to create a current of air, or to blow away the insect pests with which they are infested. They have also been seen to take a branch in their trunks to brush away flies, using it as a person would a fan. The hearing of the elephant is very acute, much more so than in man; experiment having shown that a female heard her young when the sound was inaudible to a party of Englishmen between her and the calf.

Sir Everard Home experimented with an elephant by musical sounds, and came to the conclusion that it did not possess a musical ear, though it was attracted by certain notes. He says, "I got Mr. Broadwood, as a matter of curiosity, to send one of his tuners with a piano-forte to the menageries of wild beasts in Exeter Change, that I might know the effect of acute and grave sounds upon the ear of a full-grown elephant. The acute sounds seemed hardly to attract his notice; but as soon as the grave notes were struck, he became all attention, brought forward the large external ear, tried to discover where the sounds came from, remained in the attitude of listening, and after some time made noises by no means of dissatisfaction."

The elephant is extremely fond of water; and soon after sunrise the Asiatic species can be seen sporting in the streams, floundering about, and spouting water over their huge bodies, piping and trumpeting with conflicting emotions. They are very susceptible to cold, and when obliged to enter water at night, or when it is chilly, are careful to lift their tails and trunks above the surface if possible.

So clumsy an animal would hardly be expected to excel in swimming, yet probably few land animals can compete with them in this respect. In 1875 Mr. Sanderson sent a herd of seventy-nine from Dacca to Barrackpur near Calcutta, and during the march they had to cross the Ganges and several large tributaries. In one place the entire herd swam without touching bottom for six consecutive hours: then after resting a while on a sand-bank, they swam three more, or nine in all, with but one rest. Few land animals could accomplish this without losing some of their number. But Mr. Sanderson states that he has heard of swims even more remarkable than this. Notwithstanding their fine swimming powers, elephants are sometimes drowned by very simple means; and Mr. Sanderson records such an instance: "We had left the Myanee above its junction with the Kurnafoolie, and were marching by land; but, owing to the lie of the country, we had to cross the Kurnafoolie occasionally. It was very deep, and the elephants had to swim. One morning, whilst crossing where it was about eighty yards wide and thirty feet deep in a gorge through a saddle in the hills, a tusker which was secured between two tame ones, one in advance of, and one behind, him, sank like a stone, probably from being seized with cramp from the coldness of the water, and dragged the two females with him. Their mahouts tried in vain to slash the ropes through: they had barely time to save themselves by swimming. Any thing more sudden or unexpected I never witnessed. One elephant appeared again for a brief moment, at least about two feet of her trunk did: she waved us a last farewell, when all was still save the air-bubbles which continued to rise for some time from the calm, deep pool. Every one who witnessed it was shocked. The drivers of the elephants yet to cross hesitated. We could not believe the unfortunate beasts would not come up again. The mahouts sat down, and cried like children over the loss of the faithful beasts they had tended for years. Elephants are such good swimmers, that I cannot understand how it was that the two tame ones were unable to gain the shore, which was only twenty yards distant, by towing the wild one. When they floated, we found that they were in no way entangled; and it was not owing to snags catching the ropes, nor to any undercurrent, that they were drawn down. One of the tame ones, Geraldine, was a great favorite of mine; and she and the other were worth twelve hundred dollars each. The tusker was worth twenty-four hundred, so the money lost to the government was considerable."

No subject relating to elephants is so difficult to determine by a mere casual examination, as that relating to its size. Statements from natives can never be relied upon; as in times of excitement a large bull will appear twenty feet high, and the observers are not at all unwilling to make affidavit to that effect. Asiatic elephants rarely, if ever, attain a height of ten feet at the shoulder. The largest in the Madras commissariat stud to-day measures nine feet ten inches. The next largest is owned by his Highness the Mahárájah of Mysore, and measures nine feet two inches, and is forty years old.

Females are usually smaller. Two in the collection at Dacca measure eight feet five inches, and eight feet three inches respectively; and, to show that this is exceptional, Mr. Sanderson measured one hundred and forty in 1874, and found that the largest females measured just eight feet. Mistakes and exaggerations occur from the fact that elephants are often measured by throwing a tape over the shoulders, and, when both ends touch the ground, accepting one-half as the correct height: nine inches may be gained in this way in measuring an eight-foot animal. Mr. Corse, a former superintendent of the East India Company's elephants at Tiperah, a province of Bengal, who probably saw a greater number of elephants than any European, states that he never heard of more than one Asiatic elephant that exceeded ten feet. This was a large tusker, the property of the Vizier of Oude. Accurate measurements were made, which were as follows:—

	FT.	IN.
From foot to foot over the shoulder	22	10½
From the top of the shoulder, perpendicular height .	10	6
From the top of the head, when set up . . .	12	2
From the top of the face to the insertion of the tail .	15	11

Mr. Corse says, "During the war with Tippoo Sultan, of the fifteen hundred elephants under the management of Capt. Sandys, not one was ten feet high, and only a few males nine and a half feet high. He was very particular in ascertaining the height of elephants used at Madras and in the army under Marquis Cornwallis, from the fact that the most remarkable stories were current at the time concerning large elephants. Madras elephants were reported from fifteen to twenty feet high. The Nabob of Dacca was said to have one, fourteen feet in height; and Mr. Corse took a journey to the locality

ELEPHANTS MOVING TIMBER.

Page 34.

purposely to measure it. He found, that instead of twelve feet, as he thought barely possible, the elephant was only ten. If any of my readers wish to test the accuracy of any statement as to an elephant's height, they have only to measure the distance around its foot twice, which will give nearly the exact height at the shoulder. This is as deceptive as guessing the height of a silk hat or the length of a horse's head. A party of young people were once watching some elephants, when the question was propounded how many times around the foot would equal the height. The answers were all over ten, and one was fifteen. As the circumference of the fore-foot of the average elephant is about fifty-four inches, this would have given them an animal over sixty feet high. It has been supposed by some authors, that elephants are not as tall now as formerly, that they have degenerated in size as the world grew older; but this is not borne out by facts. The Emperor Baber (a contemporary of Henry VII.) says, "They say in some islands about Hindostan, elephants grow to the height of ten gez [about twenty feet]. I have never seen one above four or five gez" [eight or ten feet].

The elephants from Hindostan are the smallest; those from Pegu and Ava being larger, as a rule. A skeleton from the latter country was presented to the Czar Peter by the King of Persia; and the taxidermist managed to give it a height, when mounted in the museum at St. Petersburg, of sixteen and a half feet.

Among the natives of the elephant country, there are many curious superstitions concerning the age, death, and final resting-place of the great animal. The age to which they may possibly attain is a matter of conjecture. One hundred and fifty years is considered the limit by persons who are familiar with the subject. Expert native hunters state that they live one hundred and twenty years, or average about eighty. Mr. Sanderson expresses the belief that they attain one hundred and fifty years, and bases his conclusions from his observations of the famous elephant Bheemruttee, owned by his Highness the Mahárájah of Mysore. It was captured in Coorg in 1805, and was then a baby elephant three years old. In 1876 she was in her prime, and did not show any of the evidences of age evinced by elephants that were known to be advanced in years; and, when it is remembered that in captivity the animals are often ill-fed and abused, it is evident that they may attain a great age. Natives can determine the age of an Asiatic elephant within a few years. They easily ascertain that of a young or very old animal, but those of middle age present more difficulties. The head of an old elephant is lean and rugged, the bones of the skull being prominent, the eyes and temples sunken; while the fore-legs, instead of bulging out at the knees, present the same general size throughout. An old elephant also has a different gait from a young one: instead of putting the foot firmly upon the ground, the heel touches it first. The surest test to the native, however, is the ear, which is almost as conclusive a telltale as are the teeth of a horse. In elephants not older than seven years, the top of the ear is not turned over at the rim; but, as they grow older, it begins to lap and curve, increasing with age; and in very old animals, the lower portion is always torn and jagged. Elephants attain their full growth at about twenty-five years of age, and are in full vigor at thirty-five.

The Strologas, a tribe of the Billiga-rungun hills, assert and believe that the elephant never dies; while the Kurrabas of Kákankoté, and many others, are firm in the belief that they have some secret place to which they retire to die. When this idea is scouted as romance by a European, the native invariably asks, "Did you ever see a dead elephant? Did you ever hear of any one who did?" and the questioner and doubter is obliged generally to answer in the negative. Not only have few sportsmen found an elephant that had evidently died a natural death, but few natives have ever seen one.

In all his rambles, covering nearly twenty years in the heart of the elephant country, Mr. Sanderson never found an elephant that had died a natural death, nor did he ever meet with a professional native elephant-hunter who had, except during an epidemic among the animals in the Chittagong forest. This seems extremely remarkable when it is remembered that, while the flesh might be devoured, the bones and tusks would last a long time. The same belief is entertained by the wild tribes of Ceylon. Sir Emerson Tennent says, "The natives generally assert that the body of a dead elephant is seldom or never discovered in the woods; and certain it is, that frequenters of the forest with whom I had conversed, whether European or Singhalese, alike are consistent in their assurances that they have never found the remains of a dead elephant that had died a natural death. One chief, the Wanyyah of the Trincomalie district, told a friend of mine, that, once after a severe murrain which had swept the province, he found the carcasses of elephants that had died of the disease. On the other hand, a European gentleman, who for thirty-six years without intermission had been living in the jungle, ascending to the summits of mountains in the prosecution of the trigonometrical survey, and penetrating valleys in tracing roads, and opening means of communication, — one, too, who has made the habits of the wild elephant a subject of constant study and observation, — has often expressed to me his astonishment that, after seeing many thousands of living elephants in all possible situations, he had never yet found a single skeleton of a dead one, except those which had fallen by a rifle." The Singhalese have a superstition in relation to the close of life in the elephant. They believe that, on feeling the approach of dissolution, he repairs to a solitary valley, and there resigns himself to death. A native who accompanied Mr. Cripps, when hunting in the forests of Anarájapoora, intimated to him that he was then in the immediate vicinity of the spot "to which the elephants come to die," but that it was so mysteriously concealed, that, although every one believed in its existence, no one had ever succeeded in penetrating it. At the corral of Kornegalle in 1847, one of the Kandyan chiefs assured him that it was the universal belief of his countrymen, that the elephants, when about to die, resorted to a valley in an unknown spot among the mountains to the east of Adams Peak, which was reached by a narrow pass with walls of rock on each side, and that here, by the side of a lake of clear water, they took their last repose. While this belief is held by some natives of Continental India, there is not a spot in the elephant country that has not been penetrated by either Europeans or natives; yet the latter are not convinced, and the mystery as to what becomes of the dead elephants is as deep as ever. The elephants that die in captivity are victims to the same troubles that affect all animals, and the wild elephant is probably no exception. At the commissariat at Bengal, one hundred and fourteen elephants died in 1874–75.

Eleven died of apoplexy, three of dysentery, five of inflammation of the lungs, thirteen of debility, one of cold, twenty-six of zahirbad, one of vomiting, three of colic, and one of congestion of the brain,—abundant proof to the superstitious native that the elephant is susceptible to dissolution. Ceylon elephants are remarkable for the numbers born without tusks. These are called mucknas, and differ in no other respect from the elephants of Continental India. They resemble ordinary females; the tusks being extremely small, and useless as defence. Sometimes they are larger than ordinary tuskers; but this may be mere accident, as is their dental defect, and it is not an hereditary trait. So rare is a good tusker in Ceylon, that one is looked upon as a curiosity. Sir Samuel Baker states that not over one in three hundred possessed them; and to show the difference between these and the continental elephant, out of one hundred and forty, fifty-one of which were males, captured by Mr. Sanderson in Mysore, Bengal, in 1874–76, only five were mucknas, or tuskless. We should expect to find theories at least to explain this strange difference in an adjoining country, where the climate and food conditions are almost identical (the food in Ceylon is easier to obtain); but I am not aware that any of importance have been expressed.

As large and powerful as the elephant is, it is easily dismayed and alarmed; and many have an especial aversion to small animals. Thus, some elephants have a great dislike for small dogs; and a mouse has been known to cause a large tusker to snort with fear. Wild hogs are particularly disagreeable to the great animals, and it appears that this was known to the ancients; as Procopius, the historian of the Persian and Gothic wars, states that at the siege of Edessa by Chosroes, the king of Persia, in the time of Justinian, the besieged Greeks imitated the cry of the pig to frighten the elephants of the enemy. In fact, elephants are like other animals. They have their likes and dislikes; and their alarm at a mouse, in justice to some of the human race, should not be used, as it often is, as an argument in proof of their supposed cowardice and lack of intelligence.

CHAPTER III.

THE INTELLIGENCE OF THE ELEPHANT.

IN determining the intelligence of an animal, we naturally take ourselves as the type of mental excellence, and grade the lower animals as they approach us. Some would place the ant next to man, arguing that it more closely resembles him in its habits, customs, and methods of showing what we consider the result of intelligent action. It keeps domestic animals (*aphis*), goes to war in organized bodies, makes slaves of other insects, erects wonderful structures, is accredited with planting seeds, and certainly stores them up after arranging them so that they cannot sprout; in fact, appears to act in many ways like a rational human being: and, contrasted to it, the elephant, dog, horse, and beaver would seem to be comparatively stupid animals; at least, such would be the verdict of the observer who mistakes instinct for reason. Such a comparison seems unfair to the other animals mentioned; and to argue that the elephant is not as intelligent as the ant because it does not build a house, and lay up a food-supply, would hardly be just, as the great proboscidian does not require such shelter: and, without instancing any more examples, it would appear, that, to establish the relative intelligence of an animal, it should be judged, not especially by the standard of another, but according to its displayal of what we term thought; and this leads us to consider how thought may be exhibited in an animal. Instinctive action is something that is done without appreciable thought: thus, a colt instinctively kicks at an enemy, as a kitten spits at a dog. The fear of this animal has been present in all the generations of cats, and is inherited, as shown by the protest in the curve of the back, the raising of the tail, and other familiar methods of expression. So we may, without multiplying instances, consider that instinctive action is the outward expression of inherited experience, and has practically nothing in common with that action of the mind which we call thought. If this kitten when it grows older,—and I know of an instance,—should without instruction climb upon a door, and lift the latch, she would be exhibiting a practical illustration of the results of thought: in other words, she would lift the latch because she knew that the door could not be opened without it, and consequently had, in her feline mind, turned over to some extent the relations that existed between the latch, the door, and the object she had in view. So if the colt should go to a pump, as a cow is alleged to have done, and take the handle in its mouth without being taught, and pump water to drink, it would show that the animal had used its powers of thought. Now, what position does the elephant take in the scale of intelligence?

The Hindoos of the present day do not consider the elephant a remarkably intelligent animal. Yet at one time its sagacity was certainly appreciated, as the Hindoo god of wisdom is figured with the body of a man and the head of an elephant; and A. W. Schlegel states that in very early times they marvelled at every thing about the animal, especially its sagacity, which made it seem to them the embodiment of the god Ganessa.

Probably Dr. Dalton expresses the latest knowledge touching this subject. He says, —

"If we examine the comparative development of the hemispheres of the brain in different species of animals, and in different races of men, we shall find that the size of these ganglia corresponds very closely with the degree of intelligence possessed by the individual. . . . Among quadrupeds, the elephant has much the largest, and most perfectly formed, cerebrum, in proportion to the size of the entire body; and, of all quadrupeds, he is proverbially the most intelligent and the most teachable. It is important to observe, in this connection, that the kind of intelligence which characterizes the elephant and some other of the lower animals, and which most nearly resembles that of man, is a *teachable* intelligence, — a very different thing from the intelligence which depends upon instinct, such as that of insects, for example, or birds of passage."

In a previous chapter I mentioned that Mr. H. H. Cross informed me that he had seen an elephant of the Barnum herd select a stick, and probe the small orifice in the temple. Since then I have seen a statement by Mr. Cross in print, to the effect that he has seen the elephant select a twig, examine it carefully with one of its keen little eyes, by holding it up in its trunk, and, if it found it was not sharp enough for the purpose, deliberately grind down the point by rubbing it upon a stone, and, when its shape suited him, use it to open the orifice.

In Africa, according to Drummond, the wild elephants

migrate south in time for certain fruits, which shows that they must remember the pleasures of the past season. The migration is not suggested by a lack of food, as the supply of mimosa and other trees does not give out. When a wild elephant takes a branch in its trunk, and uses it to brush away flies, it shows more intelligence than it is generally given credit for; while its lodging dust and sand on its back to prevent the attack of these pests, is also to be considered an intelligent act. Elephants are extremely cautious, and this has been used as an argument against their intelligence. Sanderson says that the animal is stupid because the simplest fence is often sufficient to protect grain from them; but I am inclined to think that this is owing to their extreme caution: the fence may have in their mind some association with the pitfall, or traps of some kind, which have been met in their experience. An elephant will rarely step upon a bridge that is not safe, and many instances could be cited showing that their protests and objections were founded upon an intelligent appreciation of danger. Sanderson says also that the elephant lacks originality: but the two instances I have mentioned, — namely, using a branch to brush off flies, and sharpening the stick, — will, I think, in the opinion of my young readers, free the great animal from this imputation; and I do not recall many actions performed by *wild* animals, that show more appreciation of the practical application of cause and effect. The intelligence of the elephant has been a subject of varied appreciation. Many observers have considered remarkable actions of elephants involuntary, when in truth they were merely obeying the commands of their riders or mahouts, who expressed their wishes by the pressure of their legs, or by the voice, which was not seen or

THE SIBERIAN MAMMOTH.

[*By courtesy of Ward & Howell, Rochester, N. Y.*]

Page 39.

heard by the observer. When Tavernier was travelling with the Mahommedan army of the Mogul, he was astonished to see the elephants seize the little images which stood before the pagodas, and dash them to the ground. The Hindoos readily believed that the elephant did this from a religious aversion to the idols, but the traveller knew that the mahouts were secretly directing the great animals. So, in passing in review before the king, the elephants did not salute until coming to his majesty.

Once when two elephants were at a spring, the largest violently seized a bucket carried by the smaller, and began to dip up water; upon which the other elephant drew back, and butted its companion so that it fell headlong into the pool. This story is told to illustrate the revengeful nature of the animal, when, in point of fact, the entire action was instigated by the mahout upon its back. The most remarkable trait of the elephant is its obedience: and if we were to take its aptitude to learn the tasks described in the chapter on trained elephants, as a test of intelligence, it would certainly hold its own among all animals; as, considering that it is perhaps the most ungainly, and certainly the heaviest, of all land animals, its various feats are indeed remarkable.

At the slightest pressure of its rider's foot it will salute, lift the trunk in the air, and trumpet loudly; stop, back, lie down to enable the mahout to dismount, roll over, lift the man upon its trunk, pass over his body with the greatest ease, lift stones from the ground for the driver to throw at other elephants, and even tie itself up at night; in fact, among all trained animals, dogs, horses, or birds, none compare with the elephant in their obedience, and intelligent appreciation of what is required. "Though playing 'possum" or feigning death can hardly be cited as an evidence of intelligence, it may be interesting to know that it is sometimes attempted by elephants. Sir Emerson Tennent was informed by Mr. Cripps that he was aware of an instance where an elephant adopted this ruse to secure its freedom. It had been led into a corral between two tame elephants, and upon being released sank to the ground apparently lifeless. Every attempt to revive it, or force it to show any evidence of life, failed; and the natives believed that it had died of a broken-heart,—a term that they often apply when an elephant dies without apparent cause. Finally the body was abandoned as lifeless; and, as soon as the hunters had gone a short distance, the wily brute regained its feet, and rushed for the jungle, screaming at the top of its voice; its cries of evident delight being heard long after it had disappeared. In the various chapters of this work, other instances have been cited showing that, far from being a stupid animal, the elephant in its *wild* state exhibits far more intelligence than the wild dog or horse; and when we compare the animals after their so-called education, there is little that the trained dog can do that is not accomplished by the elephant; and while it is difficult to draw exact lines, and point out the exact mental status of the elephant in the rank and file of the lower animals, I would place it well to the front among mammals.

I am glad to be able to bring to the support of my belief in the superior intelligence of the elephant, the testimony of a naturalist and careful observer, Col. Nicholas Pike, late consul at Mauritius, whose extensive travels and long residence in the East render his opinions of especial value and interest. The following is Col. Pike's letter in answer to my request for an expression of his opinion upon the subject: —

Mr. C. F. Holder.

My dear Sir, — In answer to your questions as to my opinion relative to the intelligence of the elephant, I will jot down a few notes that may interest you.

This animal is to my mind one of the most intelligent of the brute creation. I am led to this conclusion from what I have actually seen, and from reliable information given me by persons who have devoted a lifetime to studying their habits and life-history generally. I think that in elephants, as in other animals, — and we see even in man himself, — there is a great difference in the amount of intelligence they possess.

A friend of mine, who owned many of these animals, placed an old tame male that appeared sick, in a pasture, where he had also some horses and sheep feeding, thinking it would recuperate "Dick," who was a great favorite. The whole pasture was well fenced in, and the gate was securely bolted. One morning when I was visiting my friend, we were surprised to see "Dick" let himself in by the back-gate; and he warned us of his presence by trumpeting. His master went to him, and asked what he wanted. The beast at once took up a pitcher containing water which was near by, and poured some of it on the ground, attempting to sip a few drops of it with his trunk. His master, seeing what he wanted, gave him water, and told him to go back. Thinking the gate must have been left open, and perhaps the sheep and horses straying out, we followed, but to our surprise found the gate shut, and not only bolted, but the bolt turned up in the little slot so that it should not be easily opened. We waited, curious to see what Dick would do. As soon as he reached the gate, he deliberately moved the bolt, and passed into the field, then turning round, he re-adjusted the bolt as well as I could have done it, and marched off contentedly to a favorite corner under some trees.

I have seen my friend quietly call individuals by their name out of the herd; and in one instance, a female, "Maggie," was called, and told to take me on her back, which she did, helping me up carefully with her trunk. I have seen an elephant draw a cork from a bottle of claret, and drink the contents without spilling a drop. I saw four or five called singly by name from their grazing-ground, form in line, and bow, and kneel before a group of ladies, and then march back in as regular order at the word of command as a file of soldiers.

Hundreds of elephants are employed in the government service in the three presidencies of India, — Calcutta, Bombay and Madras. They go through a regular routine, and know their hours for work and recreation as well as the man who watches the clock. When the bell sounds in the morning, they take up their line of march, to the lumber-yards for instance, where vast piles of beams and planks are stored. As soon as they arrive, each takes up his work, left from the day before. Great logs and beams are rolled along by the aid of the trunk, and, when near the pile, are lifted, two elephants to each beam, and hoisted into place, when they walk round and adjust their work with as much precision as a man would use with a plumb-line. When the usual hour for quitting work arrives, nothing can induce the creatures to go on; and you can't fool them on the time either, by ringing the bell late. Off they go to get their afternoon bath, where they will lie and wallow in the muddy water for hours. Their varied works require *cute* intelligence, not mere instinct, any more than you can attribute the good paving of a roadway by a poor laborer, who knows his business, though he may not be able to read or write, to instinct.

A circumstance was related to me by my friend, Gen. E. W. de Lansing Lowe, who was all through the campaign in India during the Sepoy rebellion. He said he had a very intelligent elephant that he constantly rode on, and as it was so hot they mostly travelled morning and evening. During the war, they came about the dusk of evening to a small bridge that spanned a deep ravine with water at the bottom. As soon as the elephant came to this bridge, no inducement could make him cross it. After some delay, finding all persuasion useless, the general determined to examine the structure. They found the enemy had cut away the supports of the bridge; and, had the elephant stepped on to it, the whole party would have been precipitated into the gulf below.

We have a notable instance of the sagacity of these animals at the time Barnum's circus was in Bridgeport a few years ago. A fire broke out in some sheds adjoining the tents, and it was feared the stables would catch the flames. They began to pull down the sheds, when some one suggested to bring out two elephants. This was done, and the animals set to with a will to pull down the place. They evidently at once took in the situation. They not only tore down the place, but threw the timbers so that they should not touch the tents, and beat out the flames. Now, if this does not show almost human reason, what does? They were put to the work on the spur of the moment, and not only performed it as if used to it, but actually did it more intelligently than many men would have done in such perilous circumstances. Had they not done so, as water was short, the loss of life to man and beast, and of property, might have been enormous.

If you could only interview Barnum, he could tell you more of the intelligence of the elephant than any man living.

I could relate numerous other incidents I have seen and been informed of; but enough has been said, I think, to prove how highly I think of the intelligence, sagacity, or whatever other name you may give it, of this unwieldly pachyderm.[1]

NICHOLAS PIKE.

[1] See Plate II. for a view of elephant moving timber.

CHAPTER IV.

THE MAMMOTH.

IN one of the old Chinese histories, there is a description of a curious creature called *tyn-schu*, supposed to be a subterranean, rat-like animal. It lived, according to the old chroniclers, entirely beneath the ground; was as large as an ox; and had enormous tusks, with which it threw up the soil, or made its burrows; and the rumbling of earthquakes was attributed to them. This was naturally considered a fable by Europeans, but finally an English traveller was shown a piece of the tusk. He found it to be ivory, and suspected that the strange animal was a mammoth, as indeed was the case. The bodies of these elephantine giants were found in the far North, buried in the tundra; and the simple Chinamen believed that they lived there, and on their return from trading-trips told the story in the South; and thus it became a part of their curious and, it is needless to say, erroneous history.

The mammoth may rightly be considered the king of all elephants, and in general appearance it much resembled the African species. The full adult may have been a third more bulky than the largest existing elephants, and undoubtedly weighed at least twice as much. To protect them from the cold, they were covered with hair, which gave them a fero-

MAMMOTH HUNT.

Page 36.

cious appearance. The hair was of three kinds: first there was a thick coat of reddish wool; over this grew a coat of long, thick hair; while upon the neck was a heavy mane. The tusks of the mammoth were enormous: some measured thirteen feet in length; and, curved in a circle, gave the animal a strange and formidable appearance.

While the mammoth greatly resembled the African elephant, there are some points of difference. The skull is narrower at the summit, and the molar teeth have great breadth of crown as compared to the length: the ridges also are narrow and crowded, while the enamel is thin and straight, the crimping that is seen in others being absent. The molars number, as in other elephants, eight, at one time present; or, one and a portion of another one each side of both jaws.

This huge elephant flourished principally in the far North; and, as its remains are now found in the greatest abundance on the shores of the Arctic Sea, it must have existed in vast herds. The majority of specimens discovered are buried in the soil, that is now frozen the year round in a solid mass for many feet. The finest specimen known is a skeleton in the museum at St. Petersburg; the original having been discovered in 1799 by a poor fisherman named Schumachoff, a Tongoose, who every spring followed down the Lena River that led into the Arctic Sea. One day while engaged in following his vocation, he observed on the side of a tundra a shapeless mass, appearing like some huge monster entombed. The following year he returned to the same locality, and found that the object had weathered out still more, and was a mammoth — a veritable frozen giant. Still, he could not claim the fine tusks; and another year passed, and then his family were so superstitious that they refused to consent to his again visiting the strange animal that he had described. But finally, five years after his first trip, he determined to again visit the scene of his discovery. He sailed down the river in his small boat, and, with mingled emotions of fear and curiosity, approached the imprisoned monster. Raising his eyes on reaching the spot, he saw a great cavity in the cliff, but the mammoth was gone. The ice had melted away, but beneath where the giant had rested lay the enormous body. The tusks were still intact; and Schumachoff carried them South in triumph, where he realized fifty rubles from the sale, leaving the body — which, wonderful to relate, was as fresh as if the animal had died only a week before — to the bears and wolves.

We could hardly expect a poor fisherman to know that it was a valuable scientific discovery, and it was only by accident that the story of the strange animal reached the scientific world. Seven years later a Mr. Adams visited the spot, where he found the mammoth still in the flesh, with the exception of the fore-leg; and, even after this lapse of time, its preservation was remarkable. The pupil of the eye was still intact; and the brain rested in the cranium, the tissues being so perfect that they could hardly be distinguished from those of a living animal. During the interim between its fall upon the beach and Mr. Adams's visit, it had attracted numbers of wild animals, — bears, foxes, etc., — that devoured much of the meat, that had been preserved for perhaps thousands of years. The neck of the animal was still covered with a long mane; and next to the skin was a thick brown wool, that was evidently very valuable as a protection against the severe cold. Much of the hair and wool of the huge creature was ground into the soil, but thirty pounds of this reddish wool was recovered. Mr. Adams purchased the tusks, which were nine feet in length; and finally the entire skeleton was removed to St. Petersburg, where it may still be seen.

From the description and measurements of the skeleton, Professor Ward has made a restoration of this ancient giant, which gives a striking idea of the grandeur of its appearance. (See Plate III.)

Dr. Pallas was the first to describe the mammoth with scientific accuracy; and Blumenbach gave it its present name, *Elephas primigenius.* In the northern countries it ranged the forests at one time in vast numbers, being especially common in England and Wales, where its remains are generally found in caves and river-deposits. In Yorkshire and Wales it was evidently followed by hyenas, that dragged its bones into the caves. W. Boyd Dawkins says, that, in the spring of 1866, he accompanied Mr. Antonio Brady to the Uphall pit, England, and describes his finds as follows:—

"At the top, there was the surface-soil from one to three feet deep; then an irregularly stratified layer of brick-earth and gravel six feet; and lastly, an irregular layer of flint gravel, underneath which was a fine reddish gray sandy loam, four feet thick. All these had been cleared away, leaving a platform exposed, on which was a most remarkable accumulation of bones carefully left *in situ* by the workmen. On the right hand was a huge tusk of mammoth, eight feet long, with the spiral curvature undisturbed by the pressure of the superadjacent strata. Across it lay a remarkably fine antler of red deer. At a little distance was the frontal portion of the skull of a urus, with its horn-cores perfect to the very tips; while around, bones of various animals were scattered,—of the *Rhinoceros hemitœchus*, mammoth, urus, horse, either brown or grisly bear, and wolf. As we gazed down on this tableau, we could not doubt for a moment that the bottom of an ancient river with all its contents lay before our eyes,—a river in which all these animals had been drowned, and by which they had been swept into the exact position which they then occupied. This inference was confirmed by the examination of the thin layer of sandy gravel on which they rested, for it was full of the shells of *Corbicula fluminalis*, with the valves together just as in life. There were also specimens of the common anodon of our rivers, and of the *Helix nemoralis* of our hedge-rows. On a continuation of the same platform, now cut away, the skull of a mammoth was discovered in 1864, perfect, with the exception of the tusks, which had been broken away, with their incisive alveoli. That of the right side lay twenty feet away from the skull, while the left has not yet been discovered. Owing to the surprising skill of Mr. Davies, the skull and tusk were taken up and re-united, and now constitute by far the finest specimen of mammoth in the British Museum. In some cases, the mammoth remains have not been deposited by a river. At Lexden, near Colchester, as the Rev. O. Fisher well observes, they were overwhelmed in a bog, the small bones of the feet being found in their natural position, a fact which shows that they sank feet foremost through the peat into the subjacent clay."

That the sea has greatly encroached upon the land of England, and that the old grazing-grounds of the mammoth are now under water, is evident from the fact that the teeth of elephants are often dredged up by fishermen; and ivory-hunters in some localities have literally fished for these teeth with drag-nets. A tusk dredged at Scarborough was as fresh as when the animal was alive, and was cut up and used for the various purposes to which ivory is put.

In its day, the mammoth also wandered through the forests of France, and to the south as far as Rome. Portions of its skeleton have been found in the volcanic gravel of Ponte Molle and Monte Sacro, a fact showing that it flourished here when the site of Rome was a bed of lava that flowed from the volcanoes of Central Italy.

Germany was a famous grazing-ground for the mammoth. At Seilberg near Constadt on the Necker, a heap of thirteen tusks and teeth were found "heaped close upon each other," as if they had been packed artificially. A like find was made in the village of Thiede, four miles south of Brunswick: in a heap of soil ten feet square, there were found eleven tusks, one eleven and another fourteen and three-quarters feet long; thirty molar teeth, and numbers of large bones; "mixed with these were the bones and teeth of rhinoceros, horse, ox, and stag; they all lay mixed confusedly together; none of them were rolled or much broken; and the teeth, for the most part, separate and without the jaws: there were also some horns of stag."

The borders of the Arctic were, however, the favorite pasturage for these giants; and the store of ivory there may be said to be practically inexhaustible, though the trade in the tusks has been going on with the Jakuti and Tungusians from time immemorial.

The Siberian islands are a favorite locality for collectors, where the tusks have been found protruding from the sand in vast numbers. After Adams, the most valuable find was made by Dr. Middendorf, a famous Siberian explorer, in

1843. It was discovered in latitude 66° 30′, between the Obi and Yenesei, near the Arctic circle. Shortly after, the body of a young one was found in a bed of sand and gravel fifteen feet or so above the sea, near the river Taimyr; and in the former the eye was so perfectly preserved, that the bulb, now in the St. Petersburg museum, looks as though it had been taken from a recent animal.

One of the most interesting mammoth discoveries in late years was made by a young Russian engineer named Benkendorf, who was employed in 1846 by the government to survey the coast off the mouth of the Lena and Indigirka rivers. The discovery is of such great interest and value, that I give it in his own words, the account being an abstract from a letter written to a friend in Germany: —

"In 1846 there was unusually warm weather in the north of Siberia. Already in May unusual rains poured over the moors and bogs, storms shook the earth, and the streams carried not only ice to the sea, but also large tracts of land thawed by the masses of warm water fed by the southern rains. . . . We steamed on the first favorable day up the Indigirka, but there were no thoughts of land: we saw around us only a sea of dirty brown water, and knew the river only by the rushing and roaring of the stream. The river rolled against us trees, moss, and large masses of peat, so that it was only with great trouble and danger that we could proceed. At the end of the second day, we were only about forty wersts up the stream. Some one had to stand with the sounding-rod in hand continually, and the boat received so many shocks that it shuddered to the keel. A wooden vessel would have been smashed. Around us we saw nothing but the flooded land. For eight days we met with the like hinderances, until at last we reached the place where our Jakuti were to have met us. Farther up was a place called Ujandina, whence the people were to have come to us; but they were not there, prevented evidently by the floods. As we had been here in former years, we knew the place. But how it had changed! The Indigirka, here about three wersts wide, had torn up the land, and worn itself a fresh channel; and, when the waters sank, we saw, to our astonishment, that the old river-bed had become merely that of an insignificant stream. This allowed me to cut through the soft earth; and we went reconnoitring up the new stream, which had worn its way westward. Afterwards we landed on the new shore, and surveyed the undermining and destructive operation of the wild waters, that carried away, with extraordinary rapidity, masses of soft peat and loam. It was then that we made a wonderful discovery. The land on which we were treading was moorland, covered thickly with young plants. Many lovely flowers rejoiced the eye in the warm beams of the sun, that shone for twenty-two out of the twenty-four hours. The stream rolled over, and tore up the soft, wet ground like chaff: so that it was dangerous to go near the brink. While we were all quiet, we suddenly heard under our feet a sudden gurgling and stirring, which betrayed the working of the disturbed water. Suddenly our jäger, ever on the lookout, called loudly, and pointed to a singular and unshapely object, which rose and sank through the disturbed waters. I had already remarked it, but not given it any attention, considering it only drift-wood. Now we all hastened to the spot on the shore, had the boat drawn near, and waited until the mysterious thing should again show itself. Our patience was tried: but at last, a black, horrible, giant-like mass was thrust out of the water; and we beheld a colossal elephant's head, armed with mighty tusks, with its long trunk moving in the water in an unearthly manner, as though seeking for something lost therein. Breathless with astonishment, I beheld the monster hardly twelve feet from me, with his half-open eyes yet showing the whites. It was still in good preservation.

"'A mammoth! a mammoth!' broke out the Tschernomori; and I shouted, 'Here, quickly! chains and ropes!' I will go over our preparations for securing the giant animal, whose body the water was trying to tear from us. As the animal again sank, we waited for an opportunity to throw the ropes over his neck. This was only accomplished after many efforts. For the rest we had no cause for anxiety; for, after examining the ground, I satisfied myself that the hind-legs of the mammoth still stuck in the earth, and that the waters would work for us to unloosen them. We therefore fastened a rope round his neck, threw a chain round his tusks, that were eight feet long, drove a stake into the ground about twenty feet from the shore, and made chain and rope fast to it. The day went by quicker than I thought for; but still, the time seemed long before the animal was secured, as it was only after the lapse of twenty-four hours that the water had loosened it. But the position of the animal was interesting to me: it was standing in the earth, and not lying on its side or back as a dead animal naturally would, indicating, by this, the manner of its destruction. The soft peat or marsh land, on which he stepped thousands of years ago, gave way under the weight of the giant; and he sank as he stood on it, feet foremost, incapable of saving himself; and a severe frost came, and turned him into ice and the moor which had buried him. The latter, however, grew and flourished, every summer renewing itself. Possibly the neighboring stream had heaped over the dead body plants and sand. God only knows what causes had worked for its preservation. Now, however, the stream had brought it once more to the light of day; and I, an ephemera of life compared with this primeval giant, was sent here by Heaven just at the right time to welcome him. You can imagine how I jumped for joy.

"During our evening meal, our posts announced strangers: a troop of Jakuti came on their fast, shaggy horses; they were our appointed people, and were very joyful at sight of us. Our company was augmented by them to about fifty persons. On showing them our wonderful capture, they hastened to the stream; and it was amusing to hear how they chattered and talked over the sight. The first day I left them in quiet possession; but when, on the following, the ropes and chains gave a great jerk, a sign that the mammoth was quite freed from the earth, I commanded them to use their utmost strength, and bring the beast to land. At length, after much hard work, in which the horses were extremely useful, the animal was brought to land; and we were able to roll the body about twelve feet from the shore. The decomposing effect of the warm air filled us all with astonishment.

"Picture to yourself an elephant with a body covered with thick fur, about thirteen feet in height, and fifteen in length, with tusks eight feet long, thick, and curving outward at their ends, a stout trunk of six feet in length, colossal limbs of one and a half feet in thickness, and a tail, naked up to the end, which was covered with thick, tufty hair. The animal was fat, and well grown. Death had overtaken him in the fulness of his powers. His parchment-like, large, naked ears lay fearfully turned up over the head. About the shoulders and the back he had stiff hair, about a foot in length, like a mane. The long, outer hair was deep brown, and coarsely rooted. The top of the head looked so wild, and so penetrated with pitch (*und mit Pech so durchgedrung-en*), that it resembled the rind of an old oak-tree. On the sides it was cleaner (*reiner*); and under the outer hair, there appeared everywhere a wool, very soft, warm, and thick, and of a fallow-brown color. The giant was well protected against the cold. The whole appearance of the animal was fearfully strange and wild. It had not the shape of our present elephants. As compared with our Indian elephants, its head was rough, the brain-case low and narrow, but the trunk and mouth were much larger. The teeth were very powerful. Our elephant is an awkward animal; but, compared with this mammoth, it is as an Arabian steed to a coarse, ugly dray-horse. I could not divest myself of a feeling of fear as I approached the head. The broken, widely open eyes gave the animal an appearance of life, as though it might move in a moment, and destroy us with a roar. . . . The bad smell of the body warned us that it was time to save of it what we could; and the swelling flood, too, bid us hasten. First of all, we cut off the tusks, and sent them to the cutter. Then the people tried to hew the head off; but, notwithstanding their good will, this was slow work. As the belly of the animal was cut open, the intestines rolled out; and then the smell was so dreadful, that I could not overcome my nauseousness, and was obliged to turn away. But I had the stomach separated, and brought on one side.

It was well filled, and the contents instructive and well preserved. The principal were young shoots of the fir and pine: a quantity of young fir-cones, also in a chewed state, were mixed with the mass. . . . As we were eviscerating the animal, I was as careless and forgetful as my Jakuti, who did not notice that the ground was sinking under their feet, until a fearful scream warned me of their misfortune, as I was still groping in the animal's stomach. Shocked, I sprang up, and beheld how the river was burying in its waves our five Jakuti and our laboriously saved beast. Fortunately the boat was near, so that our poor work-people were all saved; but the mammoth was swallowed up by the waves, and never more made its appearance."

This mammoth had undoubtedly strayed into a morass, and been ingulfed; and soon after, or before the body had an opportunity to decay, it had frozen up, to be released again ages after by an unusual thaw.

The most recent mammoth-hunt has been made by Dr. Bunge, who instituted a search along the Lena delta, finding, I believe, but one specimen, which was without its head and one fore-leg. It had been exposed for ten years to the attack of foxes, native dogs, and the natives themselves, and was well-nigh ruined.

The mammoth was not confined to the Old World. Vast quantities of bones have been found in Escholtz Bay in a peaty deposit that rests on a cliff of pure blue ice, and in various parts of America. As to the causes that led to its extinction, they are equally problematical. In Kentucky, Ohio, and Central North America, there would seem to have been every thing to favor its continuance, — an abundance of food, and vast areas to range upon. The one agency that might have produced its extermination is the one now at work upon its ally in Africa, namely, man. There is little doubt that the early Americans chased the great animal, and, hunted from one part of the country to another, they finally entirely disappeared.

ST. PETERSBURG MUSEUM.

ASIATIC ELEPHANT. SKELETON OF ASIATIC ELEPHANT. EXTINCT ELEPHANT, OR MAMMOTH.

Page 48.

CHAPTER V.

THREE AND FOUR TUSKED ELEPHANTS.

THOUGH to-day we look to Asia and Africa for elephants, and consider the huge proboscidians as extremely un-American, they originally roamed this country in vast herds, and were as common on our plains and prairies as are many animals of the present day. The mastodon, in the estimation of many naturalists, existed up to five hundred years ago; and, judging from the apparent freshness of the remains, there is no great objection to the belief. They were undoubtedly hunted by the ancestors of the mound-builders and early tribes; and, while other agencies may have aided in their extermination, the aboriginal hunter was an all-powerful factor, the result being no more remarkable than that going on at present in the extermination of the bison. What sights the early American boys and girls must have witnessed, assuming this to have been the case! The mighty mastodons, with their huge bodies and pillar-like legs, presented a far more impressive spectacle than the largest elephant of to-day; and when a captive giant was brought in, or found mired in a bog, what shouts and cries arose from these children, perhaps, of the mound-builders!

The tusks of the mastodon were marvels of beauty. Those of some species were straight, turning only at the tips: others had three tusks, two in the upper jaw, and one in the lower, the latter ordinarily of small size, though occasionally they attained large dimensions. Some individuals had four of these ivory weapons, giving them a strange and ferocious appearance.

The discovery that mastodons existed in America at one time, was made over a hundred years ago. In 1714 Dr. Cotton Mather of Boston forwarded a paper to the Royal Society of London, describing some mastodon bones, and endeavoring to prove that they were those of some giant mentioned in Holy Writ. The mastodon he referred to was discovered near Albany in 1705; and some of the grinders, or teeth, weighed four pounds. Thirty-five years later, a French officer, named Longueil, while travelling through what is now the State of Ohio, found near the Ohio River in a swamp a number of bones and tusks. Some of these were carried to Paris. In 1763 Mr. George Croghan, an Englishman, made a valuable find of mastodon remains near the celebrated Big Bone Lick of Kentucky. It was estimated that the finds represented the remains of thirty individuals. Some of the tusks which were found about six feet from the surface were seven feet in length.

The next important discovery was made on the Walkill River, about seventy miles from New York, by the Rev. Robert Annan. The bones were found in digging a ditch; and, from their position, it was evident that the huge animal had died standing, or had been mired, and so met its death. In 1805 Bishop Madison of Virginia communicated to "The Scientific World" the discovery of some mastodon bones that were found about five feet beneath the ground. This find was extremely interesting and valuable; as with the body, or in a position which represented the stomach of one of the skeletons, was found a mass of ground and bruised vegetation, which upon analysis showed that it was made up of grass, shrubs, and leaves, and of a species of rose still growing in Virginia. The Indians, who, it seems, made the discovery, stated that among these there was one that flesh still adhered to, and that it had a long nose.

Quite a number of Indian tribes have traditions concerning animals with a long nose, or trunk. The most familiar is that of the Delaware tribe, and the following is the statement that the natives claim to have been handed down by their ancestors: "That in ancient times a herd of these tremendous animals came to the Big Bone Licks, and began a universal destruction of the bear, deer, elks, buffaloes, and other animals, which had been created for the use of the Indians; that the Great Man above, looking down, and seeing this, was so enraged that he seized his lightning, descended on the earth, seated himself on a neighboring mountain on a rock, on which his seat and the print of his feet are still to be seen, and hurled his bolts among them till the whole were slaughtered, except the big bull, who, presenting his forehead to the shafts, shook them off as they fell; but, missing one at length, it wounded him in the side; whereon, springing round, he bounded over the Ohio, over the Wabash, the Illinois, and finally over the Great Lakes, where he is living at this day."

Mastodon tusks and remains have been unearthed in various parts of the State of California, showing that the huge elephants roamed over the entire continent just as the African elephant originally did on that continent. In California the remains of the mastodon have been found associated with human bones, stone implements, the remains of the elephant, tapir, bison, and modern horse. Mr. Stickney, the well-known Indian agent, states that "particular persons in every nation were selected as the repositories of their history and traditions; that these persons had others who were younger, selected for this purpose continually, and repeatedly instructed in those things which were handed down from generation to generation; and that there was a tradition among the Indians of the existence of the mastodon; that they were often seen; that they fed on the boughs of a species of lime-tree; and that they did not lie down, but leaned against a tree to sleep."

Some tribes are familiar with such remains, and call them "fathers of oxen," and state that they lived long years ago with a race of gigantic men, and that the Great Spirit killed them all with fire-bolts.

According to Dr. Barton, in 1761 there were found by Indians in this country five huge carcasses with long noses above their mouths; but this lacks satisfactory proof. In some of the ancient carvings in Mexico and Yucatan, especially those at Palenque, representations of an elephant's head are to be seen; and it is assumed that the artists must have been acquainted with the animals, or have had some tradition concerning them. Mr. Latrobe relates that "near the city of Tezcuco, one of the ancient roads or causeways was discovered; and on one side, only three feet below the surface, in what may have been the ditch of the road, there lay the entire skeleton of a mastodon. It bore every appearance of having been coeval with the period when the road was used." An old Mexican hieroglyphic represents a sacrificing priest with head covered with a casque, in which the head of an animal bearing a striking resemblance to the elephant may be seen. The trunk is too distinct and plain to be an accidental resemblance; and the artist did not have the tapir in view when he produced it, the head being decidedly elephantine.

Professor Holmes found the bones of the mastodon associated with pottery on the banks of the Ashley River, near Charleston, S.C.; and, in the majority of these cases, the mastodon's remains were discovered very near the surface. Professor Winchell states that he has himself "seen the bones of the mastodon and elephant embedded in peat, at depths so shallow that he could readily believe the animals to have occupied the country during its possession by the Indians." The so-called elephant-mound, referred to in these pages, is considered by some as evidence that the mastodon was a familiar form to the early American; so with the Indian pipes (Plate XVIII.). If they are intended to represent elephants, which one can hardly doubt, the maker must either have seen the mastodon, or have had it accurately described to him. Quite recently some tracks, presumably those of the mastodon or elephant, have been discovered on the surface of a sandstone quarry at Carson City, in Nevada. They represent a series of circular depressions from three to six inches in depth, each about twenty inches in diameter, which, according to the method of measuring the height of elephants in India, would give an elephant ten feet high. The impressions have been traced for forty feet, and show distinct footprints giving a stride of about five feet eight inches.

The largest find ever made in this country, with the exception perhaps of the vast collection at the Big Bone Lick,

Kentucky, was that at Warren, N.J., in 1845, where no less than six almost perfect skeletons were found six feet below the surface. A farmer discovered them while digging out mud from a small swamp; and, as most of the huge creatures were standing upright, it is evident that they became mired in the bog, and slowly sank into it. We can imagine the scene when these six monsters were entrapped, — their trumpeting, their roars of rage and fear, their mighty struggles to escape, that, with their combined weight, only served to mire them deeper and deeper, until they finally disappeared, to remain entombed for untold ages, and to be finally found, and placed in our museums and halls of science as monuments of a lost race.

Nearly all the mastodons are found in swamps, showing that possibly these morasses appeared to be veritable traps that hastened the extinction of these monarchs of the forest. This may be considered the popular theory of one method by which mastodons were destroyed: but there is no better authority than Professor James Hall, the present geologist in chief of the State of New York; and his opinions are entirely different. His views are, that the extinction of the mastodon was hastened by the glacial period, and that most of the remains discovered have been dropped in hollows or ponds, from the ice perhaps, and the peat formed over them. He advances in favor of this the fact that several tusks have been discovered which show evidences of glacial action. There is such a tusk in the collection of the Philadelphia Academy of Sciences, worn by supposed glacial action; and Rutgers College has the extremity of a tusk, showing what is considered by Professor Hall to be glacial striæ.

Referring to the Big Bone Lick, Professor Hall says,

"With our present knowledge, it would appear that this accumulation of bones, teeth, and tusks of mastodon, in Kentucky, may have been caused by the melting of a glacier in which they had become embedded, and, being gradually pushed forward to its southern limit, had been deposited in this place. There are other similar localities of less importance and extent, where mastodon remains have been obtained in considerable numbers; and it is not improbable that a critical examination of all known collections may furnish some further evidence of conditions similar to those indicated by the specimens in the Museums of the Philadelphia Academy of Sciences and of Rutgers College.

"However heterodox these views may appear, as opposed to the generally received opinions of the age and relations of the mastodon, I feel quite sure that some other hypothesis than the one usually entertained must be adopted in order to arrive at a satisfactory explanation of the mode and conditions of distribution and inhumation of the mastodon and fossil elephant remains of this country.

"In advocating this opinion regarding the extermination of the mastodon, I have reference to the remains as they have come under my own observation: and I do not mean to be understood as opposing *in toto*, the views so generally entertained, that the mastodon has existed during the present epoch; or that the opinion held by some of our scientists, that the animal may have existed both before and since the glacial period, is untenable. I refer only to the phenomena usually accompanying these remains, and the conditions attending those which have been exhumed within the State of New York and adjacent parts of New Jersey, and to some extent in other parts of the country. The locality of Big

Bone Lick in Kentucky, which has furnished the fragmentary parts of so many skeletons (and some other Western localities), I have not visited; but the evidence already given in relation to the bones from this place, indicates very clearly that they had suffered from glacial action; and the animals were, as we infer, of the glacial period."

On the great Osage River, the mastodons were sunk in the mud in a vertical position. Perhaps the most interesting find in New-York State was what is known as the Cohoes mastodon. In the fall of 1866 a number of workmen were employed in excavating the foundation for the Harmony Mills Company, in Cohoes; and after much labor, during which several thousand loads of muck or peaty soil, and old trunks of trees, had been removed, one of the men discovered the jaw-bone of some gigantic animal. The bone was found almost at the water-level, and at a depth of twenty-five feet below the surface; the entire locality being clay and earth, which formerly had been filled in to cover a swampy depression.

The report of the find was conveyed to Professor James Hall, who immediately undertook the superintendence of the search. He soon saw that the locality had at one time been the bed of the river, and that the remains were evidently in a vast pot-hole,—a circular pit often seen in the rock-borders of rivers at the present day. The discovery of the jaw pointed to the assumption that the entire skeleton could not be far off, and careful search was immediately commenced. Loads of refuse, old trunks of trees showing the imprint of beavers' teeth, broken slate, water-worn pebbles, were removed, and finally, in the bottom of the great pot-hole, upon a mass of material similar to that which had been taken out, covered with river-ooze and vegetable soil, the principal parts of the great mastodon were found. First, the bones of the hind-legs appeared, and a portion of the pelvis; and against the sloping wall reclined the massive head with tusks complete, unbroken and undisturbed; then followed many of the other portions of the skeleton, all lodged in a pot-hole of great depth. Sixty feet were explored without finding bottom; and the supposition was, that the animal had in some way been caught in a glacier, and gradually melted out as the great mass of ice slowly moved down over the face of the country, dropping it into this natural tomb. This complete skeleton (Plate V.) was presented to the cabinet of the State Museum at Albany, and is now on exhibition there, one of the finest specimens in existence. Its dimensions are as follows:—

	FT.	IN.
Length in a direct line	14	3
Length following the curve of the spinal column	20	6
Width of the thorax at the seventh rib	3	5½
Elevation of the crest of the scapula	8	4
Elevation of the crest of the pelvis	8	4
Elevation of the head	8	11
Elevation of the spine of the second dorsal vertebra	8	10
Elevation of the spine of the eighth dorsal vertebra	9	3

In some of the mastodons found, remains of food have been discovered between the ribs: thus it has been determined that the huge creature existed when the country appeared much as it does to-day. The *Mastodon giganteus* fed upon the spruce and fir trees. The mastodons wandered over almost every country known, and their remains are very common in South America. Humboldt found them as far north as Santa Fe de Bogota, and they have been discovered as far south as Buenos Ayres. Their range in South America has been given from five degrees north to about thirty-seven degrees south; and they were probably not restricted to this area.

Like the elephants of the present day, they wandered to great elevations, even up to the borders of perpetual snow; and a tooth described by Cuvier was obtained by Humboldt, in a volcano, at an elevation of seventy-two hundred feet above the level of the sea. A fine collection of these South-American mastodons is exhibited in the museum at Santiago. They were found by a party of men in an attempt to drain Lake Tagua in the province of Colchagua, about one hundred miles south of Santiago, sixty from the Pacific, and fourteen hundred feet above the sea. A ditch was cut, to drain off the water; and, after it had been drawn off, the remains of the great animal were seen lying upon the bottom.

With these mastodons, there existed in North America an elephant, *E. Columbi*, which probably associated in herds with the mastodon, but were not as large. The mastodons were extremely ponderous, and exceeded the largest elephant of to-day in size, and, though resembling them in general appearance, differed in several marked features. The tusks often grew in a peculiar manner: two large, nearly straight ones appeared in the upper jaw, while one or two protruded from the lower. As a rule, these lower incisors were small; but in some instances they attained considerable size. Imagine an elephant eleven or more feet in height, with three or four enormous sharp ivory tusks, its trunk raised aloft, rushing at an enemy! surely, such an animal was the true king of beasts, even in these early days. The tusks of the mastodons assumed many strange shapes, and a herd

PLATE V.

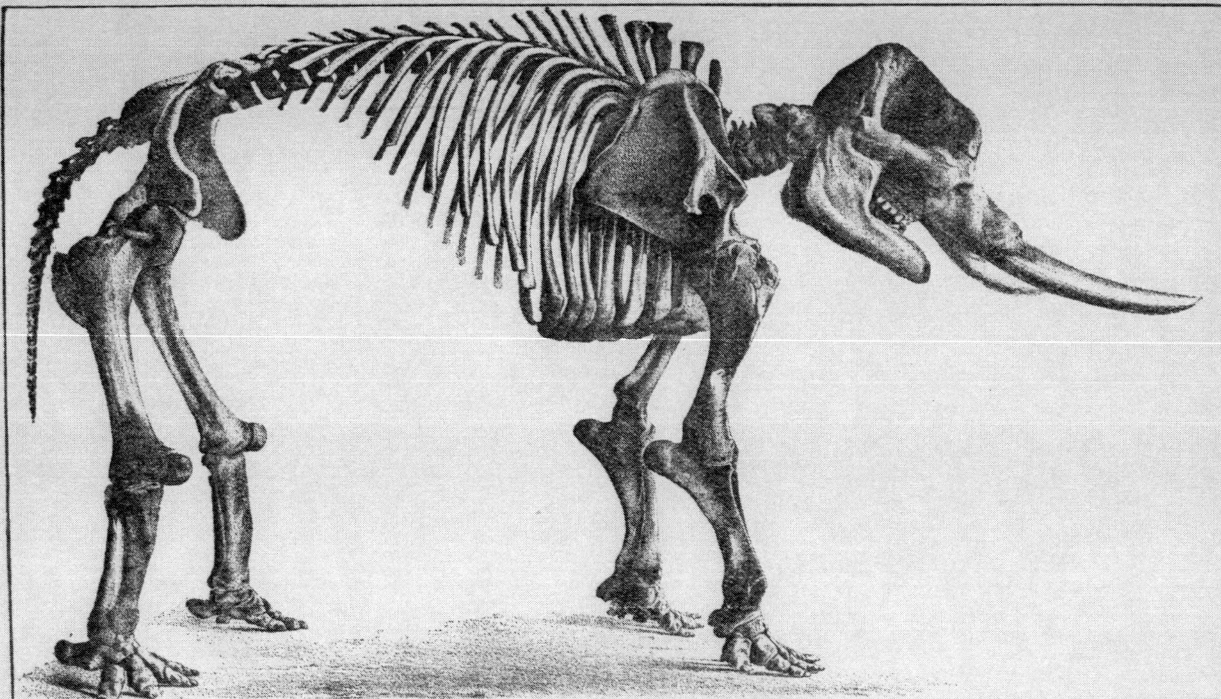

COHOES MASTODON.

Page 57.

of these great creatures must have presented a curious appearance. As in other proboscidians, the teeth consisted of incisors and molars. In the *Mastodon turiensis* of the pliocene time, found at Sismonda, the tusks of the upper jaw were nearly straight, though bending their points toward each other, long, sharp, and powerful. In a mastodon whose remains were found in Ohio (*Mastodon Ohioticus*), the tusks were long, gradually rising at the ends in a graceful curve; while in the lower jaw appeared a small single tusk. These lower incisors were present in the young of both sexes of this species, but were soon shed by the female, one being retained in the male; so that it was a three-tusked mastodon. In the *Mastodon longirostris*, there were, besides the two upper tusks, two long, slender tusks in the lower jaw, a defence more formidable than that possessed by any animal of to-day. In the elephant, the enamel is confined to the apex of the tusks; but in the huge mastodons they often had longitudinal bands of enamel, more or less spirally disposed upon their surface. The molar or grinding teeth of the mastodons appeared, much as in the elephants, in a horizontal succession: the front or worn-out teeth were pushed out or lost before the complete development of the posterior ones, which gradually moved forward to take the place of those which were worn out or ground away. The process was not as perfect as that in the present elephant, described in chapter first; as sometimes three teeth were in each jaw of the mastodon at the same time. The teeth are the chief points of distinction between the elephant and the mastodon; and they are readily recognized by the grinding surfaces of the molars, which have transverse ridges, their summits being divided into conical cusps, with smaller ones often clustered about them.

The enamel is quite thick: the cementum, which is so plentiful in the teeth of elephants, is very scanty, never filling in the interspaces of the ridges; so that the teeth present a serrated edge.

The great mastodon, many species of which are known, lived during what is known as the miocene time of geology, ranging from the middle of this period to the end of the pliocene, in the Old World, when they appear to have become extinct. In Ohio, the mastodons lived to a much later time, surviving until the late pliocene period, and were, as I have suggested, probably hunted by early man, if he was in existence at that time.

The mastodons had a wide geographical range, being found in almost every country. Nine species are known from Europe,—*M. angustidens*, *M. borsoni*, *M. pentelici*, *M. pyrenaicus*, *M. taperoides*, *M. virgatidens*, *M. avernensis*, *M. dissimilis*, and *M. longirostris*. Five species have been found in India, and four in North America. Two are from South America. Two only have been found in England.

Mastodons undoubtedly lived in Australia; a molar tooth of *M. andium*, or a similar form, having been found in New South Wales.

From this brief review of the early proboscidians, it will be seen that the elephant, as we popularly term all proboscidians, had originally as wide a range as man, appearing in almost every country; and it is even described by Pliny as being very plentiful in the forests of the so-called Atlantis.

Equally as interesting as the huge mastodon was the pygmy elephant, two species of which formerly existed. These were remarkably diminutive creatures, about the size of ordinary sheep; while their baby elephants must have been about that of ordinary cats. We can imagine a herd of these wonderful little creatures roaming about, and the strange appearance they must have presented. Their names are *Elephas melittensis* and *E. falconeri;* their bones are found in Malta and various parts of Italy. Living small or pygmy elephants are frequently referred to in old works. Bles, a correspondent of Buffon, states that he saw one in the Kandyan kingdom not larger than a heifer, and covered with hair. Bishop Heber says, that, in his journey from Bareilly to the Himalayas, he saw the Rajah Gourman Sing mounted on an elephant hardly bigger than a Durham ox, and almost as shaggy as a poodle.

It would seem that at one time a pygmy elephant existed in the Philippines, perhaps when they were connected to the Indian continent; as Professor Semper found the tooth of a fossil species at Mindanao, on the upper course of the Agusan, the most southerly of the group. The tooth, which this eminent scientist considers to have belonged to a dwarf species of the Indian elephant, was used in a remarkable ceremonial. It was worn by the Baganis, or chiefs of a cannibal race, on important occasions, strung about the neck with various objects, as images of gods, crocodile-teeth, etc. When the wearer in battle killed a foe, his breast was opened with a sacred sword, and the tooth and associated objects were dipped in the blood; and after the god of war, to which these objects are sacred, was supposed to have slaked his thirst, the Bagani indulged themselves in the human feast.

In the second book of the Æneid, Virgil refers to a tradition that at one time Sicily was a part of the main-land; and Malta was probably connected in a similar manner. Geologists even claim that Italy was united to Africa by a bridge of land, over which various animals passed.

It would be extremely interesting to trace back the early history of elephants, to follow their ancestry into the past, as we can the horse; but the present state of knowledge renders this difficult if not impossible. The present elephants stand alone and distinct, without any living allies. They are hoofed animals, in this related to the cows, etc.; and in their structure they show some affinities with the gnawing animals, or rodents; but here nearly all resemblances cease. We may follow them back to ancient elephants of the tertiary time, and to the era when mastodons reigned, but we cannot show that they are descended from the mastodons: in short, their history is shrouded in mystery.

One of the earliest proboscidians was the dinotherium, a remarkable animal larger than living elephants, with a trunk, and an enormous head, the lower jaw of which was armed with two powerful tusks which pointed downward, and tended toward the body. This strange elephantine creature lived in the upper miocene time, and has been found only in Europe. It is supposed to have been a water-loving animal, and to have uprooted trees and roots with the powerful tusks. In the accompanying picture (Plate VI.), I have attempted a restoration of the animal, which gives an idea of its general appearance. The dinotherium ranged, as far as known, from France to India, its southern limit in Europe being Greece (Pikermi).

Some authors express the opinion that the singular group of extinct animals known as dinocerata are ancestral forms of the elephant. The various species of dinoceros were animals of elephantine stature, but with shorter limbs; and their heads could reach the ground, so that there was no evident need of a proboscis. Indeed, certain animals may have possessed trunks, and not been elephants, if we may accept the restoration of Burmeister, who shows a pliocene, horse-like animal, — *Macrauchenia patagonia*, — with a proboscis.

The head of the dinoceros must have presented a remarkable appearance, being provided with two long, sharp, canine teeth, and places for four horns. Whether the latter were present, or not, is not known. All the species that are known come from the Wyoming tertiary. In fact, the question is involved in darkness. Professor Cope considers that they all branched from some primitive stock in eocene times, and at one time stated that the coryphodon, an animal as large as an ox, with a wide elephantine pelvis, was a possible ancestor; but now I believe he looks still farther back, to a group he has termed *Taxepoda.*

Professor Schmidt of the University of Strasburg says, "In entering upon a discussion of the elephants as a class, it was our wish to do away with what mystery seemed to encompass the existence of the present animal; and we have done so by pointing out their undoubted descent from the miocene mastodons." The latter forms he considers to "have originated from ancestors of the dinotherium species;" but as to the ancestor of the dinotherium, the learned professor leaves us in the dark as much as ever. It is only within a few years that the genealogy of the horse has been regarded as worked out; and it may be only a matter of time before Cope, Marsh, Leidy, or others will present the world with the original elephant.

CHAPTER VI.

JUMBO (See Plate VII.).

MANY elephants have become famous in ancient and modern times,—some by their deeds in war (for their courage and daring), others for their domestic virtues and intelligence. But Jumbo, whose fame extended to all civilized nations, was noted for his great size, and for the hue and cry raised over his departure from their country by the English people; and it is safe to say that no animal ever rose to quite such a lofty pinnacle of popularity. Probably not a boy or girl who visited the huge animal when alive, but ever after took an interest in his career, and sincerely regretted his untimely end. Jumbo was a prince among elephants, a magnificent example of the possibilities of animal life, and a type of a race that is slowly but surely passing away. Jumbo's early infancy was undoubtedly spent in the wilds of Central Africa. In 1861, when he was about four feet high, an elephantine toddler, Sir Samuel Baker saw him in the possession of some Hamran Arabs, who were taking him down the Settite River for delivery to a collector named Johann Schmidt. The latter sold him to the Jardin des Plantes; and Mr. W. B. Tegetmier says, "I saw him the day after his arrival in the Gardens, and went into his den with Mr. Bartlett. He was then about four feet high; and the

PLATE VI.

THE DINOTHERIUM.

(An extinct Elephant-like Creature.)

Page 62.

keeper, holding a long-handled broom in the usual manner, was scrubbing his back, which was far below him." This was in 1865: so that when he died, Jumbo was presumably about twenty-six years old, hardly in his prime; and I learn from Professor Ward, who mounted the skeleton, that he had not ceased growing. From 1865 to 1882 Jumbo lived in the Gardens of the London Zoölogical Society, pampered, fed, and petted by old and young; daily being marched upon the green with a load of children upon his back; and though, as Sir Samuel Baker says, he was not designed by nature as a perambulator, still the great animal was eminently successful as one.

Whether founded on fact, it is difficult to say, but rumors became current, that Jumbo had given evidence of dangerous outbursts of temper; and the keepers were afraid, so the report went, that possibly some one would be hurt. At this opportune juncture, Mr. Barnum, through an agent, offered the Zoölogical Society the sum of ten thousand dollars for Jumbo, which was immediately accepted; and, before the astonished public were hardly aware of what had occurred, the papers were signed that placed Jumbo in American hands. When this fact became known, there rose a clamor and protest from all classes. The excitement grew daily, added to by the comments of the German, English, and French press, until the question of Jumbo was the all-absorbing topic of the day. "The New-York Herald" said, "It seems a sad thought that a war between England and America is imminent, and may break out at any moment, and that no intervention will be able to stay the angry passions of two nations which ought to live in undisturbed harmony. The cause of this possible outbreak is the thoughtless sale of Jumbo, the pet elephant. Mr. Barnum vows that he will exhibit the giant to fifty millions of free Americans at fifty cents apiece. It seems a pity to rupture the amicable relations that have so long existed between us and our neighbors, but we must have that elephant."

Mr. Labouchere mentioned the matter in a humorous way in Parliament; and "The London Standard" pathetically remarked, "When a Southern slave-owner put in force his legal right of separating a family at the auction-block, the world rang with anathemas against the inhumanity of the deed. Surely, to tear this aged brute from a home to which he is attached, and from associates who have so markedly displayed their affection for him, is scarcely less cruel." Mr. Lowell, our minister at the time, is said to have observed, that the only burning question between the countries was Jumbo.

Thousands now flocked to the Garden to see the now famous elephant, that evidently had a strong hold upon their affections; subscriptions were started, to buy him back at any price; and the directors of the Garden were the butt of a vast amount of abuse.

Finally the editor of "The London Daily Telegraph" sent the following cablegram to Mr. Barnum:—

P. T. Barnum, New York.—Editor's compliments. All British children distressed at elephant's departure. Hundreds of correspondents beg us to inquire on what terms you will kindly return Jumbo. Answer prepaid, unlimited.

LESARGE.

And back went this eminently characteristic reply from the great American showman:—

My compliments to editor "Daily Telegraph" and British nation. Fifty millions of American citizens anxiously awaiting Jumbo's arrival. My forty years invariable practice of exhibiting best that money could procure, makes Jumbo's presence here imperative. Hundred thousand pounds would be no inducement to cancel the purchase. . . .

In December next I visit Australia in person with Jumbo and my entire mammoth combination of seven shows, *via* California, thence through Suez Canal. Following summer to London. I shall then exhibit in every prominent city in Great Britain. May afterwards return Jumbo to his old position in Royal Zoölogical Gardens. Wishing long life and prosperity to the British nation, "The Daily Telegraph," and Jumbo, I am the public's obedient servant,

P. T. BARNUM.

To this answer, the "Telegraph" referred in the following editorial: —

"Jumbo's fate is sealed. The disappointing answer from his new American proprietor, which we published yesterday, proves too clearly that there is nothing to expect from delicacy or remorse in that quarter. Moved by the universal emotion which the approaching departure of London's gigantic friend had aroused, we communicated with Mr. Barnum, indicating that 'money was no object' if he would only listen to the entreaties of the English children, and let the Royal Zoölogical Council off their foolish bargain. The famous showman replied — as all the world now knows — in tones of polite but implacable decision. He has bought Jumbo, and Jumbo he means to have; nor would 'a hundred thousand pounds' be any inducement to cancel the purchase. If innumerable childish hearts are grieving here over the loss of a creature so gentle, vast, and sensible, 'fifty millions of American citizens,' Mr. Barnum says, are anxiously waiting to see the great elephant arrive in the States. Then, to increase the general regret, the message depicts the sort of life which poor Jumbo has before him. No more quiet garden-strolls, no shady trees, green lawns, and flowery thickets, peopled with tropical beasts, bright birds, and snakes, making it all quite homely. Our amiable monster must dwell in a tent, take part in the routine of a circus. Mr. Barnum announces the intention of taking his 'mammoth combination of seven shows' round the world, *via* California, Australia, and the Suez Canal. Elephants hate the sea. They love a quiet bath as much as any Christians; but the indignity and terror of being slung on board a ship, and tossed about in the agony of sea-sickness, which is probably on a scale with the size of their stomachs, would appear to them worse than death. Yet to this doom the children's 'dear old Jumbo' is condemned; and it is enough, if he knew of it, to precipitate that insanity which his guardians have pretended to fear. It is true Mr. Barnum holds out hopes that we may some day see again the colossal form of the public favorite. In the summer of 1883 he proposes to bring the good beast back to England, exhibiting him in 'every prominent city;' and the message adds, 'I may afterwards return Jumbo to his old position in the Royal Zoölogical Gardens.' There is a gleam of consolation in this, which we would not darken by any remarks upon the great showman's ironclad inflexibility; but what will be the mental and physical condition of our immense friend when bereavement, sea-sickness, and American diet shall have ruined his temper and digestion and abolished his self-respect? There will be a Yankee twang in his trumpeting; he will roll about on his 'sea-legs,' with a gait sadly changed from the substantial swing so well known; and Alice herself will hardly know him.

"We fear, however, that Jumbo will never come back to her and us alive. His mighty heart will probably break with rage, shame, and grief; and we may hear of him, like another Samson, playing the mischief with the Philistines who have led him into captivity, and dying amid some scene of terrible wrath and ruin. We hope Mr. Barnum fully realizes what ten tons and a half of solid fury can do when it has a mind."

The young folks, who were the greatest losers by the sale of Jumbo, were not silent; and their attempts to move Mr. Barnum are shown in the following letters:—

9 DINGLE HILL, LIVERPOOL, March 7.

DEAR MR. BARNUM,—Please do not take Jumbo to America. I think it will be cruel if you do take him when he begs so hard not to be taken. There are plenty of other elephants—will not one of them do for you instead?—one that does not mind going. If you will only let Jumbo stay, I am sure the English children will thank you; and I do not think the people in America can be so cruel as to wish to have him when it makes him so unhappy to leave England.

GERTRUDE COX.

P. T. BARNUM. TURNBRIDGE WELLS, KENT.

Dear Sir,—You would receive the deepest and most grateful thanks of the whole of the British nation, if you would only forego your bargain about poor, dear Jumbo. You are so well known as the greatest showman in the world, do be known now as the most generous-minded man. I have always found American gentlemen to be every thing that was good, kind, and chivalrous; and I hope you will show yourself a king among them. We are all so attached to Jumbo, and he to his home, that it would be really cruel to move him. He deserves to remain, I'm sure, for his fidelity to all his surroundings, and his good temper under all his present trials. I know the American mind is so large, that I have quite expected each day to see in the papers that you would let Jumbo remain in his old home. In fact, I have all along thought it one of your jokes.

Praying that you may change your mind, and that this letter may arrive in time to assist to that end, I remain,

ONE OF JUMBO'S SINCERE FRIENDS.

P. S. — I am sure you will never regret leaving Jumbo in peace.

MR. BARNUM, — I write in behalf of our dear old Jumbo. Do be kind and generous to our English boys and girls. We do so love him! and I am sure if you have children or little friends of your own, you will be able to understand how their hearts would ache, and their tears be shed, should they lose the friend who has given them such delight, and who is one of their few pleasures in this great and sorrowful city. We all know from older and cleverer heads, that by rights Jumbo is yours, as you have paid the money for him; but, dear Mr. Barnum, you who have so many famous animals, and, among them, so many elephants, surely will think seriously and kindly before you take from us our very dear friend Jumbo. About the money for damages — I am sure all our parents in this city, who love their little ones so much, will willingly help to give you back your money, with an extra sum to make up for any expense you may have had concerning him. Do let the kindest side of your nature prevail. Think over the many hearts among us nearly breaking, and ready to do any thing to implore you to give us back Jumbo. If only you are generous to us in this, you will not lose by it, either in this world or the next. I am nearly sure if Jumbo does go, he will die when he reaches you, for he has clearly shown his great reluctance to leave us; and the voyage, and every thing taken together, will have an ill effect on him; that it will be but a poor Jumbo that will appear before you, even if a worse thing does not happen, and the grief at leaving his old friends, and such new experiences, does not turn him mad.

I think, — indeed I do not think, I am sure, — that if Jumbo had been our purchase from you, and letters had been sent to us, telling of the sorrow of American children at parting with an old favorite, every English girl and boy, man and woman, would have said with one voice, that the purchase-money should be given back, and the animal left to delight the children across the Atlantic. I am sure the wish of possessing the finest animal would not have crushed our manly and womanly feelings — and those of all true men and women are generously in sympathy with the cry of children in distress.

You say that perhaps Jumbo will return to us after you have exhibited him. I am afraid he will not be alive to come, or, if he is, all his trust in his old friends and keepers will be soured, and he will not seem like the old friend he now is.

You may think it a waste of time for a young girl to write to you, when older and wiser heads have failed; but I must tell you of the thousands of children to whom the parting from Jumbo will be a terrible grief. Be to us the generous-hearted man you are believed to be, and give us back our Jumbo.

I remain, yours truly,

A YOUNG ENGLISH GIRL.

The ninety pupils of a school in the Edgeware road memorialized the secretary of the London Zoo, who replied to them thus: —

Zoölogical Society of London, 11 Hanover Square, W.,
March 2, 1882.

Dear Friends, — Your petition has been duly received, but I fear we shall not be able to assent to your request. We must ask you to believe that our experienced superintendent knows better what elephants are suitable to be kept in the Society's Gardens than you do. There are still three elephants left in the gardens, upon which we hope you will have many rides in future.

Yours faithfully,

P. S. SCLATER, *Secretary to the Society.*

To Miss E. V. NICHOLS *and her companions.*

These appeals, — selected from the hundreds of such, — of course, had no effect upon Mr. Barnum; and in the mean time preparations had been going on to ship the giant. A huge box was constructed, six feet eight inches in width, and thirteen feet high, bound with heavy bands of three-fourths inch iron, weighing in all six tons. Feb. 18, 1882, was selected as the day for the start. To prevent any trouble, Jumbo was heavily chained by his feet; and, after a struggle to break his bonds, he was led toward the box that was to convey him to the steamer. But elephants are naturally suspicious, and Jumbo was no exception to the rule. Bracing back, he flatly refused to enter; and the attempt was then given up. The next day, another trial was made, with like success; then it was proposed to walk the great animal to the steamer, with the hope that, after the long tramp, he would enter the box readily. Accordingly, the gates were thrown open, and Jumbo marched out; and "then," says "The London Telegraph," "came one of the most pathetic scenes in which a dumb animal was ever the chief actor. The poor brute moaned sadly, and appealed in all but human words to Scott, his keeper, embracing the man with its trunk, and actually kneeling before him." In short, Jumbo refused to go, and was again returned to his house; and then the storm of public resentment broke out with renewed fury. The actions of the elephant were contorted into every possible meaning: his simplest acts and movements were given a significance which in all probability they did not have, and the press urged that some action be taken to prevent what was considered an outrage. A prominent clergyman wrote, "I trust the people of London will rise as one man, to prevent this cruel, inhuman bargain being carried out. Are there not walls in England strong enough to hold Jumbo, that we must send him away?"

Every legal obstacle was thrown in the way of the Americans. The authorities objected to the elephant being led

PLATE VII.

AFRICAN ELEPHANT, JUMBO.

Pages 66–70.

through the streets; and, according to Mr. Barnum, the superintendent of the Society for the Prevention of Cruelty to Animals never left the Garden until Jumbo did, awaiting an opportunity, according to the Americans, to use his authority in favor of public sentiment. As a last resort, an interim injunction was sworn out before Justice Chilly, restraining the Council of the Zoölogical Society from allowing Jumbo to be removed. But finally it was seen that Jumbo had been purchased fairly; and in the last of March the great elephant was coaxed into its box, and was ultimately hoisted aboard the steamer "Assyrian Monarch," and shipped to New York, where he was hauled up Broadway in triumph by sixteen horses and a large crowd who dragged upon ropes attached to the wheeled box for the purpose; and from that time to his death became the object of great attention.

One never tired looking at this stupendous animal. His enormous size, the pillar-like legs,—columns of support rather than for locomotion,—his stately movements, the pendulum-like swinging of his huge trunk, all impressed the observer that Jumbo was indeed the king among all animals, and the most remarkable one ever seen upon this continent.

Jumbo continued with the Barnum circus until Sept. 13, 1885, when he met an untimely death in St. Thomas, Canada. The final performance of the circus had been given; and Jumbo and the trick elephant Tom were marching over the track to reach their cars, guided by Scott, the former's trainer, when a heavy freight-train came rushing along from the east. The headlight was not seen until the train was within five hundred yards of the animals, and was not expected, as the railroad officials had assured the men that a train was not due for an hour. Signals were given as soon as possible, and the brakes were put on; while the elephants fled up the track, led by Scott, who stood by them to the last: but the heavy train could not be stopped, being on a down grade; and with a thundering roar it came on, striking the clown elephant, and hurling him into a ditch, then crashing into the ponderous Jumbo, the contact stopping the train, and derailing the engine and two cars.

The unfortunate Jumbo was struck in the hind-legs; and it is said, as he felt the cow-catcher, he gave a loud roar, turned and fell; the first car passing along his back, and inflicting wounds from which he died in fifteen minutes.

Jumbo's measurements after death were found to be as follows: circumference of the fore-arm, five feet six inches; height, about eleven feet two inches; length of trunk, seven feet four inches; around the tusk, one foot three and a half inches; length of fore-leg, six feet. Mr. Barnum presented the skeleton to the National Museum, and the skin to Tufts College, of Massachusetts, where they will ultimately go. The two gifts were mounted by Professor Ward of Rochester, probably the most stupendous piece of taxidermy ever attempted in any country; and, as such, it may be of interest to know something of the methods employed. Professor Ward thus describes his work in a letter to Mr. Barnum: . . . "Fortunately, we had one good life-photograph, also many measurements of his body, taken after the sad accident in Canada. The mounting was a matter involving such formidable conditions of weight and size, that no ordinary base would serve to support him. His pedestal was first built of heavy oak beams, the crossbars on which he stands being six by nine inches in thickness. In these were planted eight great standards of two-inch iron, — two of them to go through each leg, — which were bolted above into equally heavy cross-beams, which held them together, and strengthened the whole. Other beams ran lengthwise of the body, placed straight, obliquely, diagonally, and in every direction calculated to strengthen and stiffen, and all bound together with rods and bars and bolts. One great beam, reaching from rear part through the body to centre of his forehead, is calculated to sustain fully a ton's weight, if at any time his great head should need such support. The outlines of his body and legs are then obtained by properly fastening pieces of thick plank on edge, and cutting them to form required. The further final contour of the body is secured by covering these timbers with wooden coating two inches thick, and all built up, cut and chiselled to the exact form desired in every part. Thus was gradually built up an elephant of almost solid wood, of Jumbo's exact size and form. To this was applied his vast skin, weighing over three-quarters of a ton, and the same nailed and screwed in place over the entire surface and along the seams. There was no intermediate filling, and his skin now fits his wooden body in every part as closely as does the bark on a tree."

In mounting the skeleton, Professor Ward made some interesting observations, and was able to compare Jumbo's frame with that of a full-grown mastodon which was being mounted at the same time. That Jumbo was quite a young animal, was determined from an examination of his teeth and bones; and, gigantic as he was, he might have attained much larger dimensions.

To take Jumbo's place, Mr. Barnum has purchased Alice, the large African elephant of the London Zoölogical Garden, who, according to Tegetmier, "is not of an amiable temper."

Alice is an African elephant, perfect with the exception of the tip end of her trunk, which was torn off some years ago. She is about the age of the late Jumbo, and will also find a resting-place, when her term has run, in some of the American institutions of science.

CHAPTER VII.

HOW ASIATIC ELEPHANTS ARE CAPTURED ALIVE.

THOUGH the tusks of the Asiatic elephant are not large and valuable enough to make its capture for that purpose profitable, the live animal itself is greatly esteemed as a beast of burden, and as a show-animal in the pageants of the native princes, every petty court or rich man considering it necessary to his dignity to possess a number of the huge animals. To supply this demand, professional hunters are in the field during every season, using several different methods to entrap the great game. If the plan is to capture a large number of elephants at a time, kheddahs, or enclosures, are built; this method being the one now in use by the Government Hunting-Establishment in Bengal. To make it successful, about four hundred natives are required; and their duties are so different and varied, that a page from the pay-roll, and list of duties from the books of Mr. G. P. Sanderson, officer in charge of the Government Elephant-Catching Establishment in Mysore, are appended: —

No.	Detail.	Rate of pay per mensem. *Rs.*	Remarks.
1	Jemadar	25	To collect establishment, and conduct operations.
1	Interpreter . . .	10	To Hill-men.
1	Writer	9	

No.	Detail.	Rate of pay per mensem.	Remarks.
		Rs.	
1	Head tracker . . .	9	To go ahead and learn the position of herd, and send word to hunters.
2	Mate trackers . .	7½	
15	Trackers	7	
20	Head coolies . . .	9	To surround and guard herd, construct enclosure, and drive elephants in.
20	Mate coolies . . .	7½	
280	Coolies	7	
1	Havildar	9	To keep a check on circle of coolies, by going around at short intervals; also to mount guard at the department's camp. These men are furnished with guns.
1	Naik	7½	
14	Sepoys	7	
1	Head nooser . . .	9	To bind the wild elephants when impounded in the enclosure.
4	Noosers	7	
1	Head pulwán . . .	9	These men are furnished with guns, and take post at any point where the elephants show a determination to face the cordon of coolies.
4	Pulwáns	7	

These men constitute a well-organized army of elephant-hunters under the immediate command of a jemadar, or native sergeant, who in turn is responsible to a British or European officer. Besides the remuneration in the above pay-roll, each man receives free rations equal to two pounds of rice a day, two pounds of salt fish, chillies, salt, etc., per month. The total expense of a party is about twelve hundred dollars. Besides these numerous hunters, every party has a number of tame elephants, or koonkies, upon which the success of the hunt often depends. It is estimated that one tame elephant can manage two wild ones. This consists in leading the captives to water, bringing them fodder, etc. The Asiatic hunting-parties generally organize in December, and enter the field for two or three months. When the advance-guard discovers a herd, the large party comes to a stand-still some distance away, and then begins an organized system of progression. The men divide, and spread out in a circle, the object being to surround the herd; and, when complete, the natives often cover six or eight miles of ground, the men being some distance apart. When the word has been passed that the herd is in the centre, a bamboo fence is quickly put up, the material being at hand: in two or three hours, perhaps, the animals are entirely surrounded, and the men on the alert to see that they do not break out. During the day the elephants are generally not visible; and at night bonfires are built around the great circle, and the men by yells and shouts keep the terrified animals in the centre. Here they are watched, perhaps for a week, the men remaining at the posts, where they erect rude huts, and make themselves comfortable. As soon as the bamboo enclosure is completed, the important work, or the kheddah, is commenced,—a fence within the large one. To construct this, half the guard are detailed; and in a remarkably short time a stout fence is built in a circular form, about twelve feet in height, and from sixty to one hundred and fifty feet in diameter, braced and supported in the strongest manner; while all around the inside of the fence a ditch four feet wide is made. An opening about twelve feet wide is left on one side, facing one of the elephant runs, or tracts. To guide the elephants to the gate, palisades are built, diverging from it to a distance of one hundred and fifty feet. This arranged, the men close in on the herd, and, by shouting and firing, force them along the drive that leads to the funnel-shaped opening. Into this they run in a terrified throng; and, when all are in, the gate, which is a heavy affair studded with nails, is lowered by men stationed overhead, and a shout of triumph rises from the crowd of coolies. The elephants are now completely at their mercy. The fence is strong enough to prevent an outbreak; and, even if it were not, the ditch prevents their approaching it near enough to test their strength. Sometimes an elephant more plucky than the rest will make the attempt, and go through it like paper: but the elephant lacks intelligence in some things; and, when a break has been made by one, the others rarely follow the leader, a few shouting coolies being sufficient to keep them back.

The elephants do not always enter the kheddah so willingly, but break away, running over the men, and often killing numbers of them; but, as a rule, a well drilled and organized party manages the drive without great difficulty. When the herd is under control, the tame elephants are marched in, each with its mahout, or driver, upon its neck; and it is a curious fact, again showing the elephant's lack of intelligence, that the men are never touched, though they could be hauled from the tame animals with the greatest ease. Acting under the directions of the mahouts, the tame elephants separate the wild ones one by one from the herd; and, when they are surrounded, the men, or tiers, slip to the ground, and pass ropes or chains about their hind-legs, by which they are picketed until they have been reduced to subjection.

For many years elephants have been caught in Bengal, and the above plan for taking entire herds at a time is now in use by Mr. Sanderson.[1] His most successful operations were carried on near the village of Chámraj-Nuggar near the

[1] Mr. Sanderson's long residence in India, and his great experience, naturally entitle him to be regarded as authority on the elephant, notwithstanding some authors do not agree with him on certain points.

PLATE VIII.

BABY JUMBO.

From a photograph taken just after his arrival at London Zoological Gardens about 1862.

Pages 66–70.

foot of the Billiga-rungun hills. His first plan was met by much ridicule from the natives; and all the true Mussulmans were firm in the belief that no good would come of it, for the very good reason that there was a curse handed down by a former unsuccessful elephant-trapper for the benefit of any one who made the attempt to capture an entire herd after him. The natives were willing, however, to enter the employ of the official for a consideration, probably when they were convinced that the curse would fall upon him alone. Be this as it may, he had no difficulty in organizing a good band of elephant-hunters; and in a short time a plan of operations was formed on the Houhollay River. The first attempt was unsuccessful, but the next season an entire herd was captured; and since then, many large herds have been secured, the business being a valuable one to the government. The following is a description of one of these government hunts from the pen of Mr. Sanderson, the officer in charge:—

"It was past mid-day before we got all the elephants into cover, and not a minute's rest did any of us get until eleven P.M. Capt. C——, of the revenue survey, came over from his camp at Surgoor, and Major G——, and he helped to superintend the people. At one point, the supply of tools was insufficient; and Capt. C—— was superintending and encouraging a body of men who were digging with sharpened sticks, and even their bare fingers. The elephants were very noisy in the cover, but did not show themselves. At every twenty yards three or four men were stationed to keep up large fires. These were reflected in the water of the channel and river, which increased their effect. We all had a most exaggerated idea of what the elephants might attempt; and the strength of our defences was in proportion, and greater than they need have been. I was kept on the move almost all night by false alarms at different points, fortunately groundless ones. One tusker showed himself on the bank of the channel, but met with such a reception from firebrands and stones, that he retreated in haste. The river was an advantage, as the elephants had easy access to water. The lurid glare of the fires, the giant figures of the lightly clad watchers, their wild gesticulations on the bank with waving torches, the background of dense jungle resonant with trumpeting of the giants of the forest, formed a scene which words are feeble to depict, and that cannot fade from the memories of those who witnessed it. By eleven P.M. the defences were thoroughly secured; and that the elephants could not now escape, was certain, unless, indeed, they carried some of our barricades, which were, however, so strong as to be almost beyond their power. The men differed as to their number. I had seen about twenty: some declared there were fifty, but I could not believe this at the time. The number was fifty-four, as we subsequently found. The excitement of the scene was irresistible; so I betook myself to walking around the enclosure at intervals throughout the night, followed by a man carrying a basket of cheroots, which I distributed to the people. The rest of the time I lay upon my cot, which my servant had been thoughtful enough to bring from Morlay, enjoying the wildness of the sounds and scenes around, and soothed by cheroots and coffee. When the elephants approached the place where I was, the guards thrust long bamboos into the fires, which sent showers of sparks up to the tops of the trees overhead, where they exploded with a sound like pistol-shots. The first crow of the jungle-cock was the most grateful sound I think I ever heard, as it showed our anxious vigil was drawing to a close. We knew that during the day the elephants would give us no trouble. My herdsmen now joined me from the points where they had been stationed during the night, and we set about considering the next step to be taken; namely, making a small enclosure, or pound, into which to get the elephants confined. Of course, this would take some time to carry out. If driven from the east, we knew that the animals would pass between the temple and channel at the west end of the cover, with a view to crossing the river below the temple, and regaining their native hills, which, however, they were fated never to see again. I therefore laid out a pound of one hundred yards in diameter, surrounded by a ditch nine feet wide at top, three at bottom, and nine feet deep. This was connected with the larger cover by two guiding trenches which converged to the gate. It was completed in four days by the personal exertions of the amildár with a body of laborers who worked with a will, as their crops had suffered from the incursions of elephants, and they appreciated the idea of reducing their numbers.

"The last thing completed was the entrance gate, which consisted of three transverse trunks of trees slung by chains between two trees that formed gate-posts. This barrier was hauled up and suspended by a single rope, so as to be cut away after the elephants passed. The news of the intended drive attracted several visitors from Mysore. Tents were pitched in an open glade close to the river, and we soon had a pleasant party of ladies and gentlemen. The evening before the drive, all assembled within view of the point where the elephants were in the habit of drinking at sunset, and were gratified with an admirable view of the huge creatures, disporting themselves timidly in the water. On the morning of the 17th, every thing being in readiness for the drive, Capts. P., B., and I proceeded with some picked hands to drive the herd from its stronghold towards the pound. We succeeded in moving them through the thick parts of the cover with rockets, and soon got them near to its entrance. A screened platform had been erected for the ladies at a point near the gate, where they could see the final drive into the enclosure from a place of safety. The elephants, however, when near the entrance, made a stand, and refused to proceed, and finally, headed by a determined female, turned upon the beaters, and threatened to break down an open glade. P. and I intercepted them, and most of them hesitated; but the leading female, the mother of an albino calf, which had been evilly disposed from the beginning, rushed down upon me, as I happened to be directly in her path, with shrill screams, followed by four or five others, which, however, advanced less boldly. When within five yards, I floored her with my eight-bore Greener and ten drams; but, though the heavy ball hit the right spot between the eyes, the shot was not fatal; as the head was carried in a peculiar position, and the bullet passed under the brain. The elephant fell at the shot, almost upon me, and P. fired; and I gave her my second barrel, which in the smoke missed her head, but took effect in her chest, and must have penetrated to the region of the heart, as a heavy jet of blood spouted forth when she rose. For a moment she swayed about, then fell to rise no more. This was a painful sight. The elephant had only acted in defence of her young; but shooting her was unavoidable, as our lives, as well as those of the beaters, were in jeopardy.

"The next scene partook of the ridiculous. The herd dispersed, and regained its position. The little albino calf, seeing P., screamed wildly, and with ears extended, and tail aloft, chased him. He, wishing to save it, darted around the trees, but was near coming to grief, as he tripped and fell. The result might have been disastrous had I not given the pertinacious youngster a telling butt in the head with my eight-bore. His attention was next turned to a native, who took to his heels when he found that three sharp blows with a club on the head had little effect. After some severe struggles, in which a few natives were floored, the calf was at last secured to a tree by a native's waist-cloth and a jungle-creeper.

"While all this took place, the beat became thoroughly disorganized. When the elephant had charged P. and me, our men had given way; and the herd regained its original position, at the extreme east end of the cover. After a short delay, we beat it up again to the spot near the gate from which it had broken back. The elephants had formed a dense mob, and began moving round and round in a circle, hesitating to cross the newly filled-in trench, which had reached from the channel to the river, but which was now refilled to allow them to pass on into the kheddah. At length they were forced to proceed by the shots fired, and by the firebrands carried through the paths in the thicket. The bright eyes of the fair watchers near the gate were at length gratified by seeing one great elephant after another pass the Rubicon. After a short pause, owing to a stand being made by some of the most refractory, the last of the herd passed in with a rush, closely followed into the inner enclosure by a frantic beater, waving a firebrand. P. and

I came up third, in time to save any accident from the fall of the barrier. C., who was perched on a light branch of the gate-post, cut the rope; and, amidst the cheers of all, the valuable prize of fifty-three elephants was secured to the Mysore Government. I often think of the rapture of that moment. How warmly we sahibs shook hands! How my trackers hugged my legs, and prostrated themselves before P. and B.! An hour of such varied excitement as elephant-catching is surely worth a lifetime of uneventful routine in town."

Such is the account of an enthusiastic hunter, one of the best living authorities on these elephants; and few men have enjoyed his privileges. To complete the capture of this herd, seventeen tame elephants were employed; and finally they were all tamed and ready for use. They consisted of sixteen male elephants, the largest being eight feet five inches at the shoulder; three mucknas, or tuskless males; thirty females, and nine young ones. Nine were given to the Mahárájah's stud, ten to the Madras Commissariat Department, while twenty-five were sold at public auction when they were tame enough to be used by purchasers. The latter realized about $415 apiece, or in a bulk $10,425; and the amount realized from the entire catch, deducting the deaths, was $18,770. Deducting from this the total sum of expenditures from Mr. Sanderson's first attempt at their capture in 1873, or $7,780, a profit to the government remained of $10,995. Mr. Sanderson was congratulated by the chief commissioner of Mysore, and his excellency the viceroy and governor-general in council, and has since continued to capture elephants on this plan, always with marked success. His last catch that I have record of, that of 1882, was two hundred and fifty-one, and that only up to March. The first drive yielded sixty-five, and the second fifty-five, elephants. These animals were taken in the Garrow Hills.

A second method of taking wild elephants in India is by following them with females trained for the purpose. This plan is usually more successful in the capture of large tuskers than the kheddah, as the latter are often away from the herd, and do not become entrapped. The hunt is generally composed of four or five well-trained female elephants ridden by mahouts, who sit upon their necks, and are hidden by cloths or blankets of the same color as the elephant's skin. In some works, these elephants are called decoys; but this is an entirely mistaken idea. The tame elephants use no arts to attract the wild ones, in the sense of a decoy, merely obeying the commands or signs of the keeper.

When the location of a single male is determined, the tame elephants approach the spot in a leisurely manner, feeding as they move. Sometimes the wild elephant scents the mahouts, and moves off; but, as often, they do not seem to notice them; and, if not, the tame ones gradually surround him, and endeavor by command of their mahouts, who direct them by signs, to keep its attention. Generally there is an elephant in the near vicinity, loaded with ropes and other material; and, as several days are occupied, the men are relieved every day, the elephants drawing off one by one, and returning with fresh men.

This surveillance is kept up day and night; and, during the latter, the wild elephant goes into the fields to feed, being closely followed by the seemingly treacherous females with their concealed drivers. When he returns to the forest as the day approaches, they follow: and as he lies down, and tries to go to sleep, they close in about him, and, at the command of the mahouts, keep him awake by various devices; all this performance resulting in thoroughly fatiguing the old fellow, and making him sleep very soundly when he does take a nap. Sometimes an elephant is fed with sugar-cane loaded with opium, to make him sleep; and, as soon as he has fallen into a deep slumber, the mahouts slip off behind, and securely tie his legs. Then the men in the rear come up, and rudely awaken him, slapping him on his haunches, and telling him facetiously to be of "good cheer."

The struggles of the trapped elephant are terrific, and they often injure themselves fatally. The tame elephants follow them up until they are thoroughly subdued, when they are securely bound, and led to the place where their training commences; and a few months later, they are carrying their human owners about, or working in the timber district, as if they had not been wild elephants so short a time before.

A third method of taking elephants here is by the pitfall, — a barbarous custom, not now in general practice, as it always resulted in the loss by death of a large proportion of the catch. The plan was to dig pitfalls in the well-known and beaten tracts of elephants in the jungle, or under certain trees where they were known to congregate to feed. These traps, or holes, were generally ten and a half feet long by seven and a half broad, and fifteen feet deep, being purposely small, so that the imprisoned animals could not dig down the earth with their tusks, which they often did. In former years, there was, according to the government official, a perfect network of these pits in Mysore, and kept in order by the Mahárájah, the Forest Department, and others. The natives,

PLATE IX.

ASIATIC ELEPHANT.

Page 77.

as the Strolagas and Kurrabas, also made pits; and when an elephant was trapped, and they had no way of getting it out, the poor creatures often died before a tame elephant could be secured to give the required assistance. Through the endeavors of Sanderson, this inhuman practice has been given up; and all elephants caught are treated as humanely as possible.

A fourth plan of capture is by noosing wild elephants from the back of a tame one; and this affords a most excellent and manly sport, to be commended, as the animal is given fair play, and boldly met in the field. It is confined to Bengal and Napaul, not being practised in Southern India, and is not in favor for the reason that not rarely the tame elephants are badly injured, and the wear and tear upon them is too great. The sport is extremely dangerous, and is carried on something after the fashion of lariating wild cattle in the West of our own country. Fast elephants are selected, and three drivers provided each. One sits on the neck, to direct it; another sits near the tail, and, with a spike and a mallet, is supposed to hammer the unfortunate animal as hard as possible, just over the spot marked by the *os coccygis.* This is to spur the elephant on to excessive bursts of speed, and generally success. A third man sits on a pad upon the elephant's back, and holds a noose, the other end of the rope being strapped about the animal's body.

Thus fitted, a wild herd is followed; and, once sighted, the last man hammers at the creature with his spike and mallet, and away they go, over the rocks and through the bush in a wild chase. If the tame elephants are fleet enough, they soon range alongside, and give the rope-handler an opportunity to test his skill, which he does by throwing the noose over the head of the nearest elephant. Some natives are very expert at this; but men are often hauled off and crushed, or the elephants are choked, and many accidents occur.

A different kind of noosing is practised in Ceylon, where men follow the animals on foot, and throw a noose so skilfully, that they catch them about their legs when running at full speed through the jungle. As soon as this is accomplished, the men follow along, and twist the end about a tree, and soon have the great game at their mercy.

In all these cases, there is great danger, but not so much as where the animal is followed by the hunter on foot, and meets the huge creature face to face, his object being the tusks; described in a separate chapter on elephant-hunting as a sport.

CHAPTER VIII.

ASIATIC ELEPHANTS IN CAPTIVITY.

IN the previous chapter we have seen how elephants were captured in the early times in India, and how modern methods have humanized the entire system of their seizure; and now we will glance at the huge captives in confinement. The Asiatic elephant is a marketable commodity, and is bought and sold like the horse in this country. After the government has selected those needed for its use, the rest are sold. Certain places have become famous for their sales. Stōnepoor, on the Ganges, is, perhaps, the best known; and here, every year, a great fair is held, and many elephants sold and exchanged. This location is particularly favorable for the purpose, as hundreds of thousands of pilgrims meet here to worship at the famous shrine of Shiva.

The scene at this time is one of great activity: and immense numbers of elephants are exhibited, and many sharp bargains made; as the East Indian elephant-traders are not a whit behind the horse-dealers of Western countries.

Another celebrated elephant headquarters in Bengal, where these animals are sometimes sold, is at Dacca, a populous native city of seventy thousand inhabitants. It is about one hundred miles from the sea, and was once noted as a ship-building port, and headquarters for a fleet of eight hundred armed vessels, whose duty it was to protect the southern coast from the cruel Arracanese pirates. From its location on a branch of the Ganges, it is admirably adapted as the headquarters of the Bengal Elephant-catching Establishment, water, grasses, and fodder of various kinds, being plentiful; while its availability to the forests of Sylhet Cachâr and Chittagong, which abound in wild elephants, render it a comparatively easy matter for the captives to be brought to a first-class market.

The elephant depot is called a peelkhâna, and stands in the suburbs of the town. It embraces an area about a quarter of a mile square, consisting of an intrenched quadrangular piece of ground, where the pickets, to which the elephants are tethered, are arranged in regular rows. Each picket is provided with a solid floor of stone or mortar, where there is a post to which the elephants are fastened. During the heat of the day, they are removed to sheds. In the enclosures are numbers of buildings, containing the gear, and various appliances used about elephants. There is a hospital, where the invalid elephants are tended; for, if elephants do not die very often, they sometimes get sick, and are then given the best of treatment. There is also a hospital, or room, for the native doctor, who doses the elephants' attendants when they require it, as only a native doctor can do; and, as the elephants have a European to look after them when ill, they probably have the best of it. This great depot is under an English officer, who generally organizes the great hunts that have been described. The establishment is composed at all times of about fifty trained elephants, called koonkies. Besides these, there are always a number undergoing the training process; and, when ready for service, they are divided up among the various military stations, or sold, as the case may be. Stōnepoor is the scene of great public sales. Here those who wish to make a selection from many elephants, congregate; and their ideas of good points are strangely at variance with our own. The natives recognize three different castes, or breeds, based upon certain physical peculiarities; and, when about to purchase, they state which class they wish to invest in. In Bengal, these breeds are known as *Koomeriah*, *Dwásala*, and *Meerga;* meaning, first, second, and third class animals. The word *Koomeriah* implies royalty, and is supposed to possess every excellence, and is among elephants what Maud S. or St. Julian are among trotting-horses. Its points, according to Sanderson, are: barrel deep, and of great girth; legs short (especially the hind ones) and colossal, the front pair convex on the front side from the development of the muscles; back straight and flat, but sloping from shoulder to tail, as an up-standing elephant must be high in front; head and chest massive, neck thick and short; trunk broad at the base, and proportionately heavy throughout; bump between the eyes prominent; cheeks full; the eye full, bright, and kindly; hindquarters square and plump, the skin rumpled, thick, inclining to folds at the root of the tail, and soft. If the face, base of trunk, and ears be blotched with cream-colored markings,[1] the animal's value is enhanced thereby. The tail must be long, but not touch the ground, and be well feathered. A *Koomeriah* should be about nine feet and over high.

The temper of these animals of both sexes is, as a rule, superior to that of others; and, according to the above authority, while gentleness and submissiveness are character-

[1] In Burmah this would be considered a white elephant.

istics of all elephants, the *Koomeriah* possesses these qualities, and unanimity, urbanity, and courage, in a high degree. In short, the *Koomeriah* is the standard of perfection among elephants.

The *Dwásala* caste includes all those which rank just below this in point of excellence; while the *Meerga*, which is supposed to be a corruption of the Sanscrit *Mriga*, a deer, refers to all the rest; almost the reverse of the first caste in every particular, being long and thin of limb, with an arched, sharp-ridged back, a thin, flabby trunk, and long and lean neck; the head small, and eyes piggish. In fact, its whole appearance is often indicative of its nature; that is, mean and cowardly at times. The *Meerga*, however, is not without a value, being the swifter of the race; and, if speed alone is required, it is more valued than the *Koomeriah*. They can always be obtained, while *Koomeriahs* are not always in the market. The Kábul merchants make a specialty of them, as our Kentucky dealers do of blooded horse-stock. Many are attached to the various courts, and devote their entire time in hunting for first-class animals for their masters.

It sometimes happens that an elephant dies after almost reaching the city, and the merchant is nearly ruined; but in such cases an Eastern nobleman would consider it beneath his dignity to refuse to pay for the defunct animal; — an example of true Oriental munificence.

The price of elephants has increased in India of late years, though their numbers are not growing less. In 1835 they could be bought for $225 apiece; in 1855 for $375; in 1874, $660. Now $750 is the lowest figure for which even a young animal can be purchased. Though the prices are very capricious, good females of full growth bring from $1,000 to

$1,500; and $10,000 is often paid for a fine *Koomeriah.* These are all bought up by rájahs and others, who use them in their retinues, and for temple purposes.

Elephants were often in the olden times grossly treated and starved; but in the present day they are too valuable to be neglected, and are, as a rule, carefully tended when under the observation of Europeans; but, if left to the mercies of the natives to-day, they will often deprive them of food if any thing can be gained by it.

The captive elephants require much care, from the enormous amount of food they eat. In Bengal and Madras, the government decides how much each elephant shall have for breakfast, dinner, and supper; and the allowance is a liberal one. In Bengal the rations per day are four hundred pounds of green fodder, which means grass, sugar-cane, or branches of trees; or two hundred and forty pounds of dry fodder, namely, stalks of cut grain. In Madras, only two hundred and fifty pounds of green fodder, and one hundred and twenty-five of dry, are allowed; — not by any means the amount a full-grown, hearty elephant will eat. A large tusker requires eight hundred pounds of green fodder every eighteen hours, or day. In eight females which were watched by Mr. Sanderson, commencing at six P.M., they ate an average weight of six hundred and fifty pounds by twelve A.M. the next day. They also had eighteen pounds of grain a day.

The elephants are required to bring in their own green fodder; and one can conveniently carry a load of eight hundred pounds, or one day's food.

The discrepancy between this showing and that which the Madras elephants received, was made a subject of investigation by the government at the suggestion of Mr. Sanderson, and resulted in the poor creatures receiving their proper allowance. It was found by the investigating officers, that the animals which had been having two hundred and fifty pounds of green fodder, could eat seven hundred and fifty pounds of dry sugar-cane: so for years they had been worked hard and half starved, merely because the government had fixed the rate *per diem.* This is another instance of the reforms that have been instituted by Mr. Sanderson, who has the thanks of all admirers of this noble animal.

If an elephant in confinement possesses such a seemingly enormous appetite, a herd must be an expensive luxury to keep. In Bengal the expense for one elephant *per mensen* is as follows: —

	RS.	AS.[1]
1 mahout (driver)	6	0
1 grass-cutter	5	0
18 lbs. unhusked rice per day, at 64 lbs. per rupee .	8	7
Allowance for medicines, salt, etc.		13
Fodder allowance at 2 annas *per diem*	3	12
	24	0

In Madras it is forty-eight rupees.

[1] A rupee equals fifty cents.

CHAPTER IX.

HUNTING THE ASIATIC ELEPHANT.

THE lion and tiger share the time-honored term of king of beasts; their courage, intrepid natures, majestic bearing, and record for ferocity, having earned them the title, in the estimation of many. But, when compared to the elephant, these noble animals are mere pretenders. The elephant is the true king, the monarch of the land in size and strength, and capable, when thoroughly enraged, of toying with the tiger or lion. Rarely does an elephant fall a victim to either of these animals, and then only in their extreme youth. An instance is recorded by Sanderson which was considered so remarkable that he made a long trip to the place to verify it.

The elephant was a mere baby, — a calf four and a half feet at the shoulder, and weighing, perhaps, six hundred pounds. It had wandered off into the jungle, where it was pounced upon by the man-eater; falling an easy victim, as its legs were tied to each other. The tiger had sprung upon it, seizing it by the throat as it would a bullock, and dragged it twenty or thirty feet, there feasting upon its quarters.

Another instance is recorded of a hobbled, or tied, elephant being attacked by a man-eater; but the animal's cries attracted the attention of the keeper, and it was saved.

An animal so powerful as the elephant would naturally afford the grandest sport to the hunter; and, in following the great game, more dangers are incurred, and risks run, than in any known chase.

We have seen, that, in trapping elephants, every attempt is made to preserve them from injury: but, in hunting them for mere sport, this is reversed; and the animal is followed, either on foot or horseback, and shot as quickly as possible. This is often a most dangerous operation, and accompanied by the death of hunter and attendants. In trapping elephants, the men have the fences to retreat to, and tame elephants to hide behind; but the true sportsman follows the game into its own haunts, the deepest jungle, and boldly faces it, giving the noble creature an even chance for its life.

Sir Samuel Baker and Sanderson both say that elephant-shooting is the most dangerous of all sports if fairly followed for a length of time. Many elephants may be killed without the sportsman being in any peril; but, if an infuriated beast does make an attack, its charge is one of supreme danger. The risk has this charm, that, though so great unless steadily and skilfully met, it is within the sportsman's power, by coolness and good shooting, to end it and the assailant's career by one well-planted ball.

The wild elephant's attack is one of the noblest sights of the chase, and a grander animated object than a wild elephant in full charge can hardly be imagined. The cocked ears and broad forehead present an immense frontage. The head is held high, with the trunk coiled between the tusks, to be uncoiled in the moment of attack. The massive fore-legs come down with the force and regularity of ponderous machinery;

and the whole figure is rapidly foreshortened, and appears to double in size with each advancing stride. The trunk being doubled, and unable to emit any sound, the attack is made in silence, and after the usual premonitory shriek, which adds to its impressiveness. (See Plate XXIII.)

In former times the natives hunted the elephant with what are called *jinjalls*,—nothing more nor less than small cannon weighing about forty-five pounds, and mounted on a tripod-stand or carriage. The bullet used was of lead, weight about half a pound, and propelled by half a pound of native powder. Each hunting-party was fitted out with one of these, which was borne on a pole by four men,—two men carrying the gun itself, one the stand, while the fourth was the captain, who did the aiming and firing.

When the game was discovered by these pot-hunters, the gun was placed about three feet from the ground, aimed at any portion of the body, and fired. A fuze was generally used; and, igniting this, the valiant sportsmen ran away as fast as possible,—indeed, for their lives, as the cannon usually kicked completely over: and often limbs were broken, and other accidents occurred, the result of tardiness in retreating.

These guns were usually fatal at ninety or one hundred feet; and the unfortunate brutes rarely escaped if hit, often being desperately wounded. As many as five or six have been taken in this way, during the time that the Madras Government offered thirty dollars a head for them, to reduce their numbers; and elephant-hunting became a lucrative business, adopted by every one who could buy a jinjall.

The weapons now used in elephant-hunting are rifles; and the heaviest bore that can be carried with convenience is generally none too large, though Sir Samuel Baker usually used a light gun ; this being, however, because he could not shoot with a heavy one.

The larger the gun, the less opportunity there is of game escaping, to die a lingering death; and this generally decides the true sportsman. During the last decade, twelve-bore rifles were greatly used (1½ oz. ball), but these are rarely seen now. Sanderson, one of the best living authorities on the subject of hunting the Asiatic elephant, killed several of his first elephants with a No. 12 spherical-ball rifle with hard bullets and six drachms of powder. But this he discarded for a No. 4 double smooth bore, C. F., weighing nineteen and a half pounds, built by W. W. Greener. With this he fires twelve drachms of powder. Another gun, a No. 8 double rifle, firing twelve drachms, and weighing seventeen pounds, same make, he recommends, having stopped several charging elephants with it. No game in America requires such heavy arms, but the huge elephant demands weapons in proportion to its size.

In the majority of animals, a shot in any vital part is sufficient to disable them to some extent: but, in Asiatic-elephant shooting, there are only three shots that can be depended upon; and the sportsman must be somewhat well acquainted with the anatomy of the animal to successfully make them. The three vulnerable spots are the front, the bullet striking the forehead; the side, or temple; and the rear, or behind the ear. The brain of the animal is the mark; and it is so small in proportion to the rest of the skull, that a slight change of position, either raising or depressing the head, will render the shot futile. This can be seen by examining a section of an elephant's skull. (See Plate I.)

PLATE X.

HUNTING THE ELEPHANT WITH SWORDS.

Page 171.

The elephant sportsman usually makes elaborate preparations for the sport, taking a sufficient number of natives, servants, and trackers, with provisions to stay in the field some time; and only after some practice can he approach a herd, and pick out his shot, with any feeling of confidence.

The true hunter disregards the females, seeking the old tuskers; and to approach a herd without giving the alarm requires great caution, and not a little experience. The great game is generally found moving gradually in a given direction, feeding as they go. If they are approached from the wind, they scent danger from afar: but the experienced hunter creeps up against the wind, and ordinary caution enables him to approach within thirty or forty feet, —quite near enough, my readers would think, when one knows, that, upon the first shot, the entire herd will charge madly in any and every direction. The old tuskers, the heads of the family, rarely cover the retreat of a herd when an attack is made, usually starting off on their own account, leaving the others to look out for themselves.

When the presence of the hunter is realized, the one who makes the discovery informs the rest by a "peculiar short, shrill trumpet," understood by old hunters as well. The herd immediately cease feeding, all standing perfectly still, probably using their ears and scent, or perhaps making up their minds which way to go. The next movement differs in different cases. Sometimes the herd charge wildly in any direction; sometimes in a body; or, again, they move with such remarkable celerity and silence, that even old hunters have been deceived.

This peculiarity of the elephant, the largest of living land animals, is extremely remarkable. How such a huge body can make its way through bamboo and jungle so gently, is hard to imagine; but often, after the first rapid rush, there is absolute silence; and the novice comes to a stand-still, thinking that the game has followed suit. On the contrary, the headlong charge of the herd has been changed to a rapid walk, so silent, that persons in very close proximity to a band making off in this way, have failed to hear even the boughs and bushes scraping against the thick hide.

A charging herd will soon overtake a man, especially if he runs up-hill; and the appearance of a mass of bobbing heads and elevated ears moving forward through the jungle, is quite sufficient to unnerve the majority of men. When a charge is made, the natives rush for trees or clumps of bamboos, or often escape by standing still, so small an object being passed by in the fury of the rush.

Exactly what a herd will do when attacked, it is impossible to say. If they have never heard a shot before, they often huddle together in the greatest alarm, and do not break and charge until the continued firing and appearance of smoke thoroughly alarms them. They perhaps think the noise is thunder until the continued repetition disabuses them of the idea.

Elephants, when standing in this undecided manner, are liable to outbursts of fury if not treated in a certain way. Sanderson says, "At such times no one should shout to turn them, as a charge by one or more is sure to be made if startled in this peculiar way. I have seen and experienced several instances of the danger of this. In Chittagong, whilst driving elephants into a stockade on one occasion, they approached the guiding line of beaters too closely, when a man who was behind a small bush shouted at them within thirty yards. A female at once charged him. The man fell; and with the pressure of her foot she split him open, and killed him on the spot. This elephant had a very young calf, from solicitude of which she became a perfect fury."

Contrary to general belief, the single, or solitary, tuskers afford the greatest sport. They are generally found away from the herd before nine o'clock in the morning, and at this time the hunter endeavors to find them. When a great distance from a herd, the solitary elephant ceases feeding at about ten, then stands listlessly a while under cover, and finally lies down and goes to sleep. As a rule, it snores quite loudly; the sound, which has a metallic ring to it, coming from the trunk. Besides this, they often, perhaps involuntarily, raise their upper ear, and let it fall with a resounding slap upon the neck. All these sounds are well known to the trackers; and, by them, they can tell just what to expect, and how far away the game which is concealed in the jungle is.

If a bed recently used is found by the trackers, they immediately look for tusk-holes, or the impressions of the tusks in the soil, made when the animal is lying down. If they can put five fingers in the hole, they consider that the tusks will weigh thirty pounds apiece, and are well worth following.

Sanderson thus describes a hunt organized for his benefit in the Billiga-rungun hills, not far from Mysore: "I kept my eye on the tusker, who was in the middle of the line, and was wondering how I could get a shot at his brain, when, as luck would have it, some vegetable attraction overhead tempted him, and he raised his head to reach it with his trunk. I had beforehand fixed the fatal spot in my mind's eye; and, catching sight of his temple, I fired. For a moment I could see nothing, for the smoke, but heard a tremendous commotion amongst the elephants that were in company with the tusker. Stepping a little aside, I saw their huge heads all turning towards me, their ears outspread, and their trunks coiled up in terrified astonishment. Being a novice in the sport, I felt for the moment that I was in real danger. I stood my ground however, determined, that, if any of them charged, to fire at the foremost, and to run to Jaffer for the second rifle: that failing, the case would have been rather bad. However, charging was far from their thoughts: right about! quick march! was more to their fancy; and with shrieks and trumpets, away they went, some to the right, some to the left, joined by the whole herd in one headlong race, up or down the nullah. But my tusker remained stone dead upon his knees. The triumph of such a success, utterly unassisted, and in my first inexperienced attempt, quite transported me. My bullet had reached the tusker's brain: and, in sinking down, he must have been supported by the bodies and legs of the elephants between which he was wedged in; thus he still remained on his knees, though quite dead. He retained this kneeling position for some minutes, when, by a gradual subsidence of the carcass, he heeled over, and fell heavily on his side. I narrowly escaped being crushed between him and the bank as he sank, just springing out of the way in time. It would have been a fine thing indeed, if, after bagging my first elephant, I had fallen a victim to the collapse of his carcass."

The largest elephant shot by this sportsman measured as follows:—

	FT.	IN.
Vertical height at shoulder	9	7
Length from tip of trunk to tip of tail	26	2½
Tusks, each showing out of gum	2	4
When taken out, right	5	0
" " " left	4	11
Circumference at gum	1	4½
Weight (right, 37½, left, 37)	74½ lbs.	

At the end of a successful trip, when such an elephant has been shot, the sportsman is disposed to be liberal to the trackers; and the following is what Sanderson gave his men:—

	RS.[1]
Present to nine Kurrabas	36
Blankets to ditto	15
Present to gun-bearers	30
Hologas for cleaning skull	3
Warm clothes for servant	20
Two carts to Kákankoté	20
Tobacco, arrack, and rice	20
Sundries	6
Total	150 rupees, or $75

On one occasion, this hunter was following a herd, when two Kurrabas ahead of him began to gesticulate furiously; and, running ahead, he almost lost his life. He says, "Not knowing what to make of this, except that there was an elephant somewhere in the grass, I ran on, and almost fell into an old and disused pitfall, which now contained an elephant. His head was a little above the level of the ground. As I stepped back quickly, he threw his fore-feet on to the bank, and tried to reach me with his tusks. The whole occurrence

[1] A rupee equals two shillings.

was so sudden and unexpected, and his rush so startling, that I instinctively pulled the trigger of my four-bore rifle from my hip as I stepped back: there was no time to bring it to my shoulder. The shot went through the base of his right tusk, and buried itself deeply in his neck. He fell backwards; but, recovering himself, he commenced dashing his head with great violence against the sides of the pit in his stupefaction. I therefore took a light gun from Jaffer, and killed him." The elephant had fallen into the pit some time before, and the herd had immediately deserted it, as, says Sanderson, they always do.

In following wild elephants, sportsmen often have favorable opportunities to observe the habits and customs of the great game in their native wilds; and on such an occasion a fight between two tuskers was witnessed. Such an instance is recorded in the following: "We ran towards the place where the sounds of contest were increasing every moment: a deep ravine at last only separated us from the combatants, and we could see the tops of the bamboos bowing as the monsters bore each other backwards and forwards with a crashing noise in their tremendous struggles. As we ran along the bank of the nullah to find a crossing, one elephant uttered a deep roar of pain, and crossed the nullah some forty yards in advance of us to our side. Here he commenced to destroy a bamboo clump (the bamboos in these hills have a very large hollow, and are weak and comparatively worthless) in sheer fury, grumbling deeply the while with rage and pain. Blood was streaming the while from a deep stab in his left side high up. He was a very large elephant, with long and fairly thick tusks, and with much white above the forehead: the left tusk was some inches shorter than the right. The opponent of this Goliath must have been a monster indeed, to have worsted him.

"An elephant-fight, if the combatants are well matched, frequently lasts for a day or more, a round being fought every now and then. The beaten elephant retreats temporarily, followed leisurely by the other, until, by mutual consent, they meet again. The more powerful elephant occasionally keeps his foe in view till he perhaps kills him: otherwise the beaten elephant takes himself off for good on finding he has the worst of it. Tails are frequently bitten off in these encounters. This mutilation is common amongst rogue elephants, and amongst the females in a herd. In the latter case, it is generally the result of rivalry amongst themselves.

"The wounded tusker was evidently the temporarily beaten combatant of the occasion; and I have seldom seen such a picture of power and rage as he presented, mowing the bamboos down with trunk and tusks, and bending the thickest part over with his fore-feet. Suddenly his whole demeanor changed: he backed from the clump, and stood like a statue. Not a sound broke the stillness for an instant. His antagonist was silent, wherever he was. Now the tip of his trunk came slowly round in our direction, and I saw that we were discovered to his fine sense of smell. We had been standing silently behind a thin bamboo clump, watching him; and, when I first saw that he had winded us, I imagined that he might take himself off. But his frenzy quite overcame all fear for the moment. Forward went his ears, and up went his tail, in a way which no one who has once seen the signal in a wild elephant can mistake the significance of; and in the same instant he wheeled about with astonishing swiftness, getting at once into full speed, and bore down upon us. The bamboos, by which we were partly hidden, were useless as a cover, and would have prevented a clear shot: so I slipped out into open ground. The instant the elephant commenced his charge, I gave a shout, hoping to stop him, which failed. I had my No. 4 double smooth bore, loaded with ten drachms, in hand. I fired when the elephant was about nine paces off, aiming into his coiled trunk about one foot above the fatal bump between the eyes; as his head was held very high, and this allowance had to be made for its elevation. I felt confident of the shot, but made a grand mistake in not giving him both barrels. It was useless to reserve the left, as I did, at such close quarters; and I deserved more than what followed for doing so. The smoke from the ten drachms obscured the elephant, and I stepped quickly to see where he lay. Good Heavens! he had not been even checked, and was upon me. There was no time to step to right or left. His tusks came through the smoke (his head being now held low) like the cow-catcher of a locomotive, and I had just time to fall flat to avoid being hurled in front of him. I fell a little to the right. The next instant down came his ponderous foot within a few inches of my left thigh; and I should have been trodden upon had I not been quick enough, when I saw the fore-foot coming, to draw my leg from the sprawling position in which I fell. As the elephant rushed over me, he shrieked shrilly, which showed his trunk was uncoiled; and his head also being held low, instead of in a charging position, I rightly inferred that he was in full flight. Had he stopped, I should have been caught; but the heavy bullet had taken all the fight out of him. Jaffer had been disposed of by a recoiling bamboo, and was now lying almost in the elephant's line. Fortunately, however, the brute held on. I was covered with blood from the wound inflicted by his late antagonist in his left side: even my hair was matted together when the blood became dry. How it was that I did not bag the elephant, I can't tell."

A good idea of the excitement and sport of elephant-hunting is obtained from the following account, from the pen of Sir Victor Brooke, of a hunt participated in by him and Col. Douglas Hamilton in the Billiga-rungun hills. The adventure is particularly interesting, as the tusks were the largest ever taken in India: —

"In July, 1863, Col. Douglas Hamilton and I were shooting in the Hássanoor hills, Southern India. We had had excellent sport, but, until the date of the death of the big tusker, had not come across any elephants. Upon the morning of that day, in the jungles to the east of the Hássanoor bungalow, we had tracked up a fine tusker, which, partly from over-anxiety, and partly, I must confess, from the effect on my nervous system of the presence of the first wild bull elephant I had ever seen, I failed to bag. About mid-day I was lying on my bed, chewing the cud of vexation, and inwardly vowing terrible vengeance on the next tusker I might meet, when two natives came in to report a herd of elephants in a valley some three or four miles to the north of our camp. To prepare ourselves was the work of a few seconds. As we arrived on the ridge overlooking the valley where the elephants were, we heard the crackling of bamboos, and occasionally caught sight of the track of an elephant as it crossed a break amongst the confused mass of tree-tops upon which we were gazing. Presently one of the elephants trumpeted loudly, which attracted the attention of some people herding cattle on the opposite side of the valley, who, seeing us, and divining our intentions, yelled out, '*Ánay! ánay!*' (elephants) at the top of their voices, in the hope, no doubt, of receiving reward for their untimely information. The effect of these discordant human cries was magical. Every matted clump seemed to heave and shake, and vomit forth an elephant. With marvellous silence and quickness the huge beasts marshalled themselves together; and, by the time they appeared on the more open ground of the open valley, a mighty cavalcade was formed, which, once seen, can never be forgotten. There were about eighty elephants in the herd. Towards the head of the procession was a noble bull with a pair of tusks such as are seldom seen in India nowadays. Following him in a direct line came a medley of elephants of lower degree, — bulls, cows, and calves of every size, some of the latter frolicking with comic glee, and running in among the legs of their elders with the utmost confidence. It was truly a splendid sight; and I really believe, that, while it lasted, neither Col. Hamilton nor I entertained any feeling but that of intense admiration and wonder. At length this great exhibition was, we believed, over; and we were commencing to arrange our mode of attack when that hove in sight which called forth an ejaculation of astonishment from each one of us. Striding along thoughtfully in the rear of the herd, many of the members of which were doubtless his children and his children's children, came a mighty bull, the like of which neither of my companions after many years of jungle experience, nor the natives who were with us, had ever seen before. But it was not merely the stature of the noble beast that astonished us; for that, though great, could not be considered unrivalled. It was the sight of his enormous tusks, which projected like a gleam of light through the grass, through which he was slowly wending his way, that held us rooted to the spot. With an almost solemn expression of countenance, Col. Hamilton turned to me, and said, 'There's the largest tusker in India, old boy; and, come what may, you must get him, and take his tusk to Ireland with you.' It was in vain that I expostulated with my dear old friend, recalling my morning's mishap, and reminding him, that, in jungle laws, it stands written, 'Shot turn and turn about at elephants.' It was of no avail. 'You must bag that tusker,' was all the answer I could get.

"It took us but a short time to run down the slope, and to find the track which swept like a broad avenue along the bed of the valley. Cautiously we followed it up, and, after about a quarter of a mile, came upon the elephants. They were standing in perfect silence around the borders of a small glade, in the middle of which stood the great tusker, quite alone, and broadside to us. He was about fifty yards from us, and therefore out of all elephant-shooting range; but the difficulty was to shorten the distance. The approach direct was impossible, owing to the absolute want of cover: so, after some deliberation, we decided on working to the right, and endeavoring to creep up behind a solitary tree, which stood about twenty yards behind the elephant. When within ten yards of this tree, we found to our annoyance a watchful old cow, who was not farther than fifteen yards from us, and to our right, and had decided suspicions of our proximity. To attempt to gain another foot would have been to run the risk of disturbing the elephants. Seeing this, and knowing the improbability of our ever getting the bull outside the herd again, Col. Hamilton recommended me to creep a little to the left, so as to get the shot behind his ear, and to try the effect of my big Purdy rifle, while he kept his eye on the old cow in case her curiosity should induce her to become unpleasant. I should mention that we now, for the first time, perceived that the old bull had only one perfect tusk, the left one being a mere stump, projecting but little beyond the upper lip. I accordingly followed Col. Hamilton's instructions. At the shot, the old bull, with a shrill trumpet of pain and rage, swung around on his hind-legs as on a pivot, receiving my second barrel, and two from Col. Hamilton. This staggered the old fellow dreadfully; and, as he stood facing us, Col. Hamilton ran up within twelve yards of him with a very large single-bore rifle, and placed a bullet between his eyes. Had the rifle been as good as it was big, I believe this would have ended the fray; but, though its shock produced a severe momentary effect, the bullet had, as we afterwards ascertained, only penetrated three or four inches into the cancellous tissue of the frontal bone. After swaying backwards and forwards for a moment or two, during which I gave him both barrels of my second rifle, the grand old beast seemed to rally all his forces, and, rolling up his trunk, and sticking his tail in the air, rushed off trumpeting, and whistling like a steam-engine.

"Col. Hamilton followed, and fired two more barrel-shots, while I remained behind to reload the empty rifles. This completed, I joined my friend, whom I found standing in despair at the edge of a small ravine overgrown with tangled underwood, into which the tusker had disappeared. For some little time I found it difficult to persuade Col. Hamilton to continue the chase. Long experience had taught him how rarely elephants once alarmed are met with a second time the same day. At length, however, finding that I was determined to follow the tracks of the noble beast until I lost them, even should it involve sleeping upon them, my gallant old friend gave way, and entered eagerly into a pursuit which at the time he considered almost, if not absolutely, useless. It would be tedious, even if it were possible, to describe all the details of the long, stern chase which followed. After emerging from the thorny ravine into which the elephant had disappeared, the tracks led over a series of extensive open grassy glades, crossed the Mysore-Hássanoor road beyond the seventh milestone, and then followed the deep, sandy bed of a dry river for a considerable distance. At length, when about nine weary miles had been left behind us, we began to remark signs of the elephant having relaxed a little in its direct onward flight. His tracks commenced to zigzag backwards and forwards in an undecided manner, and finally led down a steep, grassy slope into a densely matted, thorny jungle bordering a small stream at its foot. I was the first to arrive at the edge of the thicket, and without waiting for my companions, who were out of sight, followed the tracks cautiously into it. I soon found that it was almost impossible to track the elephant any farther. The entire thicket was traversed by a perfect labyrinth of elephant-paths, and on each path were more or less recent footprints of elephants. Giving up the idea of tracking for a moment, I was on the point of commencing a further exploration of the thicket, when a low hiss attracted my attention; and, looking around, I saw a native who had accompanied us, beckoning to me, and gesticulating to me in the most frantic manner. Upon going to him, he pointed eagerly in front of him; and, following the direction of his finger, my eyes alighted, not on the elephant as I expected, but upon Col. Hamilton, who, from behind the trunk of a small tree, was gazing intently towards the little stream, which ran not more than thirty yards from where he was standing. With the greatest care I stole to his side. 'There he is, in front of you, standing in the stream. You had better take him at once, or he will be off again,' were the welcome words which greeted my ears. At the same moment my eyes were gratified by the indistinct outline of the mighty bull, who, already suspicious of danger, was standing perfectly motionless in the middle of the stream, which was so narrow that the branches of the low bamboos on its banks nearly met across it. The distance, twenty-seven yards, was too great for certainty: but there was no choice; as, even if the elephant had been utterly unaware of our vicinity, the tangled, thorny nature of the dense jungle surrounding him would have rendered it impossible to approach nearer without discovery. As it was, the perfect immobility of all save his eye, and every now and then the quickly altered position of his tattered ears, showed undeniably that the chances of flight and battle were being weighed in the massive head, and that there was no time to lose. Covering the orifice of the ear with as much ease as if the shot had been at an egg at a hundred yards, I fired. A heavy crash, and the sudden expulsion of the stream from its bed ten or twelve feet into the air, followed the report; and I have a dim recollection of my old friend hugging me the next minute in his delight while he exclaimed, 'Splendid, old boy! he's dead, and the biggest tusker ever killed in India.' But our work was not over yet. With one or two tremendous lurches from side to side, the old bull regained his feet, but only to be again felled by my second barrel, and this time to rise no more. The shades of evening were closing in fast, and a long journey lay between us and home, so we had but a few moments to admire the grandest trophy it has ever fallen to the lot of a sportsman to secure."

This hunt not only shows the endurance required, but the remarkable faculty of the elephant in travelling great distances when so desperately wounded, and the necessity of the heaviest ammunition to prevent prolonged suffering in the noble animals. When an elephant has been shot in the manner described by Sir Victor, the tusks are secured as trophies, and sometimes the head and other parts. They are either cut out with an axe, or left for ten or twelve days, when they can be easily drawn out of the alveole. The lowest Mysore inhabitants will not eat elephant flesh, though they have no objection to carrion; but the Chittagong hill people eat it with avidity. The tail is also used as a trophy; while the feet are taken and upholstered as footstools, and presented to the sportsman's lady friends. The feet of calves are converted into cigar-boxes, for the fortunate hunter's gentleman acquaintances; while tobacco-boxes, inkstands, and various articles are also made as mementoes of the hunt.

As the elephant shot by Sir Victor Brooke had the largest tusk ever observed in an Asiatic elephant, I give the measurements:—

RIGHT TUSK.

	FT.	IN.
Total length, outside curve	8	0
Length of part outside socket or nasal bones (outside curve)	5	9
Length of part inside socket (outside curve)	2	3
Greatest circumference	1	4.9
Weight	90 lbs.	

LEFT TUSK.

	FT.	IN.
Total length, outside curve	3	3
Outside socket, outside curve	1	2
Inside socket, outside curve	2	1
Greatest circumference	1	8
Weight	49 lbs.	

CHAPTER X.

THE WHITE ELEPHANT.

MENTION of the white elephant is found in the very early histories of Oriental countries. In a work called the "Mahaw Anso," the animal is described as forming a part of the retinue attached to the Temple of the Tooth at Anarajapoora in the fifth century after Christ; but it commanded no religious veneration, being merely considered as an emblem of royalty.

White elephants were so valued in the sixteenth century, that the nations of Pegu and Siam waged a war for many years about one; and, before it was settled, five successive kings were killed, and thousands of men.

Horace mentions the white elephant in his "Epistles." Democritus would laugh at the populace,—

> "Whether a beast of mixed and monstrous birth
> Bids them with gaping admiration gaze,
> Or a white elephant their wonder raise."

Ælian refers to a white elephant whose mother was black. In the eleventh century Mahmood possessed one, and when mounted upon it in battle he felt assured of victory.

The question whether the white elephant was worshipped, or is at the present time, in Burmah or Siam, is of considerable interest; and authorities vary so, that the seeker after information is often puzzled. I think that the status of the animal may be fairly expressed in the following.

By the most intelligent and refined Burmese and Siamese, it is merely considered as an invaluable adjunct to royalty. It is an important part of the retinue of a court; and its presence is considered a lucky omen, this superstition having an extremely strong hold upon the princes and kings. The lower classes in some cases may have worshipped the white elephant, and the attention paid to it by royalty may have easily been misunderstood by the uneducated as reverence.

The fact that the white elephant is mentioned in the mythology of the countries, and associated with Buddha, shows that it was undoubtedly reverenced if not worshipped by some; and, if the veneration had not its source in religious feeling, it was so nearly akin to it that it amounted to the same thing.

The Siamese are extremely superstitious; but, before we condemn them, we must remember how many of our sailors refuse to sail on Friday. How a broken mirror or spilled salt alarms many otherwise intelligent Americans! so that, when we learn from Major Snodgrass that in his time in Burmah a mere grunt from the white elephant was supposed to have some important significance, we need not be surprised. Any extraordinary movement or noise made by the animal was quite enough at this time to interrupt the most important affairs, and to cause the most solemn engagement to be broken. Crawford thinks this was merely superstition, and says, "I had here an opportunity, as well as in Siam, of ascertaining that the veneration paid to the white elephant had been in some respects greatly exaggerated. The white elephant *is not* an object of worship, but it is considered an indispensable part of the regalia of sovereignty. Royalty is incomplete without it; and, the more there are, the more perfect is the state of the kingly office considered. Both the court and the people would consider it as peculiarly inauspicious to want a white elephant, and hence the repute in which they are held. The lower orders, however, it must be observed, perform the "shiko, or obedience of submission," to the white elephant; but the chiefs view this as a vulgar superstition, and do not follow it."

On the other hand, Vincent states that the white elephant has been happily termed the Apis of the Buddhists. "It is held to be sacred by all the Indo-Chinese nations except the Annamese. It is revered as a god while living, and its death is regarded as a national calamity. . . . Even at the present day the white elephant is worshipped by the lower classes; but by the king and nobles it is revered and valued not so much for its divine character, being the abode of a transmigrating Buddha, as because it is believed to bring prosperity to the court in peace, and good fortune in war. The more there are of them, the more grand and powerful the state is supposed to be."

From this somewhat conflicting statement, we may infer that the white elephant was formerly worshipped; but, at the present day, the estimate that I have given may be applied.

The association of the white elephant with the religious sects of India is well known; but how much it was reverenced from the association, it is impossible to tell. Sir John Bowring gives the following reasons for believing that the animal was held sacred, principally, "because it is believed that Buddha, the divine emanation from the Deity, must necessarily, in his multitudinous metamorphoses, or transmissions through all existences, and through millions of æons, delight to abide for some time in that grand incarnation of purity which is represented by the white elephant. While the *bonzes* teach that there is no spot in the heavens above, or the earth below, or the waters under the earth, which is not visited in the peregrinations of the divinity, — whose every stage or step is towards purification, — they hold that his tarrying may be longer in the white elephant than in any other abode, and that, in the possession of the sacred creatures, they may possess the presence of Buddha himself. It is known that the Singhalese have been kept in subjection by the belief that their rulers have a tooth of Buddha in the Temple of Kandy; and that, on various tracts of the East, impressions of the foot of Buddha are reverenced, and are the objects of weary pilgrimages to places which can only be reached with difficulty: but with the white elephant some vague notions of a vital Buddha are associated, and there can be no doubt that the marvellous sagacity of the creature has served to strengthen their religious prejudices. Siamese are known to whisper their secrets into an elephant's ear, and to ask a solution of their perplexities by some sign or movement. And most assuredly there is more sense and reason in the worship of an intelligent beast than in that of stocks and stones, the work of men's hands.

Kircher says that "the veneration which, in the Burman Empire, is paid to the white elephant, is in some degree connected with the doctrine of metempsychosis. Xaca sustained seventy thousand transmigrations through various animals, and rested in the white elephant." Hindoo mythology

PLATE XI.

THE WHITE ELEPHANT, TOUNG TALOUNG.

Property of Barnum, Bailey & Hutchinson.

Page 117.

teaches that the earth is supported by eight elephants; and that this was believed, is shown by Bernier, who witnessed a dialogue between an aga at the court of Delhi, and a Pundit Brahmin. The harangue concluded with these words: "When, my lord, you place your foot in the stirrup, marching at the head of your cavalry, the earth trembles under your footsteps; the eight elephants, on whose heads it is borne, finding it impossible to support the extraordinary pressure."

In the Rámáyana, one of the most celebrated sacred books of the Brahmins, is a very curious account of the journey of a party of men who penetrated to the interior of the earth, and had an audience with the famous elephants. It will be seen from the following, that the white elephant is an important member of this subterranean band:—

"The sixty thousand descended to Patala, and there renewed their digging. There, O chief of men! they saw the elephant of that quarter of the globe, in size resembling a mountain, with distorted eyes, supporting with his head this earth, with its mountains and forests, covered with various countries, and adorned with numerous cities. When, for the sake of rest, O Kakootstha! the great elephant, through distress, refreshes himself by moving his head, an earthquake is produced. Having respectfully circumambulated this mighty elephant, guardian of the quarter, they, O Rama! fearing him, penetrated into Patala. After they had thus penetrated the east quarter, they opened their way to the south. Here they saw that great elephant Muhapudma, equal to a huge mountain, sustaining the earth with his head. Beholding him, they were filled with surprise; and, after the usual circumambulation, the sixty thousand sons of the great Sugura perforated the west quarter. In this, these mighty ones saw the elephant Soumanuca, of equal size. Having respectfully saluted him, and inquired respecting his health, these valiant men, digging, arrived at the north. In this quarter, O chief of Ruzhoo! they saw the snow-white elephant Bhudra, supporting this earth with his beautiful body."

The Persians have, according to Chardin, a festival in honor of the inspiration of an elephant, when Abraha, a prince of Yemen, marched an army to destroy the Kaaba of Mecca, the sacred oratory which Abraham built in that city. Prior to the birth of Mohammed, the Arabians reckoned from this epoch, which they called the year of the coming of the elephants. The tradition is thus told in Sale's Koran: "The Meccans, at the approach of so considerable a host, retired to the neighboring mountains, being unable to defend their city or temple. But God himself undertook the defence of both. For when Abraha drew near to Mecca, and would have entered it, the elephant on which he rode, which was a very large one, and named Mahmud, refused to advance any nigher to the town, but knelt down whenever they endeavored to force him that way, though he would rise and march briskly enough if they turned him towards any other quarter: and while matters were in this posture, on a sudden, a large flock of birds, like swallows, came flying from the seacoast, every one of which carried three stones, one in each foot, and one in its bill; and these stones they threw down upon the heads of Abraha's men, certainly killing every one they struck."

In many old works, reference is made to the fact that the elephant was a religious animal. Kircher, in his description of China, gives a plate showing a white elephant worshipping the sun and moon, which was copied from the Chinese. It was supposed that all elephants worshipped the sun. Pliny says, "We find in him qualities which are rare enough amongst men,—honesty, prudence, equity, religion also, in his worship of the sun and moon. Authors say, that, in the forests of Mauritania, the elephants, at the sight of the new moon, descend in troops to a certain river called Anelo, where they solemnly wash themselves, and, having rendered their homage to the star, return to the woods, supporting the young ones that are fatigued."

According to Vincent, in Pali Scriptures it is duly set forth "that the form under which Buddha will descend to the earth for the last time, will be that of a beautiful young white elephant, open-jawed, with a head the color of cochineal, with tusks shining like silver sparkling with gems, covered with a splendid netting of gold, perfect in organs and limbs, and majestic in appearance."

It would seem from the above, that there was at least little doubt that among some classes in ancient times the white elephant was worshipped. The term white is deceptive. The pure white elephant figured on the arms and flag of Siam has conveyed the impression that the Siamese and Burmese possessed pure white proboscidians; but this is a gross error. A pure white elephant probably never existed, at least was never captured. All the so-called sacred elephants of the present and former days possessed very few characteristics to distinguish them from ordinary elephants to be met with any day in Bombay. Mr. Barnum's white elephant is an exceptionally fine example, being whiter than many owned in Siam, and much more so than the late white elephant of Theebaw. In fact, the white elephant is not white at all, the term being applied to any elephant who shows the slightest evidence of albinism. There are two terms applied to abnormally white or black animals,—albinism and melanism. The former is given to animals, including men, who have a deficient supply of coloring matter; while the latter is associated with those who have an excess of pigment. Men and women with white hair and pink eyes, the white rabbit, etc., represent the albino phase; and the white elephant belongs to this category, being simply an ordinary elephant, who, to a greater or less extent, lacks coloring matter; and, as a result, it is often a dark mouse color, a little lighter than the ordinary elephant, and has numerous pinkish splashes about the head, or on various parts of the body. The eyes in some are pink; and the toe-nails, when scraped, are perhaps some lighter, and in some cases a yellowish white. The blotches of the white elephant are not hereditary. It is the offspring of black parents, and the condition does not affect the health of the animal in any way.

In India, the white elephant is not appreciated; but the Singhalese are fond of elephants having the pink blotches which constitute a white elephant in Siam or Burmah; and they are liable to be found in any elephant country.

While we assume that the white elephant is not worshipped or revered by the nobles of Siam and Burmah of the present day, the honor that is paid it is somewhat astonishing. Thus, the King of Cambodia, who claims that his ancestors owned seventy thousand elephants, is called the "first cousin of the white elephant;" the prime minister of Siam, "general of the elephants;" the foreign minister of Cochin China, "mandarin of elephants;" while the late Theebaw and the King of Siam enjoyed the distinction of being called "lord of the celestial elephant," and "master of many white elephants."

The animal appears upon various objects, as the national emblem, the coat of arms, medals, the buttons of officials, etc. The late white elephant of Theebaw held a high rank and position at court, taking precedence of the heir-apparent; or, assuming it to have been connected with the British court, it would have been given precedence before the Prince of Wales.

The Order of the White Elephant is one of the most honorable conferred, and few have received it. Among them is Edward Arnold, author of "The Light of Asia;" and it was reported some time before the Burmese war, that the King of Siam was about to visit England for the sole purpose of conferring it upon Queen Victoria.

The following is a copy of the parchment which accompanied the one conferred upon Mr. Arnold. It is beautifully executed in gold, red, and black, and is a curiosity in itself: —

SOMLECH PHRA PARAMINDR MAHA CHULALOUKORU, CHULA CHOM KLAO, King of Siam, fifth sovereign of the present dynasty, which founded and established its rule, Katana Kosindr Mahindr Ayuddhya, Bangkok, the capital city of Siam, both northern and southern, and its dependencies, Suzerain of the Laos and Malays and Koreans, etc., etc.

To all and singular, to whom these presents come.

KNOW YE, we deem it right and fitting, that Edwin Arnold, Esq., author of "The Light of Asia," should be appointed an officer of the most exalted Order of the White Elephant, to his honor henceforth. May the Power which is most highest in the universe keep and guard him, and grant him happiness and prosperity!

Given at our palace, Parania Raja Sthit Maholarm, on Tuesday, the

11th waning of the lunar month Migusira, the first month from the cold season of the year Toh Ekasole, 1241 of the Siamese era, corresponding to the European date 9th of December, 1879, of the Christian era, being the 4046th day, or 12th year of our reign.

(MANU REGIÂ) CHULALOUKORU, R.S.

Queen Victoria has, I believe, not yet received the order; but she is not unacquainted with the veneration entertained by the Siamese for the animal, as the following will show. Some years ago she sent an embassy to the kingdom of Siam, consisting of several noblemen and officers of rank, to conduct some diplomatic business; and, according to custom, they carried some valuable presents to the king. Upon their return, the latter, not wishing to be outdone by the Queen, delivered to Sir John Bowring a gold box locked with a gold key, containing the most valuable gift he could devise. Sir John, naturally thinking it a gem, perhaps of great price, bore it carefully from Siam to England, and personally presented it to her Majesty. Doubtless there was some curiosity in the royal mind to know what was so precious as to require a solid gold box and key; but it was not a gem, — though it may have been in the eyes of the Siamese monarch, — and was simply a few hairs taken from the king's white elephant!

A Siamese ambassador, during a visit to London, thus referred to Queen Victoria in language intended to be highly flattering: "One cannot but be struck with the aspect of the august Queen of England, or fail to observe that she must be of pure descent from a race of goodly and warlike kings and rulers of the earth, in that her eyes, complexion, and, above all, her bearing, are those of a beautiful and majestic white elephant."

As these pink-splashed elephants are so esteemed, it is not

to be wondered at that there is constant search for them in the jungle; and the fortune of him is made who discovers one. They are, however, comparatively rare; and in thirteen hundred and fifty-two years, between A.D. 515 and 1867, only twenty-four were captured, making about one in every fifty-six years. The last one was captured in 1885, and was conducted to the court of the King of Siam by His Royal Highness Somdetch Chowf Mahamalah Bamrahp Parapako, amid much parade. His Majesty accepted it, and made the fortunate finder, a poor native, a present of a sum of money, as well as his mother and son. The Siamese officials who brought the elephant to Bangkok, were honored with an audience by His Majesty, and also given valuable presents.

In former days the ceremonies attending the capture of a white elephant were very impressive. The discoverer, were he the humblest man in the kingdom, was immediately made a mandarin: he was exempted from taxation for the remainder of his life, and presented with large sums of money, the king himself giving him one thousand dollars. As soon as the capture was made, a special courier was despatched to the king, and a posse of nobles with gifts and robes started immediately for the scene of action. The ropes which the captors used in binding the royal victim were replaced by stout cords of scarlet silk. Mandarins attended to the slightest wants of the animal. Rich feather-fans with gilt handles were used to keep the insects from it during the day, while a silk embroidered mosquito-net was provided at night. To remove it to the capital, a boat was built especially for the purpose, and a magnificent canopy erected over it, ornamented and bedecked as were the king's palaces. Silk draperies, heavy with gold and silver, enclosed the royal prisoner;

and in this state he floated down the river, receiving the acclamations of the people. When near the city, it was landed, the king and his court going out to meet and escort it to the city, where a place had been built for it within the royal palace-grounds. A large tract of land was set apart for his country-place, chosen from the best the kingdom afforded. A cabinet of ministers was appointed, and a large retinue of other nobles, to attend to its wants. The priest of the king was ordered to administer to its spiritual needs, and it had physicians to see to its physical requirements. Gold and silver dishes were supplied to feed it from, and every want was attended to as became one of the royal family. The city devoted three days to festivities, and the rich mandarins made it rare presents.

When a white elephant died, the ceremonies were the same as those of a king or queen. The body lay in state for several days; and then it was placed upon a funeral pyre, and cremated. This pyre often cost thousands of dollars, being made of the choicest sandal, sassafras, and other valuable woods. After the body had been thoroughly cremated, it was allowed to remain three days more; then the ashes were collected, and placed in costly urns, and buried in the royal cemetery, a magnificent mausoleum being erected over the spot.

A friend of the author, who visited the land of the white elephant a few years ago, states that, when he observed a white elephant, about twenty natives were standing around, whom he was informed by the guide were mandarins and nobles of the highest class, who formed the cabinet of the elephant: in fact, they were a body selected for their dignity and rank. One was chief minister of the cabinet, and the others held different offices. Other nobles were attached directly to the person of his celestial highness. One fed him with bananas and rare fruits difficult to obtain: another gently brushed away the flies from its head, and created a breeze. About the room were various objects which bespoke its royal nature. The ropes, umbrellas, and blankets were of the finest description, many being ornamented with seeming gems. Later he witnessed the ceremony of the bath; and no spectacle, he said, that he had ever observed in America, began to compare with it. The entire city seemed to turn out and make a holiday of the occasion. When the march was taken up, the elephant stepped out heavily caparisoned. Elegant silks, trimmed with scarlet, silver, white, and gold, depended from its back: over its head was held the royal umbrella, a gorgeous affair, supported by gilded rods held in the hands of eight mandarins, four of whom marched on each side. On the animal's tusks were bands of solid gold; and as he moved solemnly along, surrounded by other nobles, his ministers, and attendants, all in rich garbs, with a shouting but respectful crowd all about it, it was certainly an impressive and wonderful sight. At the river the trappings were taken off, and the elephant plunged in and enjoyed himself after the manner of plebeian elephants. When the bath was finished, its feet were re-washed, and dried on a silken towel: the silks and rich stuffs were then replaced, a band of music struck up, and the procession took up the return march. Once at court, the newly captured white elephant is honored by titles which are conferred upon him by the king, some of which are "Gem of the Sky," "Glory of the Land," "Radiance of the World," "Leveller of the Earth," etc.

The king often took advantage of the capture of an elephant, to replenish the royal treasury; and, when the animal was housed in the palace, an invitation was sent out to the rich merchants to come and pay their respects. This meant literally to make presents to the white elephant, which, of course, were used by the king. People who wished to obtain favors from His Majesty, took this occasion to offer valuable gifts. In some cases, it was money; in others, objects of art; and one present was a vase of solid gold weighing four hundred and eighty ounces.

Zachard, an old traveller, saw a white elephant in Siam which was said to be over two hundred years old, over which there had been much blood shed. It lived in a magnificent pavilion, and had one hundred attendants, who fed it from vessels of gold. When Mr. Crawford was in Siam, the king had six white elephants; and the King of Ava possessed only one, which was fastened directly in front of the palace. While Mr. Crawford was in Ava, a report was sent to the king that a white elephant had been captured, but it could not be forwarded without the destruction of ten thousand baskets of rice. To which the king replied, "What signifies the destruction of ten thousand baskets of rice in comparison with the possession of a white elephant!" and the order for the beast was immediately given.

The white elephant now in the possession of the King of Ava, who styles himself "Lord of the White Elephant," is, according to Vincent, a vicious brute of medium size, with white eyes, and the forehead and ears spotted white (pink), appearing as if they had been rubbed with pumice stone or sand-paper; but the remainder of the body is as black as coal. The animal is kept chained in the centre of a pavilion, surrounded by the adjuncts of royalty, which consist of gold and white cloth umbrellas, an embroidered canopy, a bundle of spears, dishes, etc. Mr. Vincent was informed that a young white elephant had recently been captured in the north-eastern part of British Burmah, near Tounghoo; but it died, and the king had been "out of sorts" ever since.

Mr. Vincent also inspected the white elephants at Bangkok, and found them fastened to posts in large sheds, covered with gilt canopies very much as were those at Mandalay. The keeper fed the animals with bananas in his presence, and caused the Apis of Buddha, as they call the animal, to salute an American, probably for the first time. The salaam, or salutation, consisted in raising the proboscis to the forehead, and then lowering it slowly and gracefully to the ground.

With these white elephants were several white monkeys, which were kept to ward off evil spirits. White animals of all kinds are considered abodes of transmigrating souls by Buddhists. Sir John Bowring saw the white monkey honored with special attention. The veneration received by white elephants may perhaps be explained by the fact that all white animals are believed to be the abiding-place of some mighty Buddha; and by possessing such an animal, having the deity in the family, as it were, they may receive any advantages that may accrue from the association.

Curiously enough, with the downfall of the infamous Theebaw came that of his white elephant. The king left Mandalay, Nov. 29, 1885, accompanied by his queen, Soopyalot. The day the city fell, the white elephant died; and its body was dragged out of the palace-yard by the British troops on the following day. It was reported that the king ordered its destruction rather than have such a prize fall into the hands of the British.

This elephant, which was no whiter than the Barnum specimen, lived in great pomp in the palace enclosure, eating and drinking out of huge silver buckets.

The finest white elephant caught in late years is described by Mr. Carl Bock, who states that it was brought into Bangkok with all the pomp and ceremony of an emperor. According to Mr. Bock, it was quite an albino, the whole body being of a pale reddish-brown color, with a few white hairs on the back. The iris of the eye, the color of which is held to be a good test of an albino, was a pale Naples yellow. The animal was blessed and baptized in presence of the king and the nobility. One of the high priests presented it with a piece of sugar-cane, on which was written the elephant's name in full, and which it very readily ate. The following is a translation of its description painted on a red tablet, hung over one of the pillars of its stall: "An elephant of beautiful color; hair, nails, and eyes are white. Perfection in form, with all signs of regularity of the high family. The color of the skin is that of lotos. A descendant of the angels of the Brahmins. Acquired as property by the power and glory of the king for his service. Is equal to the crystal of the highest value. Is of the highest family of all in existence. A source of power of attraction of rain. It is as pure as the purest crystal of the highest value in the world."

As the white elephant is so highly esteemed in the Oriental countries, it would be surprising if obstacles were not laid in the way of their being taken to foreign lands. Hence a white elephant was never seen in a Western country before the advent of Mr. Barnum's now famous Toung Taloung, whose passage from its native country to America was highly exciting and dramatic.

The first white elephant ever seen out of its native land was one that was exhibited in Holland in 1633. The second was the Barnum elephant, which was brought to England in 1884, and from there shipped to America.[1]

Sir John Bowring states that it is almost impossible to put a price upon a white elephant; and he mentions fifty thousand dollars as a sum that might buy one; adding that a single hair from the tail of a white elephant was worth a Jew's ransom. The Barnum white elephant, it is said, cost two hundred thousand dollars by the time it was landed in America, — probably the most expensive pachyderm that ever lived. The agents sent to Siam and Burmah by Mr. Barnum had instructions to obtain the finest white elephant that money could buy. They crossed the Pacific, sailed down the coast of China, and finally reached Siam, where they endeavored to gain an interview with the first king. By him they were referred to the second, who indignantly refused their offer to purchase one of the white elephants. Some of the people, hearing of it, became enraged; and the men narrowly escaped injury. For months they followed up various clews, but at last found an elephant owned by the estate of a nobleman, whose widow agreed to part with the animal, which to her was an expensive luxury. Finally all arrangements were made; and the elephant was placed in a boat, and floated down the Irrawaddy to Rangoon. At almost every village they had difficulty, the people seeming to have a strong objection to the creature leaving the country: finally some fanatical natives secreted themselves

[1] See Plate XI.

in the steamer, and, it is believed, poisoned the noble animal, for it died suddenly before reaching Singapore. I have seen photographs of it, and the tusks are now in the possession of Mr. J. H. Hutchinson of New York. The elephant was, if any thing, a finer specimen than Toung Taloung.

The white-elephant hunters became so discouraged, that they returned home, but were, however, sent out again, and went through almost a repetition of their former experience. Through the influence of some English residents, they finally secured a typical white elephant. The permission of King Theebaw was essential before it could leave the country, and this was obtained with the condition that the white elephant should always receive the same attention that it did in Burmah. This was readily consented to, as it was to Mr. Barnum's interest to exhibit the animal with the same surroundings that characterized its life in Siam. The following is the bill of sale sworn to by H. Porter, Esq., notary public at Rangoon: —

NINTH DECREE OF TA SUNG MONG 1245 (BURMESE ERA). AT KAREN VILLAGE, DOANG DAMEE.

We who have signed below, Moung Tsaw, Kyah Yoe, Shoay Att Hpaw, these three having heard the statement of the American master, a rich man's agent from a distant country who wishes to have and possess the Nyan Zone [sacred elephant] Toung Taloung, which we now own, from the estate of Htan Yoe Ban, who is dead. We having sworn him [the agent] before God, and under the holy tree on the hill, he promises he will take him [elephant] straight to his master, to love and protect him from all misery. If not, he knows he cannot escape the evil abode. We have got from American master 30,000 gold rupees [about $200,000] to repair our gods, images, and monasteries.

We write and give this document under our own free will and to sign.

MOUNG TSAW.
KYAH YOE.
SHOAY ATT HPAW.

MOUNG H. PAY, *District Elder.*

A CERTIFICATE OF IDENTITY.

In the year 1245, month of Ta Sung Mong, fifth increase at Mandalay, I, Moung Thee, minister of royal elephants, hereby certify that the elephant named Toung Taloung is the species of white sacred elephant, and possesses the qualifications and attributes of such.

By order of

HPOUNGDAW GYEE HPAYAH,
King and Lord of all White Elephants, Moung Thee.

(Signed) W. MALLING,
Translator.

Other papers and testimonials from prominent people accompanied these documents, testifying to its identity; and, every thing being in readiness, the march was commenced from Mandalay overland to Rangoon, a distance of seven hundred miles. This trip was one of no little danger. They were continually stopped in native towns; and rumors followed them to the effect that King Theebaw had changed his mind, fearing that ill luck would follow the loss of one of the animals. But finally the little band, which consisted of several white men and natives, Toung Taloung, and four black elephants, upon which were three white monkeys, the images of the Buddhist god Gautama, the golden umbrellas, etc., reached the Irrawaddy River, four hundred miles from Mandalay. In one village they were nearly mobbed; in another imprisoned, and a lawsuit commenced. But finally they were released; and the white elephant was placed on the steamer "Tenasserim," and, guarded day and night, crossed the Bay of Bengal, and safely reached Liverpool, from where it was shipped to the United States. I was invited to go down the bay on the special steamer to be among the first to see a white elephant on American shores; and I well remember the smile of satisfaction that illumined the face of the genial Barnum, when an ex-United-States minister to one of the Eastern countries, who was of the party, spoke up, and said, as we all stood around the sacred beast in the hold of the "Lydian Monarch," "I have seen all the white elephants of the kings of Burmah and Siam, and consider this an exceptionally fine example of what is known as the sacred white elephant."

The general public, however, expected to see a pure white elephant, and naturally much criticism was provoked. I believe that Mr. Barnum now claims as much credit in educating the American public as to what constitutes a white elephant, as he did in bringing the historic animal from its native country.

Toung Taloung is a finely formed elephant, about eight feet in height, with perfect and finely developed tusks three feet in length. Its nails are ivory-hued, and its general color a light gray, which presents some contrast to ordinary elephants. Upon the head, trunk, and ears are several pink blotches, white by courtesy, or, rather, because King Theebaw chose to consider them so.

Toung Taloung has a mild and peaceful disposition, and does not object in the slightest to being fed upon delicacies, and waited upon by native attendants. He is now about sixteen years old.

A second so-called white elephant, the "Light of Asia," was imported into this country by Adam Forepaugh of Philadelphia soon after the advent of Toung Taloung. It is a male, about seven years old, and a little over five feet in height, its tusks just appearing.

CHAPTER XI.

ELEPHANTS IN CEYLON.[1]

WHILE the elephant of Ceylon does not differ specifically from its cousins of Continental India, there are certain facts of interest about it that would seem to warrant special attention. In 1847, according to Tennent, they were found over nearly the entire island, with the exception of a narrow but densely inhabited belt of cultivated land that extends along the seaboard from Chilaw on the Western coast to Tangalle on the south-east: this is, to some extent, true to-day, their great tracks being found in forests and plains where the surroundings are adapted to their requirements. There has, however, been a noticeable diminution of their numbers in certain localities.

Thus, Le Brun, who visited Ceylon in 1705, says that then they were very abundant in the country about Colombo, and that he had seen one hundred and sixty at a time in a corral. It is also known, that, in olden times, it was necessary in some localities to keep fires burning at night, in order to keep them away from the rice-fields. The opening up of the country, and the clearing off of the mountain forests of Kandy by coffee-planters, has also restricted their range; while sportsmen and others have greatly reduced their numbers.

[1] See Plate XII.

From the date of the first Punic war, the natives have been aware of their value, and have captured them to send to India for various purposes, — formerly for use in war, and to-day as laborers in the great lumber-yards, and in other positions where great strength is required.

The number of elephants exported from Ceylon between the years 1863 and 1876 was sixteen hundred and fifty-seven, a showing that has no comparison with Africa. The Ceylon elephants are remarkable for the absence of tusks. So marked is this, a Ceylon elephant with these sexual weapons is something of a curiosity, not one in a hundred having them, and then only the males being the fortunate possessors. They are not totally unarmed; as nearly all have stunted tusks, generally about a foot in length, and two inches in diameter. With these they loosen earth, strip the bark from trees, and tear down climbing-plants. That the tusks are in general use, is shown by the fact that nearly all have a groove worn in the extremities.

Many ingenious theories have been advanced to explain this lack of development. The most feasible explanation would seem to be, that, in Ceylon, the elephants had less use for weapons of defence than on the main-land.

The Ceylon elephant leads a quiet, pastoral life compared to its ally of Africa, who, if not attacked, is menaced by rhinoceros and lion; while the tiger, though not the master of the Asiatic elephant, infuses it with a wholesome dread, and will attack it if the true king of beasts is at a disadvantage.

In the chapter on Continental Asiatic Elephants, the distinguishing points of elephants are given. In Ceylon, they differ again; and in a Singhalese work, the "Hastisilpe," which treats of the management of these animals, the author says an inferior elephant (one that corresponds probably to the Meerga caste) has "eyes restless like those of a crow, the hair of the head mixed shades, the nails short and green, the ears small, the neck thin, the skin freckled, the tail without a tuft, and the fore-quarters lean and low." The perfect type, corresponding to the Koomeriah grade of India, is characterized by "softness of the skin, the red color of the mouth and tongue, the forehead expanded and hollow, the ears broad and rectangular, the trunk broad at the root, and blotched with pink in front, the eyes bright and kindly, the cheeks large, the neck full, the back level, the chest square, the fore-legs short, and convex in front, the hindquarter plump, and five nails on each foot, all smooth, polished, and round." An elephant with these perfections, says the same author, "will impart glory and magnificence to the king: but he cannot be discovered among thousands; yea, there shall never be found an elephant clothed at once with all the excellences here described."

The noises which Ceylon elephants utter, while undoubtedly identical with those of India and Bengal, seem to have a rather different meaning imputed to them. The shrill cry uttered through the trunk is indicative of rage, and is generally given when the animal is rushing upon its adversary. When the attention of an individual elephant of a herd is attracted by any unusual object, the intelligence is conveyed to the others by a low, suppressed sound, uttered by the lips, and compared by hunters to the word "prut," or the twittering of a bird. Major Macready, military secretary of Ceylon, describes a sound that he heard made by a wild elephant as "a sort of a banging noise, like a cooper hammering a cask," produced, he believes, by the animal striking its sides rapidly with its trunk. It may have been made, as has been previously described, by striking the tip of the trunk against the ground.

In size the Ceylon elephants average about the same as the continental animals, about nine feet. Wolf, a chaplain, who resided in Ceylon many years, states that he saw one that was taken near Jaffna which was twelve feet in height. Perhaps this animal was measured by throwing a rope over its back, and accepting one-half as the height, which would be at least twelve inches in excess of what it should be. The herds in Ceylon are generally families, and, as a rule, greatly resemble each other. The most powerful tusker is the leader, though a strong-minded female is often implicitly obeyed. Tennent considers that a herd recognizes the tusker-in-chief as a leader, and will support him in danger. He cites an instance where a tusker was wounded, and the rest of the herd crowded about him, covering his retreat to the forest. I am inclined to think, however, that the observers misinterpreted the actions of the herd, and that the tusker's presence in the centre was accidental, or the result of his superior strength.

That elephants have a method of communication, no one can doubt. An interesting instance of this was reported to Sir Emerson Tennent by Major Skinner of the British army, who spent many years in the jungle, and was a competent and intelligent observer. He says, "The case you refer to struck me as exhibiting something more than ordinary brute instinct, and approached nearer to reasoning powers than any other instance I can now remember. I cannot do jus-

HERD OF ELEPHANTS, CEYLON.

Page 137.

tice to the scene; although it appeared to me at the time to be so remarkable, that it left a deep impression in my mind. In the dry season in Nenera-Kalawa, you know the streams are all dried up, and the tanks nearly so. All animals are then sorely pressed for water; and they congregate in the vicinity of those tanks, in which there may remain ever so little of the precious element. During one of these seasons, I was encamped on the bund, or embankment, of a very small tank, the water in which was so dried that its surface could not have exceeded five hundred square yards. It was the only pond within many miles, and I knew that of necessity a very large herd of elephants which had been in the neighborhood all day must resort to it at night. On the lower side of the tank, and on a line with the embankment, was a thick forest, in which the elephants sheltered themselves during the day. On the upper side, and all about the tank, there was considerable margin of open ground. It was one of those beautiful, bright, clear, moonlight nights, when objects could be seen almost as distinctly as by day; and I determined to avail myself of the opportunity to observe the movements of the herd, which had already manifested some uneasiness at our presence. The locality was very favorable for my purpose, and an enormous tree projecting over the tank afforded me a secure lodgement in its branches. Having ordered the fires of my camp to be extinguished at an early hour, and all my followers to retire to rest, I took up my post of observation on the overhanging bough; but I had to remain for upwards of two hours before any thing was to be seen or heard of the elephants, although I knew they were within five hundred yards of me. At length, about the distance of three hundred feet from the water, an immensely large elephant issued from the dense cover, and advanced cautiously across the open ground to within one hundred yards of the tank, where he stood perfectly motionless. So quiet had the elephants become, although they had been roaring, and beating the jungle, throughout the day and evening, that not a movement was now heard.

"The huge vidette remained in his position still as a rock for a few moments, and then made three successive stealthy advances of several yards (halting for some minutes between each, with ears bent forward to catch the slightest sound); and, in this way, he moved slowly up to the water's edge. Still, he did not venture to quench his thirst; for, though his fore-feet were partially in the water, he remained for some minutes, listening in perfect silence. He returned cautiously and slowly to the position he had at first taken upon emerging from the forest. Here, in a little while, he was joined by five others; with them he again proceeded, as cautiously, but less slowly, to within a few yards of the tank, and then posted his patrols. He then re-entered the forest, and collected around him the whole herd, between eighty and one hundred, led them across the open ground with the most extraordinary composure and quietness till he joined the advance-guard, when he left them for a moment, and repeated his former *reconnaissance* at the edge of the tank. Having apparently satisfied himself that all was safe, he returned, and obviously gave the order to advance; for in a moment the whole herd rushed into the water with a degree of unreserved confidence so opposite to the caution and timidity which had marked their previous movements, that nothing will ever persuade me that there was not rational and preconcerted co-operation throughout the whole party, and a degree of responsible authority exercised by the patriarch leader."

The caution exhibited by the elephants here mentioned is characteristic of these animals; and so suspicious are they, that a fence of the simplest kind is often sufficient to prevent their inroads. Near Anarájapoora, there was formerly a pond, in which elephants drank; and near by, enclosed in a very frail fence, was some vegetation growing, especially attractive to the elephant; yet the latter was a complete protection to it.

From caution or curiosity, elephants often pull up the tracing-pegs put down by surveyors; and this has also been noticed in the continental elephants.

Some of the bravest elephant-hunters are found in Ceylon. They follow the animal as a profession, and are called panickeas, and live in the Moorish villages in the northern and north-eastern part of the island. Their remarkable skill in following the huge game calls to mind that of the Indians of our own continent. Frequently two panickeas will chase an elephant, and capture it single-handed. Their method is to keep to the leeward of the animal, and creep upon it when feeding, and fasten a slip-noose about the leg, that is often lifted, or kept in motion. This accomplished, the elephant turns, and endeavors to break away; but the rope is secured to a tree, and the monster is caught. A man now rushes in front, and shouts the monosyllable, "*Dah! dah!*" that seems to have some irritating effect. This attracts attention from the other man, who now throws a noose about the other leg; and soon the elephant is completely in the toils. A covering is then built over it, a camp formed, and the initiatory training performance commenced.

The animals are generally trained, however, by Arabs, and go to the rajahs and native princes in India, whose agents were formerly, and to some extent at present, sent to Ceylon for the purpose.

So brave are these men, that they seem to have absolutely no fear of the elephant; and, if the white hunter is known to them as a good shot, they will go up to an elephant, and slap him on the leg to make him turn, and present to their employer a vulnerable spot.

Most of the captured elephants of Ceylon are taken to Manaar: that is an important elephant depot, from which they are bought, and shipped to India. Arabs resort here, buying horses to exchange for elephants, and to trade in them in many ways.

Elephants have been captured by the herd in Ceylon from very early times; the process, as late as 1847, differing but little from that employed in India to-day. The animals were driven into a corral, and often two thousand men were employed in the hunt. Formerly the natives were forced to join in the hunt; but, in later years, they have been only too willing, as the elephants destroy their crops. The priests also encourage the hunters, as the elephants devour the sacred Bo-trees; and they are also desirous of obtaining the animals for use in the processions of the temples.

In the drive, the men stretch out, and surround the elephants; and, when they are encompassed, fires are built ten paces apart, and kept burning all day and night. Gradually they close in on the victims; and in every direction, except that of the corral, a fusillade of guns is kept up, accompanied by shouts, and beating of drums, until finally the terrified animals rush into the corral, and are caught. When the elephants are entrapped, female elephants with riders enter the corral; and soon the captives are noosed, and tied to trees. Then commence the struggles that often continue for hours; the huge beasts assuming the most seemingly impossible positions, — standing on their heads, twisting their bodies into various shapes, breaking down trees, and venting their rage in a variety of ways, — until, utterly wearied, they lie or stand, and throw dust over their bodies with their trunks, then insert the latter into their mouths, and withdraw enough water to convert it into mud.

The wonderful sagacity, if obedience to the mahouts can be called such, exhibited by the female elephant, is remarkable. They seem to understand just what is required of them, — butting over fractious captives, assisting to tie them, kneeling upon them when they attempt to rise too quickly, holding their trunks when they are directed to the approaching noose, and in every way assisting their drivers, and showing what would generally be considered great intelligence. "The whole scene," says Sir Emerson Tennent, "exhibits the most marvellous example of the voluntary alliance of animal sagacity and instinct in active co-operations with human intelligence and courage; and nothing else in nature, not even the chase of the whale, can afford so vivid an illustration of the sovereignty of man over the brute creation, even when confronted with force in its most stupendous embodiment."

The process of training the elephants is not so difficult as is generally supposed. For a few days, or until they eat freely, they are allowed to rest, a tame elephant being tied near to re-assure them; and, where a large number are being educated, wild ones are placed in stalls between half tame ones, until they take their food regularly. In the first lesson, the head stableman, or "Cooroowe vidahn," takes his place in front of a wild elephant, bearing a long, sharp, iron-pointed stick. Two other men station themselves on each side, assisted by the tame elephants, and hold their crooks toward the wild elephant's trunk; while others rub his back soothingly, chanting such epithets as, "Ho! my son," or, "Ho! my father." This irritates the animal, who immediately strikes out with his trunk, the men receiving it upon their weapons; and, in a very short time, the elephant learns not to strike at a man.

This lesson having been inculcated, number two is begun, which consists in taking it to bathe between two tame elephants. The feet are tied as closely as possible, and the great beast is made to lie down in the water by pressing its backbone with the crooks. This is extremely painful, and is met by furious protests; but finally the animals learn to kneel at the slightest prick of the sharp weapons, and having once succumbed to the power of man, as shown in a number of ways, rapidly become domesticated. Kind treatment does much toward conciliating them; but, like people, each elephant has its own peculiar disposition.

In two months a wild elephant may be led without a tame companion; and in three months they are generally put to work, at first in treading clay in brick-fields, or harnessed to a wagon with a tame companion, and finally in the lumber-yards, where all their intelligence is brought to play.

The Ceylon elephants attain an age equal to that of the Indian animals. Trained elephants have been kept in use one hundred and forty years; and, according to Tennent, one employed by Mr. Cripps was represented by the Cooroowe people to have served the king of Kandy in the same capacity sixty years before. Among the papers left by Col. Robertson, who held a command in Ceylon in 1799, shortly after the capture of the island by the British, there is a memorandum showing that a decoy (female) was then attached to the elephant establishment at Molura, which the records proved to have served under the Dutch during the entire period of their occupation (extending to upwards of one hundred and forty years). It was said to have been found in the stables by the Dutch on the expulsion of the Portuguese in 1650.

CHAPTER XII.

ROGUE ELEPHANTS.

THE popular opinion concerning the elephant is, that it is treacherous, quick to avenge an insult, and possesses a specially retentive memory regarding injuries received. This is an exaggeration: when compared to other animals, the elephant excels in its good qualities. Vices are found only in exceptional cases; the average males being, as a rule, safe, and not susceptible to sudden changes of temper; while the females are particularly mild and gentle. Sanderson says, "Among hundreds that I have known, only two have had any tricks. One of these would not allow herself to be ridden by a strange mahout, and the other had a great aversion to any natives but her own two attendants approaching her."

In the management of these animals, strict discipline always has to be maintained. Mr. P. T. Barnum tells me, that while his herd of twenty or more are treated with the greatest kindness, yet fear is the secret of their obedience. The keeper never relaxes his power over them; and, if not in sight, the steel hook and pointer of their trainer, though, perhaps, concealed, is always at hand, and ready for use. Even the most gentle elephants, particularly the males, are liable in confinement to outbursts of fury; becoming ungovernable, and doing great damage before they can be subdued or killed.

Without warning, an elephant, which for years had been a quiet and docile member of the East Indian commissariat stud, became possessed of a veritable demon, broke loose, and fled trumpeting to the woods. For many weeks, it was a constant terror to the entire country in the vicinity; — rushing into villages, destroying houses; and, before it was killed, thirty-five human beings fell victims to its fury.

Such instances are comparatively rare; and it should be said to the credit of the elephant, that while it is really the king of beasts, and capable of greater destruction than any in India, it has less casualties laid to its door than any so-called dangerous animal. The following table indicates this more plainly, and shows the number of persons and domestic animals destroyed by wild mammals in India during the year 1875, the numbers being about the same every year: —

ANIMALS.	PERSONS KILLED.	DOMESTIC ANIMALS KILLED.
Elephant	61	6
Tiger	828	12,423
Leopard	187	16,157
Bears	84	522
Wolves	1,061	9,407
Hyenas	68	2,116

The Philadelphia elephant Dom, who was named in honor of Dom Pedro of Brazil, occasionally gave way to fits of rage, became unmanageable; and people flocked to the garden to see it disciplined. This consisted of securing each foot at a time, and hauling them apart by strong tackles, so that the huge beast was utterly powerless.

Travelling around the country seems to irritate elephants, and reports are often seen of their outbursts of rage. The famous Chief, owned by Robinson, became enraged at Charlotte, N.C., a few years ago, and, without the slightest warning, killed its keeper. The latter was attempting to illustrate to the audience how the elephant climbed into the special car provided for it, when the animal lost its patience, and hurled the unfortunate man against the car with terrific force, killing him before the very eyes of the people.

Tom, the pet elephant of the Duke of Edinburgh, who was brought from India in 1870 in H. R. H's yacht, "Galatea," killed its keeper in very much the same way.

The greatest elephant panic ever seen in this country was that created by Barnum's Emperor, who suddenly developed all the characteristics of a rogue, while the circus was exhibiting in Troy, N.Y. The trouble commenced when an attempt was made to drive Emperor and Jumbo to the train. The former had decided objections to continuing the tour; and he suddenly bolted, and shuffled furiously up the street in the direction of the iron-foundery of Erastus Corning. The large door being open, the excited animal rushed in, and in a moment was trampling upon the red-hot coal and metal, uttering fierce shrieks. And now utterly enraged and mad, he rushed from the building into the crowded streets, trampling upon men, hurling others down an embankment with his trunk, breaking one man's leg in his flight, throwing another twenty feet into the air, while a woman was taken from the stoop of a house and hurled into the street. In fact, the demon of rage seemed to possess the huge creature, that ran amuck until he had destroyed four thousand dollars' worth of property.

Another rogue elephant was Romeo, owned by the Forepaugh Company, who died in Chicago in 1872, having killed three men, and destroyed property valued at fifty thousand dollars.

Almost equally vicious was Mr. Barnum's Albert. This elephant killed its keeper at Keene, N.H.; and, after being loaded with chains, it was led out into the woods, followed by a large crowd, and a company of Keene riflemen. Its trainer, Arstinstall, marked the location of the heart upon the dark hide of the unsuspecting giant; and at the word, the great animal fell.

These fits of frenzy are sometimes periodic, and the elephant is then said to be *must*, or mad. The paroxysms vary in different animals. Some are lethargic, or sleepy; while others go mad, and endeavor to wreak vengeance upon any thing within reach. In the chapter on the anatomy of the elephant, reference is made to a pore in the temple of the animal; and, when expert elephant-men see an oily liquid exuding from this orifice, they accept it as a warning that the period of *must* is approaching; the elephant is immediately shackled, and keepers and strangers are warned to keep out of reach.

After this secretion has flowed for a while, the temples swell, and the animal is avoided by every one; its food being tossed at it, or pushed toward it on the end of a pole. If, during this time, the elephant escapes, destruction of human life is almost sure to follow. They attack every living creature, including their own kind. Sanderson says, "I once saw one of our tuskers, which was then only under suspicion of an approaching fit, break away from the control of his mahout, as he was being ridden to water, and, despite severe punishment, attack, knock down, another elephant near by; and, had his tusks not been cut, he would, without doubt, have killed her on the spot. He was at last driven off by spears thrown at his trunk and head. Then he stalked across the open plain with his mahout on his neck, fury in his eye, master of all he surveyed, and evidently courting battle from any created being. The men had a difficult and dangerous task to secure him. His hind-legs were at last tied from behind the trunk of a tree, near which he stood; and the mahout having drawn up a chain by a cord, and secured it around his neck, he was moored fore and aft. I shall never forget the mahout's fervent ejaculation of 'Allah! Allah!' as he slipped over the elephant's tail when he was made fast." According to Mr. Sanderson, the flow of *must* is observed in both male and female elephants, but never in the tame females.

Besides the elephants which are supposed to have bad tempers, and occasionally exhibit them, there are certain animals which are by nature ugly, and more or less untrustworthy. These are called rogues, and by some, from their seeming love of a solitary life, "solitaries." The rogue elephants, or solitaries, are popularly supposed to be soured individuals, who have been driven from a herd by rivals or companions; but this is a mistake, as investigation has shown that supposed solitaries were often old tuskers grazing some distance from a herd.

Certain elephants undoubtedly prefer a solitary life: but the so-called solitar is generally a young male who has not been able to assert his position in the herd, and is grazing along the outskirts; or is an old and bold tusker, who wanders about careless of its safety.

All seemingly isolated elephants are looked upon with suspicion, as, when met, they often rush to the attack, and prove dangerous enemies. The real rogue is usually a vicious tusker, such as *Mandla*, an elephant that was owned near Jubbulpore, Central Provinces. This brute was supposed to be mad, and, in 1875, suddenly developed a taste for human victims, — rushing at them at sight, attacking houses, or any object that excited its ire, and ultimately killing a large number of persons. This monster not only killed its victims, but is said to have eaten them, tearing the bodies limb from limb, and was known before its death as the man-eater. This is probably an exaggeration; the fact being, that the elephant took the victim in its mouth while it tore him in pieces, the demoralized natives thinking that it was eating him. An organized hunt was made for this elephant, and it was finally killed by two English officers.

A few years ago elephants in various parts of India, especially about Morlay, became so fearless, that they entered fields adjoining the towns, and did great damage; some, showing the disposition of the typical rogue, could hardly be driven away. In one case in India, a number of Oopligas drove a herd into the hills with their horns and tomtoms; and, a heavy rain coming on, they thought it hardly necessary to keep up the guard, so retired from the field. In the morning, they found that a valuable lot of the Indian maize (*Sorghum vulgare*) had been destroyed, the entire herd returning as soon as the noise had ceased. Mr. Sanderson caught this entire herd in 1874.

About thirty years before the man-eating elephant was heard of, a male rogue elephant created great devastation in the fields of the Morlayites. It was continually breaking into their rice; but one morning, being seen near a village, the entire population turned out, and with hue and cry gave chase. The rogue, who was also a coward, dashed away, rushing blindly into a marsh, or morass, and soon sank to its knees in soft mud, and was almost completely at the mercy of the pursuers. They surrounded it, and rained stones and other missiles upon it; and finally, one native, more revengeful and cruel than the others, threw some lighted straw upon the poor creature's back. The terrible wounds seemed to spur it to greater exertions; and it finally escaped, and ultimately recovered, being often seen and recognized by its scars.

Sanderson mentions two tuskers which travelled about together, "twin solitaries." They were extremely vicious, had killed people, and were finally proscribed by the government. One of the tuskers was killed by Mr. Sanderson in 1870. Referring to rogue elephants which he had observed, he says, "I had just finished dinner, and was enjoying a smoke before a blazing camp-fire, which lit to their topmost branches a pair of magnificent tamarind-trees, under which my tent was pitched, when I heard a distant shout of 'Ánay!' (elephants). At once, lights began to flit over the plain, moving towards one point; tomtoms were beaten, and rattles made from split bamboo sounded. An elephant trumpeted shrilly, the men yelled in defiance, till the intruders retreated to the jungle. The cover bordering on cultivation was so dense as to afford secure shelter to elephants close at hand, even during the day. After some little time, when the tomtomming and noise had ceased, a similar commotion took place at another point: again the Will-o'-the-wisp lights moved forward, with a repetition of the shouting and trumpeting.

The villagers who were keeping up my camp-fire told me that it was only on occasional nights that the elephants visited cultivation. The watchers were evidently in for it now, and they became thoroughly alert at all points.

"Once the elephants came within two hundred yards of my camp; and, long after I went to bed, I heard the shouting and rattling of the watchers. These men were the Strolagas from the hills: they were hired annually for a month or two, at a fixed payment in grain, for watching their crops, by the low-country cultivators, who are themselves less able to stand the exposure on a rice-flat, and less bold in interfering with elephants. The watchers provide themselves with torches of light split bamboos in bundles, about eight feet long, and eight inches in diameter. These are lighted at one end, when required, and make a famous blaze. Armed with them, the men sally forth to the spot where the elephants are feeding. Some carry the torches; the others precede them, so as to have the light behind them. The elephants can be seen on open ground one hundred yards, should they wait to let the lights get so close. Some troublesome rogues get beyond caring for this; though the men are very bold, and approach within forty or fifty yards. Natives have often told me of particular elephants letting them get within a few yards, and then putting their trunks into their mouths, and withdrawing water, squirting it at the lights. I hardly need say that the latter part of the statement is purely imaginary; the idea doubtless arising from the attitude elephants often assume when in uncertainty or perplexity, putting the trunk into the mouth, and holding the tip gently between the lips."

The large area of rice-fields on the bed of the Honganoor Lake was assessed long ago at one-third the usual rates, on account of the depredations of elephants. Mr. Sanderson adds, however, that the actual damage done to crops by elephants is much less than popularly supposed.

In capturing wild elephants, numbers of tuskers which have escaped, often follow the herd, and wander about the camps at night. On one occasion, a large female charged a tame elephant and rider. The latter was warned by a native, and slipped around his elephant's neck just in time to save his life; but the jaws of the old rogue struck his thigh, and she endeavored to crush him with her single tusk. He drove his goad into her mouth, when she drew off, and came on again at full speed. The rider again dodged over his elephant's neck, and a second time the single tusk struck his leg. This was repeated several times; and the rider, whose elephant was in the midst of a herd of wild ones in a corral, was in despair, when one of his assistants hurled a spear, striking the rogue in the head. A moment later, the latter's elephant struck her a terrific blow, head on, almost knocking her over, and completely turning the scales.

Tame tuskers, under the direction of a mahout, soon outwit wild elephants in a battle. Females rarely fight among themselves; but, when they do, their spite is vented upon one another in a ludicrous and aggravating manner, by biting off each other's tails.

Sanderson had a singular adventure with a rogue elephant who attempted to enter his tent at night. He started to his feet, first seeing his tent rip, and, on looking out, discovered that a wild elephant was tearing it with its tusks. The next day, it was found torn in two, with two tusk-holes in it. The next night a guard of men and a tame elephant was established; but at midnight, he was awakened by feeling the tent shake. Leaping to his feet, he looked out, saw the men asleep, and the tame elephant some distance off. While he stood, there came a crash, and the small tent fell in; when he found that probably the same elephant was investigating again; but, before he could clear himself from the canvas, it had made off, startled by the noise. The attack was probably made out of mere curiosity, or, perhaps, in a spirit of mischief. They have been known to trample down embankments, overturn telegraph-poles, haul up surveying-pins; and once, when a surveying-party left their chain over night in a jungle, it could be heard jingling occasionally, the elephants evidently being pleased with the sound it made.

A famous rogue elephant for months devastated the country about Kákankoté. It first destroyed the crops; and gradually becoming bolder and bolder, it finally actually took possession of a strip of the country about eight miles long, including a part of the main road between Mysore and the Wynaad. No one dared to travel in the road; the monster charging every one, finally killing two natives. This aroused the populace; and the amildár, or native official, appealed to the government elephant-keeper for protection. A few days later, he was on the ground, and, with a party of Kurrabas trackers, was ready to slay the rogue. So great was the alarm, that the hunter found native policemen at the entrance of the jungle, to warn travellers of the elephant; and all who went through were preceded by natives, who, with tomtoms and other instruments, endeavored to frighten the brute, who was well known to every one by his large size, black color, and peculiar, up-curved, short tusks. For several days the professional hunter followed the great animal, and came up with him; but, by an unfortunate stampede, he lost him, and the hunt had to be given up for the time. Five months later it was renewed: and, after a long chase, the rogue was found in a bamboo thicket; then, after waiting for a fair shot, the hunter fired a heavy bullet, putting it just behind the shoulder.

For a second, there was a deathly silence, then, with a terrific scream, the monster dashed away; and the men, in full pursuit, were soon covered with blood that flowed from the wounds. The rogue ran for two hundred yards, and, when the Kurrabas came upon him, presented a terrible appearance. He was facing his foes, his trunk doubled, head elevated, and blood rushing from his mouth; yet the animal's eyes were gleaming with fury, and it was ready to sell its life dearly. The hunter fired with a four-bore rifle; the bullet penetrating the brain, and killing him upon the spot. As the huge creature rolled over, the men crawled upon its upper side, which was six feet from the grass. The head and feet were taken; the former being placed on the main road for some time, to inform the natives that the end of the rogue had come.

The tusks of this elephant were small, being ten inches in circumference at the gum, and weighed twenty-two and a half pounds, curving up in a curious way.

Capt. Dunlop, of the British army, refers to a rogue elephant in the Doon, named Gunesh. It was the property of the government, but escaped, and for years caused a reign of terror in the country. It had a chain upon its leg, and the clank of this in the jungle near a village demoralized the entire populace. For fifteen years this brute wandered about, destroying rice-fields; and, during that time, it killed over fifteen persons.

Another rogue followed a courier of the English postal service, and trampled him to death.

While the canal of Beejapore was being made, a rogue elephant charged upon the men from some bushes, and seized one; then, pressing the body under its ponderous feet, the fiend deliberately pulled away the upper portion of it, and with a remnant in its trunk ran back into the bush.

Some woodmen engaged in cutting trees in the jungle about Chandnee-Doon, had an almost identical experience. One day three of them remained at home; while, during the day, one of the men went to a neighboring spring to draw some water. As he did not return, one of his companions went after him; and that evening they were both found dead, their bones being crushed and broken. The rogue had seized and thrown them to the ground, crushing them by a tread of its ponderous foot.

In Ceylon, the rogue is called a *hora*, or *ronkedor;* the Singhalese, according to Tennent, believing it to be an individual that has either lost its associates by accident, and, from its solitary life, become morose and savage; or a naturally vicious individual, that, being more daring, has separated itself from its companions. Whatever may be the reason for the savage temper exhibited by these solitary brutes, they constitute a characteristic of elephant life, and, in Ceylon, seem to possess the same likes and dislikes that mark the African and Asiatic rogues.

More daring than the peacefully disposed elephants, they come out of the jungle at night, and prowl around the towns and villages, trampling down cultivated tracts, devouring the standing rice and young cocoa-palms, becoming so bold in some places, that one has been known to enter a field, and seize a sheaf from a pile in the very midst of a party of workers, who fled in terror. As a rule, however, they remain concealed by day, committing their depredations by night. In some sections, as the low country of Badulla, the villagers build moats or ditches about their huts to protect themselves from the rogues.

Certain localities seem to be infested by these creatures. Thus, in 1847, a dangerous rogue frequented the Rangbodde Pass on a mountain road, that led to the Sanitarium at Neuera-ellia, and demoralized the entire country so that people were afraid to undertake the pass unless in numbers. Its method of attack was to seize natives, as it did a Caffre of the Caffre Corps of pioneers, with its trunk, and beat the victim to death against the bank.

Some years ago a native trader and party were travelling near Idalgasinna, when they suddenly heard the shrill trumpeting of a rogue. The entire company took to their heels; the coolies casting away their goods, and making for the jungle. The trader himself hid behind a large rock, and saw the elephant seize one of the coolies, and, after carrying him a short distance, dash him to the ground, and trample upon him; then turning to the goods they carried, he tore them in pieces, after which he walked into the jungle. This elephant was a noted rogue, and in its time destroyed the lives of a number of people. He was finally killed by an English sportsman.

A native made a statement to a Singhalese gentleman, who in turn imparted the information to Sir Emerson Tennent, that once, when he was on his way to Badulla, and walking around a hill, a large elephant rushed upon his party without warning, trumpeting loudly. In a moment, he had seized the native's companion, who, it happened, was in the rear, and killed him by hurling him to the ground. Dropping the first victim, he then seized the narrator of the incident, and hurled him aloft with such force that he landed in the branches of a cahata-tree, and lodged there, thus escaping with only a dislocation of the wrist. The elephant returned to the body upon the ground, and tore it limb from limb, mutilating it as much as possible.

Rogue elephants in Ceylon are often very mischievous. In some sections, the tracing-pegs that have been put down by surveyors during one day, are pulled up the next by elephants. Rogues, like other elephants, are very suspicious. Col. Hardy, at one time deputy quartermaster-general in Ceylon, was travelling to an outpost in the south-eastern portion of the island, and one day became lost, and was attacked at dusk by a rogue. He ran for cover, but was almost caught, when he happened to think of his dressing-case; and, throwing it down, his pursuer came to an immediate standstill, stopping to examine it carefully, while the officer escaped.

Other rogues destroy every thing they can find. In "The Colombo Observer" of March, 1858, there was a reward of twenty-five guineas offered for the destruction of an elephant that had taken up its residence in the Rajawallé coffee-plantation near Kandy. The huge animal terrified the people for miles about; its plan being, to come out of the jungle at night, and pull down buildings and trees on the plantation. It seemed to have an especial spite for the pipes of the water-works, the pillars of which it tore down; while the tops were all destroyed by this curious animal, who was finally shot.

Some years ago a rogue elephant was wounded near the town of Hambangtotte by a native, and followed the latter into the town in a wild race, catching him in the bazaar in the midst of the town, and trampling him to death before a crowd of people, then making good its escape.

Often tame elephants, excited by some means, become rogues for the time. During one of the attempts by the government to capture an entire herd in Ceylon, a fine tame tusker became intensely excited, and finally, in a frenzy of rage, broke down the bars of the corral with its head and tusks, and ran into the jungle. A few days later, its driver went after it with a decoy; when it approached, he courageously leaped upon the back of the maddened beast, and with a pair of hooks subdued it, until it was firmly chained, when it allowed itself to be led away.

That elephants do not easily forget, is shown in case of one that turned rogue, and escaped to the jungle, and, when recaptured ten years later, immediately obeyed the mahout's command to kneel.

That rogue elephants are sometimes the result of inhuman treatment, is shown in a terrible catastrophe, reported by an Indian correspondent of "The Pall Mall Gazette" as occurring in April of the present year, in which seventeen human beings lost their lives, and much valuable property was destroyed.

"While an elephant was being ridden by its keeper in the District of Sultanpore, in Oude, the animal resented 'prodding' with a spear, by pulling the man from his back, and throwing him some distance away. Fortunately the man fell in a hollow, and remained there undiscovered by the elephant, who went to a neighboring village. There he chased an old man into a house, then broke down the walls, pulled the man out, and dashed him to pieces. The same night the elephant knocked down several houses in quest of human beings, in the villages of Sardapur, Bargaon, and Jaisingpur. He killed six men in Bersoma, three in Sota, four in Gaugeo, and four in Mardan. He likewise killed a bullock and a pony, and also completely destroyed a new carriage. The animal used to stand at the door of a house, force his entry by demolishing the walls on either side, and would then kill as many of the inmates as he could, pursuing others who tried to run away. He mangled the corpses terribly. After securing a victim, he sometimes returned to the spot to see if life were extinct, and would commence mutilating the body afresh. He carried several bodies long distances, and threw them into ravines, etc. The elephant found his way to the Dehra Rajah's palace, where he tried to enter the house of a gardener; but some men mounted on three elephants, assisted by spearmen, drove him off. He then returned to Bebipur, where he tried to break down his master's house, in which several persons had taken refuge. The police got into the house from a back window, and were obliged to send for help to the Dehra Rajah, who sent three elephants and some spearmen. The animal received two gun-shots on the head at Bebipur, which, however, only temporarily drove him off. He was ultimately captured at imminent risk, by the rajah's three elephants and men."

CHAPTER XIII.

HUNTING THE AFRICAN ELEPHANT.

FROM the huge size of its body and tusks, the African elephant affords, if any thing, a better opportunity of testing the skill and endurance of the hunter than its Asiatic ally. In former years, the great game was found from the Southern limit of Sahara to Cape Town; but so insatiate has been the greed for ivory, that it has been gradually driven from the more exposed tracts, and is now confined to the most unfrequented parts of the great continent; and as it is only with great difficulty and incalculable hardship that it can be followed, the animal is rarely hunted at the present day for pure sport, the ivory tusks alone being the desideratum. As about one hundred thousand elephants are killed every year, and they are slow breeders, their utter extermination seems only a matter of time. If the present depletion of the numbers of the African species continues, it will be but a memory of the past in a comparatively few years.

The African elephant is followed in several ways. Some hunters, as Baldwin, prefer to depend upon horses, and, so mounted, follow the herd at full speed, leaping from the saddle, firing quickly, and avoiding the charge by the fleetness of the horse. Others, as Selous, prefer shooting on foot. The latter met with an extraordinary adventure while following a fine elephant, and narrowly escaped. The following is his account:—

"My horse was now so tired that he stood well; so, reining in, I gave her a shot from his back between the neck and the shoulder, which I believe just stopped her from charging. On receiving this wound, she backed a few paces, gave her ears a flap against her sides, and then stood facing me again. I had just taken out the empty cartridge, and was about to put a fresh one in, when, seeing that she looked very vicious, and as I was not thirty yards from her, I caught the bridle, and turned the horse's head away, so as to be ready for a fair start in case of a charge. I was still holding my rifle with the breech open, when I saw that she was coming. Digging the spurs into my horse's ribs, I did my best to get him away; but he was so thoroughly done, that instead of springing forwards, which was what the emergency required, he only started at a walk, and was just breaking into a canter when the elephant was upon us. I heard two short, sharp screams above my head, and had just time to think it was all over with me, when, horse and all, I was dashed to the ground. For a few seconds I was half stunned by the violence of the shock; and the first thing I became aware of, was a very strong smell of elephant. At the same instant, I felt that I was still unhurt, and that, though in an unpleasant predicament, I had still a chance for life. I was, however, pressed down on the ground in such a way that I could not extricate my head. At last, with a violent effort I wrenched myself loose, and threw my body over sideways, so that I rested on my hands. As I did so, I saw the hind-legs of the elephant standing like two pillars before me, and at once grasped the situation. She was on her knees, with her head and tusks in the ground; and I had been pressed down under her chest, but luckily behind her fore-legs. Dragging myself from under her, I regained my feet, and made a hasty retreat, having had rather more than enough of elephants for the time being. I retained, however, sufficient presence of mind to run slowly, watching her movements over my shoulder, and directing mine accordingly. Almost immediately I had made my escape, she got up, and stood looking for me with her ears up and head raised, turning first to one side, and then to the other, but never wheeling quite round. As she made these turns, I ran obliquely to the right or left, as the case might be, always endeavoring to keep her stern towards me. At length I gained the shelter of a small bush, and breathed freely once more.

"All this time I never saw my horse, which must have been lying amongst the grass where he had been thrown to the ground. I thought he was dead; or perhaps, to speak more truly, I was so engrossed with my own affairs that I did not think about him at all. I stood now just on the highest ground of a gentle rise, which sloped gradually down to an open glade, in which, from where I was, I could see two dead elephants. Just then I saw a Caffre coming across the opening, and went down to meet him, leaving my elephant still standing on the spot where she had knocked me down. Being unarmed, — for my gun had been dashed from my hand when I fell, — I dared not go near her to look for it. Upon meeting the Caffre, I hastily told him what had happened. The elephant was not now visible, being just beyond the crest of the rise, about two hundred yards distant; but I only stopped to take some cartridges from my trousers

PLATE XIII.

AFRICAN ELEPHANT.

LEANING AGAINST A TREE.

Pages 17 and 165.

pocket, and put them in my belt, and then, accompanied by the boy, returned to the scene of the accident to look for my rifle, and see what had become of my horse. On topping the rise, we saw him standing without the saddle; but the elephant had walked away, and was no longer visible. Going up to my horse, I found that he had received an ugly wound in the buttock from behind, from which the blood was streaming down the leg: otherwise, barring a few abrasions, he was unhurt. Whilst the boy was searching for my rifle, I looked round for the elephant, which I knew had only just moved away, and, seeing a cow standing amongst some bushes not two hundred yards from me, made sure it was the one that had so nearly made an example of me. The Caffre now came up with my rifle and saddle, the girth of which was broken. The rifle, having been open at the breech when it fell to the ground, was full of sand; so that it was not until I had taken the lever out, using the point of the Caffre's assegai for a screw-driver, that I managed to get it to work. I then approached the elephant, which all the time had been standing where I first saw her, and, cautiously advancing to within fifty yards of her, took a careful aim, and gave her a shot behind the shoulder, which brought her to the ground with a crash. Pushing in another cartridge, I ran up, and gave her a shot in the back of the head to make sure of her."

Hunters do not always escape so fortunately as did Mr. Selous. One of the native hunters employed by him, named Quabeet, followed a bull elephant into the bush, and was never seen alive again. The brute must have laid in wait for him, and rushed out, taking him unawares. The bushes around the locality were levelled to the ground; and, when finally the body was discovered, it was torn in three pieces.

'The, chest, with head and arms attached, which had been wrenched from the trunk just below the breast-bone, lying in one place; one leg and thigh, that had been torn off at the pelvis, in another; and the remainder in a third. The right arm had been broken in two places, and the hand crushed; one of the thighs was also broken; but otherwise the fragment had not been trampled on. There is little reason to doubt," continues Selous, "that the infuriated elephant must have pressed the unfortunate man down with his foot or knee, and then, twisting his trunk round his body, wrenched him asunder. This feat gives one an idea of the awful strength of these huge beasts, and how powerless the strongest of men."

Sometimes the elephant is attacked with javelins, or spears, and so killed. Dr. Livingstone thus describes an instance that he witnessed:—

"I had retired from the noise, to take observations among some rocks of laminated grit, when I beheld an elephant and her calf at the end of a valley, about two miles distant. The calf was rolling in the mud, and the dam was fanning herself with her great ears. As I looked at them through my glass, I saw a long string of my own men approaching on the other side of them. I then went higher up the side of the valley, in order to have a distinct view of their mode of hunting. The goodly beast, totally unconscious of the approach of an enemy, stood for some time suckling her young one, which seemed about two years old: then they went into a pit containing mud, and smeared themselves all over with it; the little one frisking about his dam, flapping his ears, and tossing his trunk incessantly in elephantine fashion. She kept flapping her ears, and wagging her tail, as if in the height of enjoyment. Then began the piping of her enemies, which was performed by blowing into a tube, or the hands closed together, as boys do into a key. They called out, to attract the animal's attention,—

> 'O chief, chief! we have come to kill you:
> O chief, chief! many others will die beside you;
> The gods have said it,' etc.

Both animals expanded their ears, and listened, then left their bath. As the crowd rushed towards them, the little one ran forward to the end of the valley, but, seeing the men, returned to his dam. She placed herself on the dangerous side of her calf, and passed her proboscis over it again and again, as if to assure it of safety. She frequently looked back to the men, who kept up an incessant shouting, singing, and piping; then looked at her young one, and ran after it, sometimes sidewise, as if her feelings were divided between anxiety to protect her offspring, and desire to revenge the temerity of her persecutors. The men kept about a hundred yards in her rear, and some that distance from her flanks, and continued thus until she was obliged to cross a rivulet.

"The time spent in descending and getting up the opposite bank allowed of their coming up to the edge and discharging their spears at about sixty feet distance. After the first discharge, she appeared with her sides red with blood, and, beginning to flee for her own life, seemed to think no more of her young. I had previously sent off Sekweba with orders to spare the calf. He ran very fast, but neither young nor old ever enter into a gallop: their quickest pace is only a sharp walk. Before Sekweba could reach them, the calf had taken refuge in the water, and was killed. The pace of the dam gradually became slower: she turned with a shriek of rage, and made a furious charge back among the men. They vanished at right and left angles from her course; and, as she ran right on, she went through the whole party, but came near no one, except a man who wore a piece of cloth on his shoulders. She charged three or four times, and, except in the first instance, never went farther than one hundred yards. She often stood, after she had crossed a rivulet, and faced the men, though she received fresh spears. It was by this process of spearing, and loss of blood, that she was killed; for at last, making a short struggle, she staggered round, and sank down dead, in a kneeling position."

While this method is certainly a fair one,—the natives exposing themselves, and meeting the elephant in the open field, —it seems a murderous operation to torture such a noble animal, especially when she is defending her young.

Among the narrow escapes of elephant-hunters in Africa may be mentioned Mr. Oswold. He was fleeing from an elephant, near the shores of the Zonga, when his horse stumbled, and he fell in a thicket, face to the huge brute who was coming like an avalanche—a veritable mountain of flesh. He gave himself up as lost; but, by a miracle, the animal passed within a few inches, missing him in its blind rage.

Elephants are remarkable for their scent, and hunters always try to keep to the leeward. Charles Volk, a Dutchman, while hunting, concealed himself in the brush, hoping to take an elephant unawares. But he was in the wrong direction: the great game scented him, and a moment later was upon the unfortunate hunter, and had crushed him into a shapeless mass. On another occasion, a party came upon two large elephants in an open spot. They immediately made for cover, the hunters wounding a female as she ran. Hoping to cut off her retreat, they put spurs to their horses, and were well upon her, when the male, a large tusker, charged upon them from a thicket. Some of the men had dismounted to fire; and, though taken by surprise, they succeeded in reaching their horses, with the exception of a young man, who was standing with his arm through the bridle, and loading his gun. The infuriated animal caught him before he could move, drove both his tusks through his body, and tossed him dead and bleeding a great height into the air; then, returning to its mate, both animals made off.

Karol Kreiger's name is often mentioned by the Dutch African colonists as a bold hunter, who killed many elephants in his day, and was extremely fortunate in avoiding their rushes. He finally met his death while engaged in the sport of his choice. He was following a wounded elephant, when the latter suddenly whirled about as if on a pivot, took him in its trunk, and tossed him like a ball into the air, and, when he fell, trampled him underfoot in a frenzy of rage. When the body was recovered, it was completely torn in pieces.

While Europeans are remarkably courageous in facing a charging elephant, they are exceeded in daring by the Hamran Arabs, who, without any of the appliances of a modern sportsman, face the largest and most ferocious elephants with a simple sword and shield. The Hamran Arabs are skilled horsemen, and are distinguished from their countrymen of other tribes by the length of their hair, which is worn in long curls, and parted in the centre. Their sole method of defence and attack is the sword and shield. The latter is of two kinds: one is circular in shape, either of rhinoceros or giraffe hide, stiffened by a stout piece of wood that passes down the centre. The shield is about two feet in diameter, and resembles, according to Baker, a broad hat with a low crown terminating in a point. In the crown, there is a bar of leather used as a grip; while the outside is protected by a piece of scaly crocodile-hide. The swords, which are manufactured at Sollingen, are all of one pattern, being longer or shorter according to the strength of the owner. The blade is long and straight and two-edged; the guard being a simple bar, or cross, a fashion presumably adopted after the Crusades. Some of the wealthy Arabs decorate the handles with silver; and a good sword is highly prized, and handed down from generation to generation. Metal scabbards are not used; the case being two thin strips of an elastic, soft wood covered with leather, all of which is to preserve the edge; for this double-edged weapon is so delicate and keen, that it will cut a hair, and could be used as a razor. On the march, the sword is looked after with the greatest care, and is slung from the pommel of the saddle, passing beneath the thigh. When the Arab dismounts, he invariably draws it, and, after examining both edges, strops it upon his shield, and, having shaved a hair from his arm, returns it to the scabbard.

The swords are about three feet five inches in length; and about nine inches of the blade is bound with cord, which is grasped with the right hand, the left seizing the handle, so that it becomes a two-handed weapon. Thus armed, four aggageers, as the professional elephant-hunters are called, are ready to attack the largest elephant. Their method is, if they have no horses, to follow the great game on foot, and endeavor, between the hours of ten A.M. and twelve M., to find one sleeping. If this can be accomplished, they steal upon it, and with one blow of the terrible sword sever the trunk, producing a wound from which the elephant will die in an hour. A well-equipped party, however, consists of four aggageers on horseback. When the trail of a herd is struck, they dash in pursuit; and when the animals are discovered, endeavor to single out the largest tusker, generally an old bull. Galloping after the fleeing elephant, they soon gain on it, and endeavor to make it turn and charge, — a matter of little difficulty. The men now have each a duty to perform. One places himself immediately in front of the animal, and tries to attract its attention, as does the matador in the bull-fight. This is a most dangerous position; as, if the horse stumbles before the desperate charges of the enraged animal, both horse and rider will be crushed to death. But, while the nimble aggageer in front is tantalizing the great beast, the others are watching their opportunity. Galloping up behind the fleeing animal until within a foot or so of its heels, one springs to the ground lightly, sword in hand, though at full speed, and, racing along on foot for a few seconds, strikes the elephant a terrific blow, severing the back sinew of the foot, so that the first pressure after the stroke dislocates the joint. As the hunter leaps to the ground, his companion seizes his horse, and, as soon as the blow is made, he remounts: two or three ride near the unfortunate elephant's trunk, to give the third aggageer an opportunity to sever the sinew of the other hind-foot, which is soon done; and the huge animal, thus helpless, is literally killed by two blows of a sword.

The force of the blow given in this way can be imagined when it is known that a native has been seen to sever the spine of a wild boar at a single stroke. The aggageers often meet with terrible accidents. One employed by Sir S. W. Baker had his leg almost severed by his own sword. Another Arab, Roder Sherrif, had had his horse killed from under him by an elephant, whose tusk at the same time entered his arm, rendering it useless for life. Yet this maimed man was considered the finest hunter, and always chose the most dangerous post, running ahead of the elephant's trunk to attract its attention; and it was in doing this that he had met with the terrible wounds.

The wonderful daring of these hunters, of whom Sir S. W. Baker said that he felt like taking off his hat to, is well shown in the following account given by that well-known hunter and explorer:—

"Having the wind fair, we advanced quickly for about half the distance, at which time we were within a hundred and fifty yards of the elephant, which had just arrived at the water, and had commenced drinking. We now crept cautiously towards him. The sand-bank had decreased to a height of about two feet, and afforded very little shelter. Not a tree nor bush grew upon the surface of the barren sand, which was so deep that we sank nearly to the ankles at every footstep. Still we crept forward, as the elephant alternately drank, and then spouted the water in a shower over his colossal form; but, just as we had arrived within about fifty yards, he happened to turn his head in our direction, and immediately perceived us. He cocked his enormous ears, gave a short trumpet, and for an instant he wavered in his determination whether to attack or fly; but, as I rushed towards him with a shout, he turned towards the jungle, and I immediately fired a steady shot at the shoulder with the 'Baby.' As usual, the fearful recoil of the rifle, with a half-pound shell and twelve drachms of powder, nearly threw me backwards; but I saw the mark upon the elephant's shoulder in an excellent line, although rather high. The only effect of the shot was to send him off at great speed towards the jungle. But at the same moment the three aggageers came galloping across the sand, like greyhounds in a course, and, judiciously keeping parallel with the jungle, they cut off his retreat; and, turning towards the elephant, they confronted him, sword in hand. At once the furious beast charged straight at the enemy. But now came the very gallant but foolish part of the hunt. Instead of leading the elephant by the flight of one man and horse, according to their usual method, all the aggageers at the moment sprang from their saddles; and upon foot, in the heavy sand, they attacked the elephant with their swords.

"In the way of sport, I never saw any thing so magnificent, or so absurdly dangerous. No gladiatorial exhibition in the Roman arena could have surpassed this fight. The elephant was mad with rage; and, nevertheless, he seemed to know that the object of the hunters was to get behind him. This he avoided with great dexterity, turning, as it were, upon a pivot with extreme quickness, and charging headlong, first at one, and then at another, of his assailants, while he blew clouds of sand in the air with his trunk, and screamed with fury. Nimble as monkeys, nevertheless the aggageers could not get behind him. In the folly of excitement, they had forsaken their horses, which had escaped from the spot. The depth of the loose sand was in favor of the elephant, and was so much against the men, that they avoided his charges with extreme difficulty. It was only by the determined pluck of all three, that they alternately saved each other; as two invariably dashed in at the flanks when the elephant charged the third, upon which the wary animal immediately relinquished the chase, and turned round upon his pursuers. During this time, I had been laboring through the heavy sand; and, shortly after I arrived at the fight, the elephant charged directly through the aggageers, receiving a shoulder-shot from one of my Reilly No. 10 rifles, and, at the same time, a slash from the sword of Abou Do, who, with great dexterity and speed, had closed in behind him, just in time to save the leg. Unfortunately, he could not deliver the cut in the right place, as the elephant, with increased speed, completely distanced the aggageers: he charged across the deep sand, and reached the jungle. We were shortly upon his tracks; and, after running about a quarter of a mile, he fell dead in a dry water-course. His tusks, like the generality of Abyssinian elephants, were exceedingly short, but of good thickness."

The tactics employed in shooting Asiatic elephants are not always successful when applied to the African species; and the forehead-shot, referred to in the chapter on hunting the Asiatic elephant, is rarely made. The only forehead-shot that Sir S. W. Baker ever made was on the Settite River; the ball entering the base of the trunk, and lodging in the vertebræ of the neck, — a chance shot. At fifty feet, the temple-shot is often made; but the old hunters generally aim at the shoulder, or just behind it.

The flesh of the elephant is greatly esteemed by some native Africans, especially the fat; while the feet, when well cooked, are considered delicacies by some European hunters.

When the Bechuanas obtain a dead elephant, they not only enter the body, and literally mine for the fat, — hacking it out, and passing it to their comrades, — but besmear themselves with the blood from head to foot, considering that it will bring them good luck.

The native Africans have never been known to tame or utilize the elephant: though, in what is known as the fly country, they are the only animals perfectly free from attack, and would be of the greatest value, and a great saving of life, as it is estimated that every tusk that comes out from the interior of Africa, causes the death of at least one slave or native.

That the African elephant was hunted in very early times, is very evident. On an Egyptian tomb at Qournah, of the time of Thothmes III., there is a representation of the elephant, telling the story of the tribute brought by the people of the upper Euphrates to that prince in 1500 B.C. The celebrated black obelisk (now in the collection of the British Museum) of Shalmaneser II. (858–823 B.C.) bears a delineation of an elephant which formed part of a tribute brought by the Muzri, a people of Kurdistan at the head waters of the Tigris, to the Assyrian monarch. The human figures on the stone are shown bearing elephants' tusks upon their shoulders.

These inscriptions and figures, while they may be considered a part of the adornment of obelisks and tombs, are, in reality, the historical records of the time; and the representations of the elephant are often of value in showing its geographical distribution in former times. Thus, according to the stele of Amenemheb, an officer of the time of Thothmes III. and Amenophis II., translated by M. Chabas, the elephant was hunted near Nineveh, in the reign of Thothmes III.; and that there were found in great numbers, is shown by the statement, that the king "captured one hundred and twenty elephants for the sake of their tusks in the country of Nineveh." Later than this, according to an Assyrian inscription on the prism of Tiglath-pileser I. (1120 B.C.), now in London, the elephant was hunted on the Tigris. The account translated reads, "I killed ten full-grown elephants in the country of Harran; and on the banks of the Khabour [an affluent of the Tigris], I captured four elephants alive. I brought their skins and their tusks, with the living elephants, to my city of Alassar" [Asshur].

CHAPTER XIV.

BABY ELEPHANTS.

THE adult elephant attracts attention because of its great size and massive proportions; but the baby elephant is sure of the undisguised admiration of the young folk, for an exactly opposite reason; and perhaps no animal excites quite so much interest among all classes.

At least two Asiatic elephants claim America as their birthplace. The first one was born in Philadelphia in 1880, where, with its mother, it attracted great attention, people going from far and near to visit it. The second baby elephant was born in Bridgeport in 1882, its mother being Mr. Barnum's Asiatic elephant Hebe. This infant proboscidian was named after the city of its birth, and has probably been watched, fed, and petted by hundreds of thousands of children in the United States.

It is rare that elephants display any great affection for their young. Sir Emerson Tennent quotes Knox as saying that "the she's are alike tender of any one's young ones, as of their own." Mr. Sanderson, in charge of the government elephants in India, contradicts this, and states that "much exclusiveness is shown by elephants in the detailed arrangements amongst themselves in a herd; and if the mothers and young ones be closely watched, it will be seen that the latter are very rarely allowed familiarities by other females, nor, indeed, do they seek them. I have seen," he says, "many cases in the Kheddahs where young elephants, after losing their mothers by death or other causes, have been refused assistance by the other females, and have been buffetted as outcasts. I have only known one instance of a very gentle, motherly elephant, in captivity, allowing a motherless calf to nurse along with her young one."

The baby Bridgeport weighed at birth two hundred and forty-five pounds, and commenced nursing an hour and forty minutes later, — not with its trunk, as was supposed in the days of Buffon, but with its mouth, like all other mammals. The young elephants are nourished upon milk until they are six months old, when they eat a small quantity of tender grass; but for several months they depend principally upon milk. A single elephant is usually born at a time, though occasionally twins are seen among wild elephants. Sometimes three small elephants are observed about the mother; but they are generally of different ages, or are twins and a brother or sister two years and a half older.

The new baby Bridgeport, when I first saw it, was one of the most interesting creatures possible to imagine. Its diminutive stature, just about the size of the adult pygmies, described in Chap. IV.; its short trunk and tail; its pinkish skin, and small, solemn eyes, made it the most grotesque and comical little fellow in the world. Like all young animals, it was quite playful, and its attempts at frisking about were very amusing. It would seize its mother's tail or her trunk, or dart between her colossal legs in a veritable game of hide and seek, while she looked on with evident pride, displaying not the slightest alarm when the keeper lifted the baby in a

HEBE AND BABY BRIDGEPORT.

(ASIATIC FEMALE ELEPHANT AND YOUNG.)

Page 179.

variety of positions so that Mr. James C. Beard could sketch it. This is a peculiarity that few mothers in the lower animal kingdom have; and even the partly wild elephants seem to have perfect faith in man, trusting their young with them, and not resenting any familiarity that does not harm them.

Among many animals, especially sea-lions, the mortality of the young, resulting from carelessness or clumsiness on the part of the parent, is very great; but it is very rarely, if ever, that a baby elephant is killed or injured. This is true in the great herds when they are stampeded by various enemies. When on the march, the mothers and young go in advance; but when the note of alarm is sounded, they immediately fall back, the tuskers, or males, going to the front; and an observer at this time would be astonished at the sudden disappearance of the young. At the first alarm, they run to their mother, and place themselves beneath her, shuffling along in this way; yet so careful are these enormous parents, that even in travelling at a rapid rate, and crowded by one another, the babies are never harmed. To this great care on the part of elephants is, undoubtedly, due the safety of men who handle these animals; the great brutes being instinctively careful of all smaller attendants.

In wild Asiatic elephants, the greatest number of births are during September, October, and November. When a baby elephant is added to the herd, they remain about the mother for two or three days, to give the little one an opportunity to gain strength. The greatest care is given the youngsters by the mothers. They are assisted over rough places, pushed up hills, and are never an encumbrance to the movements of the body.

Perhaps the most amusing sight is witnessed when a herd with young have to swim deep streams. When the mothers are once off bottom, very little of their great bodies shows above the surface; and they often swim or walk with only the tip of the trunk showing. If the infant is very young, or there is danger of its taking cold, the old one takes it in her trunk, and holds it above the water as she swims: others are supported at the surface. Older babies scramble upon the mother's back, and ride along with only the curious cushions of their feet in the water; while some sit astride the old one's back, holding on with their legs.

The baby elephant does not lack courage. Sir Emerson Tennent states that once when a herd of elephants was captured, two tiny elephants were entrapped with them, — one about ten months old, whose head was covered with brown curly hair, and the other a little older. They both kept with the herd, trotting in and out between the legs of their elders, being caressed by all. According to the same writer, when the mother of the youngest was singled out by the noosers, and was dragged along, the little one followed, showing great indignation at the proceedings, and prevented them from putting a second noose over the mother; running in between her and the natives, trying to seize the rope, and pushing and striking them with its diminutive trunk, until it became so annoying that it had to be captured and carried away by main force. Even then it resisted, shrieking loudly, stopping to look back at every step; but finally it attached itself to a large female, and stood by her fore-legs, and moaned continually. After a while, however, it made its escape, and returned to its dam; and, when recovered, both babies shrieked lustily, struck at the men with their trunks, and twisted their little bodies into many curious contortions.

Perhaps the most laughable part of this scene was, that the babies would eagerly seize any article of food that was thrown them, and still keep on screaming all the while they were eating.

These interesting infants were afterwards sent down to Colombo, to the house of Sir Emerson Tennent, and became great pets. "One," he says, "attached himself especially to the coachman, who had a little shed erected for him near his own quarters at the stables. But his favorite resort was the kitchen, where he received a daily allowance of milk and plantains, and picked up several little delicacies besides. He was innocent and playful in the extreme; and, when walking in the grounds, he would trot up to me, twine his little trunk around my arm, and coax me to take him to the fruit-trees. In the evening the grass-cutters, now and then, indulged him by permitting him to carry home a load of fodder for the horses, on which occasions he assumed an air of great gravity that was highly amusing, showing that he was deeply impressed with the importance and responsibility of the service intrusted to him. Being sometimes permitted to enter the dining-room, and helped to fruit at dessert, he at last learned his way to the sideboard; and on more than one occasion, having stolen in during the absence of the servants, he made a clean sweep of the wineglasses and china, in his endeavors to reach a basket of oranges. For these and other pranks, we were at last obliged to put him away."

CHAPTER XV.

TRICK ELEPHANTS.

THE readiness of the elephant to familiarize itself with various tricks has been recognized from very early times, and the list of accomplishments which these unwieldy creatures have acquired is a long and interesting one. To the circus of the present day, the elephant is invaluable. People tire of the old jokes of the clown, and of the time-worn bare-back riding, but the elephant possesses a peculiar fascination; and, the more it is observed, the more there is to admire. This was, I think, particularly true of Jumbo, who, though he had no tricks to display, was a never-failing source of interest. I remember on one occasion, when afforded an opportunity of entering his stable alone, I stood for a long time noting the monotonous, pendulum-like movement of the enormous head and trunk as it swayed from side to side; and so huge did he appear, and withal so wonderful, such a giant of flesh and bone, that I could have extended my visit a long time without becoming wearied with its monotony. I think this is true to a great extent with all elephants. They are so wonderful and stupendous, that they do not wear upon the public patience.

The education of the elephant is quite an important matter; and in nearly all the large herds, like Barnum's, there are what might be called elephant schools, where the elephants are not only taught, but kept in practice. Kindness is a feature of this education; but fear is the motive, after all, on the part of the elephant; and were it not for the dread which the hook of the trainer inspires, there would be little discipline maintained.

The trainer of the Barnum herd informed me that he had often seen elephants, especially young ones, practising their lessons out of school. On one occasion he looked through a crevice into the pen of the elephants who were fastened up for the night, and there was one trying to stand on its head. While he watched, it made the attempt several times, just as if he had been standing by, and finally succeeded. Some of my young readers may possibly think that this is a remarkable evidence of intelligence, but I am inclined to think that it was merely the result of the force of daily habit.

As long ago as the time of Pliny, elephants were observed studying their lessons, if so we may term it. This ancient author tells us that an elephant, having been punished for his inaptitude in executing some feat which he was required to learn, was observed at night endeavoring to practise what he had vainly attempted during the day; and Plutarch confirms this by mentioning an elephant who practised his theatrical attitudes, alone, by moonlight.

The elephants of to-day are trained to march like soldiers, to wheel and counter-march at command, to salute their superior by throwing up the trunk and whistling loudly, to build pyramids and climb upon eminences; and one small elephant has been taught to walk upon a rope, — a very broad and flat one. Elephants upon the see-saw, upon a rolling ball, elephants upon their hind-legs, and dancing elephants,—all are familiar to the circus-goer; and to show to what perfection the art of animal-training has attained, quite recently two small Indian elephants, which were erroneously advertised as mammoths in New York, from the fact that they had some hair upon their heads and bodies, were educated to do some comical tricks, one of which was to ride a tricycle, in which position they presented a most ludicrous appearance. (See Plate XVI.)

Perhaps the most remarkable exhibition is that afforded by the little elephant, Tom Thumb, of the Barnum circus, the one who was in the accident which killed Jumbo. This elephant comes walking upon his hind-legs upon a mimic stage, with an alleged German, and both take seats at a table; the elephant being dressed in hat, coat, and trousers. The clown elephant now takes a bell in its trunk, and rings it; a waiter coming in and taking the order, which is evidently for some intoxicant. When he returns with a bottle and two glasses, the elephant seizes the former while his companion is not looking, and drinks the contents. This act is repeated a number of times, the elephant ringing the bell and ordering another bottle before the German discovers the fraud. Then the elephant appears to be overcome with the wine, and, taking a fan in its trunk, uses it vigorously. In all its movements the curious animal acts exactly as if it understood all that was going on, and fully appreciated the sport.

It is not often that an elephant is employed as a witness in court, but such an instance occurred in Cleveland some time ago. The famous trick elephant Pickaninny had been exhibited there; and, as some discussion had been raised as to its speed, a test was given, the trainer affirming that the elephant could travel three miles in thirty minutes. It accomplished a mile in eight minutes; and the officers of the Society for the Prevention of Cruelty to Animals very properly interfered, and arrested the driver, charging him with having prodded the animal with an iron until the blood came.

The next day the parties appeared in court, and the trainer subpœned his elephant in his defence. As the animal could not squeeze up the stairs to the police court, the latter was held in the corridor below. When asked if he had been injured, Pickaninny moved his head negatively; and when the inquiry was made if he was treated well, he bobbed his head up and down, and grunted his assent in a very decided manner. It is unnecessary to say that his trainer was not far off during this performance; and as examination failed to show any wounds, the man was discharged, and the elephant complimented upon his success by being presented with loaves of bread, fruit, and other delicacies.

The elephant has figured in the circus of England for at least two hundred and fifty years; and in 1681 a fine specimen was accidentally destroyed by fire in Dublin. The exhibition price had been so high that comparatively few persons had seen it; and at the time of the fire, the poorer classes hunted for pieces of the flesh as relics, which shows what a novel spectacle an elephant must have been at this time.

Among the first trained elephants exhibited in Europe, was a fine Asiatic animal, employed at the Adelphi Theatre, London. It took part in an Eastern play, and evoked much applause by marching in a procession, kneeling before the king, and saluting the true prince without apparent orders.

One of the first elephants seen in London was kept in the Tower of London in the seventeenth century, and was a gift to Henry III. from Louis IX. of France. It was probably obtained from Africa when the French king invaded that country. The order relating to this elephant is still extant among the old archives, and reads thus: "We command you, that, of the farm of our city, ye cause, without delay, to be built at our Tower of London, one house of forty feet long, and twenty feet deep, for our elephant."

It was evidently quite the custom among monarchs to send elephants to one another. Emmanuel of Portugal sent a fine one to Pope Leo X.; and Cardan describes one that he saw in the sixteenth century, at the court of the Queen of Bohemia, the daughter of Charles the Fifth. As early as 802, Haroun-al-Raschid, caliph of the Saracens, sent one to Charlemagne.

The elephants of Germanicus were trained to perform many remarkable feats, as hurling javelins into the air with their trunks, and catching them. Pliny says that these elephants danced upon a rope, and their steps were so practised and certain, that four of them walked upon the rope, bearing a litter, which contained one of their companions who feigned to be sick. This would seem an exaggeration, but an elephant upon the tight-rope has been seen in this country; and ancient writers agree with Pliny that the elephants exhibited at ancient Rome could not only walk upon the rope, but retreat backwards without falling off. This performance, wonderful as it appears, is credited by nearly all the old writers. Seneca describes an elephant, who, at the command of its keeper, would bow its head, kneel, and walk upon a rope. Of course, it is impossible for an elephant to walk upon a slack rope; and those alluded to were probably of very large size, perhaps flat upon the sides, and stretched to the greatest tension, and placed near the ground.

It is evident, however, that, in some cases, the rope was high above the spectators; as one writer mentions an elephant exhibited in the presence of the Emperor Galba, which ascended to the roof of the circus, on a rope stretched in an incline, and came back in safety, bearing a man upon its back.

This performance is extremely wonderful when we remember the natural timidity of the animal, and the almost impossibility of forcing it upon a structure that is in the least unstable or frail. When elephants are marched over a bridge, they exercise the greatest caution, often trying the boards before taking the step, and displaying much sagacity.

We have seen the elephant of to-day fire a gun, play upon the hand-organ, or ring a bell: and Arrian mentions seeing an elephant who played upon the cymbals, having one attached to each knee, and bearing the third in its proboscis; thus beating a measure with great exactness, while other elephants danced about him. Busbec, ambassador from Germany to Constantinople in 1555, saw an elephant which he describes as an extremely graceful dancer and ball-player, throwing the ball, and catching it, as easily as could a man with his hands.

It is a common thing for parrots to be taught to scream out the name of prominent people, and elephants have been trained to perform a somewhat similar trick. Thus, an elephant saluted Domitian when he passed; and when the elephant presented by Emmanuel of Portugal saw Leo X., to whom he was sent as a gift, it fell upon its knees, and made a profound obeisance.

By far the best-trained elephant which was ever exhibited in London, was owned by the Duke of Devonshire, who obtained the animal in a curious manner. On being asked by a lady *en route* for India, what she should bring him, he replied jokingly, "Ah! nothing less than an elephant." A few months later, he was astonished at receiving the animal, whose actions and intelligence were the admiration of the country.

The elephant was kept in a large enclosure, and treated with every kindness and attention, and developed a remarkable intelligence, soon learning to assist in many ways the man who was employed to take care of it. At his request it would go to him, take a broom, and sweep the paths or grass wherever he indicated, using her trunk to perform the work, with as much ease as a man would his hands. When he was watering the garden, it would follow him around, carrying the water-pot; always being rewarded for its faithful services with a carrot, or some other vegetable. The keeper soon found that the elephant was adroit at work of any kind. When given a bottle, it uncorked it itself, by pressing it against the ground with its foot, and holding it at an angle of forty-five degrees, carefully pulling the cork out with its trunk. When this feat was often tried for the entertainment of the duke's friends, a soda-water bottle was used, in which the cork projected a very little above the edge. When the bottle was uncorked, she would turn her trunk around, so as to reverse it, and drink the contents with much gusto, then handing the bottle to the attendant.

Another trick it performed was equally applauded. This

was to take off its blanket without the aid of its trunk. When the attendant rode it, he covered its back with a large cloth; and, when he wished to dismount, it would kneel, then rise, and, at the word of command, begin to agitate the muscles of its loins in such a manner that the housing was soon wriggled off, upon which it would take and fold it with exactness, and then toss it upon the centre of its back.

Such an animal naturally became a great favorite, and, at the time, was as famous as Jumbo. It displayed great affection for its keeper; and it is needless to say, that it was returned. The first keeper attended it for eight years; and, when he left, it seemed to mourn, and showed a disposition to resent the advances of the new attendant, but was gradually won over by kindness, and finally would cry lustily for him if he remained away what it considered too long a time. This famous elephant died of consumption in 1829, in the prime of life, being about twenty-one years of age.

CHAPTER XVI.

ELEPHANTS AND THEIR FRIENDS.

ALL animals have their favorites or friends, — it may be some attendant or some animal to which they have formed an attachment, — and the elephant is no exception to the rule. Most of the latter's friends are made in confinement; but the wild animal has a number of little companions, which are of great value, at least, in adding to its comfort. These are birds; and chief among them is a beautiful crane, which is often seen — and, indeed, numbers of them — perched upon the back of the great animal, and riding about, presenting a strange and decided contrast to the dark-skinned proboscidian. The presence of these shy birds moving about on so curious a roost would seem a mystery; but, should we watch them, we should see that they were performing a most friendly act. They walk over the great, wrinkled back, and with their sharp eyes spy out all the insects which infest the great pachyderm, picking them out, and so securing a dinner and serving their friend at the same time, who probably is often driven to desperation by the myriads of insect-torments which abound in the dark continent. Besides the cranes, there are several smaller birds which are equally friendly to the king of beasts, and often congregate upon its back in great numbers; running about without fear, clinging to the huge ears, now dangling by the tail, and performing a still more friendly act at times in warning their friend of danger by rising in a flock, and uttering shrill cries, which arouse the drowsy elephant to a sense of its danger.

In confinement particularly, the elephant is famous for its friendships, attaching itself to certain persons or animals, showing its affection for them in various ways. One of the Barnum elephants formed a strong friendship for a large dog, which was fully reciprocated; the dog sleeping with its great friend, and always remaining about its feet. If it strayed away at any time, the elephant would look after it, and on its return show its delight and pleasure in many ways.

Elephants often become attached to children, and seem to display the greatest solicitude for them. They have been employed as nurses to extremely small children, performing the duties as care-taker with perfect satisfaction.

Though, as a rule, elephants obey their keepers from fear, there are cases where a decided friendship exists; and even when furious with rage, an elephant will often obey its keeper's voice. An affecting instance of this was seen in the case of the famous elephant Chuni, who was believed to have gone mad. The animal was taken out to be shot; and its keeper was obliged to order it to kneel, that the soldiers might shoot it. The man reluctantly gave the order; and the elephant obeyed the command, and fell, pierced by many bullets.

A mad elephant in Germany, which had destroyed much property, yielded immediately to the voice of the man who owned it, or had been its friend and keeper. The works of the ancient writers abound in instances of attachment and friendship between the huge animals and human beings. Ælian relates a story of an elephant who became passionately attached to a little girl who sold flowers in the streets of Antioch, and had occasionally given it a part of her store. Athenæus tells of one which became so fond of a little child, that it would eat only in its presence; but I fear that this story will not stand the test. Strabo states that elephants were known to have pined away and died when deprived of their keepers to whom they were attached. Lieut. Shipp gives, in his memoirs, a very minute account of an elephant, who, upon killing its keeper, was seized with what was considered a fit of remorse, which ultimately killed the animal. In other words, it died of "a broken heart," a term that is applied to-day to elephants in India who die of no apparent cause.

In Purchas's collection of travels, there is an account of an elephant who mourned for its master, the King of Ava, who was slain in battle, for many days; and, as the same is known to have occurred among dogs and cats at the present day, it is not at all improbable.

That the elephant should become attached to its keeper, is not strange. It is perfectly familiar with all his movements, receives all its food from him, is caressed and petted; and it is not surprising that at times the animals rebel when provided with an utter stranger to replace the one in whom they have learned to trust.

CHAPTER XVII.

TUSKERS AT WORK.

WE have seen how the elephant is trapped, glanced at it in confinement, and now come to the question of its actual value; in other words, how it is utilized by man. The simplest answer to this would be, that the elephant is a patient and faithful servant, quick to oblige, and, though not the most valuable of all animals as a helpmate to man, it certainly stands first in this respect in India.

In the chapter on elephant intelligence, the traits of the great animal are dwelt upon; and it is its quickness to obey orders, the celerity with which it seems to understand them, its great strength and docility, which make it so valuable. There is hardly any service in India, requiring heavy work, in which the elephant is not employed. All the native nobles keep large herds of them, and in early times the numbers employed for simple purposes of show were remarkable.

The tuskers are valued the most; as with their stout tusks they lift lumber, and do much heavy labor, the trunk being used less than is generally supposed. In lifting a heavy burden by a rope, the male elephant does not haul by its trunk, but places it over one tusk, and takes the end with its teeth, and thus has a purchase that the female, who relies upon her teeth alone, does not possess. Long tusks are not necessary:

in fact, in confinement they are cut once a year at least, to prevent the animals from injuring themselves. This operation is performed by making the animal lie down in the water, and sawing the tusk off; the rule being, according to Sanderson, to measure from the eyes to the insertion of the tusk in the lip; this length measured from the latter point along the tusk, will give the spot where it should be cut. In young animals, a little more should be allowed; as the above measurement may approach to nearly the medullary pulp of the tusk.

Before the introduction of the railway in India, the elephant was used entirely to transport troops. Both male and female are now employed as laborers. In hunting, the tuskers are chiefly selected, on account of their superior courage; and in following the tiger in India, they are almost invariably of great value, especially in Bengal, where the places frequented by this animal are often covered by high grass. In these hunts, only elephants whose courage has been tested are used, the hunters riding in the howdah upon their backs.

There is danger, however, in having an elephant which is too courageous. Such a one will, if not under perfect control, become enraged at the very sight of a tiger, and charge it, often with lamentable results to the hunters in the howdah, who are liable to be shaken out, and crushed to death. In 1876, at Dacca, an elephant acted in this way. A gentleman had taken his courageous wife on a tiger-hunt, both being in the howdah on a female elephant. Suddenly a large tigress ran across an open place; and the elephant, despite the commands of the mahout, charged immediately, under the influence of terror and excitement, or rage. The hunter fired, and rolled the tigress over in front of the elephant, who began to kick at the prostrate brute, who, in turn, grasped the hind-leg of the elephant, and scratched, bit, and pulled with such vehemence that the elephant was fairly pulled over upon it, fortunately killing the tigress instantly.

When the elephant went down, the sportsman was thrown violently out, his rifle flying in another direction, and going off, fortunately without damage to any one. His wife managed to retain her place, and was safely helped out by her husband, both running to another elephant, and so escaping without harm.

This calls to mind the method of an English major, also a reputed famous hunter of former days. It is saïd that he had killed twelve hundred elephants in his time. He made a wager that he could kill two of these animals at one shot, and won, by shooting a female so that it fell upon its calf and killed it.

The elephant, as we have seen, is very solicitous of its trunk, and, when attacked by a tiger, holds it high in air; and if by any accident this member is injured, the mahout sometimes loses command. Mr. Williamson thus describes such an occurrence which happened to two officers of the Bengal army:—

"They had been in the habit of killing tigers with only one elephant, on which being mounted, they one day roused a tiger of a very fierce disposition. The animal, after doing some mischief among the dogs, which baited him very courageously, at length darted at the elephant's head, and, though foiled in the attempt to get upon it, nevertheless scratched her trunk severely. No sooner did she feel the tiger's claws penetrating her proboscis, than she turned round, and set off at full speed, roaring most vehemently. She seemed to have lost her senses, and to be bent on mischief; for whenever she saw a living object, she pursued it, totally heedless of the mahout's endeavors to guide or restrain her. She was at length, by fatigue and management, brought into a governable state; but she was spoiled for tiger-hunting."

The same author chronicles a narrow escape for both elephant and riders from a tiger: —

"The tiger had satiated himself upon a bullock he had killed, and lay lurking in the grass, — which was as high as the backs of the elephants, and very thick, — not far from the remains of the bullock. He was extremely cunning, and crouched so close as to render it, for a long time, doubtful whether he was in the jungle, or not. The symptoms displayed by the elephants, on approaching the place where he lay concealed, induced the party to persevere in their efforts to rouse him. One gentleman, particularly, urged his mahout to make his elephant beat the spot where the scent was strongest; which being done, in spite of the tremendous tones of the agitated animal, the tiger, finding himself compelled either to resist, or to submit to being trodden upon, sprang upon the elephant's quarter, and so far succeeded as to fix his claws in the pad; his hind-legs were somewhat spread, and their claws were fixed into the fleshy membranes of the elephant's thigh. Actuated by the excess of fear, occasioned by so sudden and so painful an attack, the elephant dashed through the cover at a surprising rate; the tiger holding fast by its fore-paws, and supported by its hinder ones, unable, however, in consequence of the rapid and irregular motions of the elephant, either to raise himself any higher, or to quit the hold he had so firmly taken with his claws. The gentleman, who had much ado to keep his seat, was precluded from firing at his grim companion, as well from his unprecedented situation, as from the great danger of wounding some of the numerous followers, who were exerting the utmost speed of their respective elephants to come up to his assistance. The constant desire felt by the elephant to get rid of his unwelcome rider, which produced a waving and irregular pace, gave the opportunity for those who were mounted on light and speedy animals to overtake the singular fugitives. Another gentleman of the party, coming up close, was enabled to choose his position; when, taking a safe aim, he shot the tiger, which fell to the ground, and required no further operations."

An elephant has been known to fling a tiger twenty feet through the air, and well-trained animals will catch a leaping tiger upon its tusks. This, however, is rarely done, perhaps from lack of opportunity. Much preparation is required in training an elephant for tiger-hunting. A stuffed skin is generally thrown to them, and they are taught to kneel and crush it; and, when thoroughly familiar with the appearance of the big cat through the dummy, they are taken into the field.

In India the elephant has often been used as a public executioner. Shah-Jehan terrified the Portuguese at Hoogly some years ago by announcing, that, if they did not renounce the Christian faith, he would throw them beneath his elephants' feet. Knox, in his account of Ceylon, states that "the king makes use of them for executioners," and that the animals would run their tusks through the bodies of the victims at the word of command. These elephant executioners were provided with sharp iron spikes with a socket with three edges, which at such times were fitted upon their tusks. This custom was kept up until the British conquered the island.

Bishop Heber says, "I preached, administered the sacrament, and confirmed twenty-six young people, in the audience-hall of the late King of Kandy, which now serves as a church. Here, twelve years ago, this man, who was a dreadful tyrant, and lost his throne in consequence of a large party of his subjects applying to Gen. Brownrigge for protection, used, as we were told, to sit in state to see those whom he had condemned trodden to death and tortured by elephants trained for the purpose."

In very early times the elephant formed an equally important factor in the hunt. Marco Polo has recorded the manner of the Grand Khan's proceeding to the sport: —

"On account of the narrowness of the passes in some parts of the country where his Majesty follows the chase, he is borne upon two elephants only, or sometimes a single one, being more convenient than a greater number. But, under other circumstances, he makes use of four, upon the backs of which is placed a pavilion of wood, handsomely carved, the inside being lined with cloth of gold, and the outside covered with the skins of lions, — a mode of conveyance which is rendered necessary to him during his hunting excursions, in consequence of the gout, with which his Majesty is troubled. In the pavilion he always carries with him twelve of his best gerfalcons, with twelve officers, from amongst his favorites, to bear him company and amuse him. Those who are on horseback by his side give him notice of the approach of cranes, or other birds, upon which he raises the curtain of the pavilion, and, when he espies the game, gives direction for letting fly the gerfalcons, which seize the cranes, and

ELEPHANT CARRYING LOGS.

Page 195.

overpower them after a long struggle. The view of this sport, as he lies upon his couch, affords extreme satisfaction to his Majesty."

The Nawaub of Oude, Vizier Ally, or Asophul-Doulah, who was elevated to the throne through the British, was even more prodigal than the Grand Khan:—

"He generally took the field in the month of March, accompanied by ten thousand cavalry and as many infantry, and from seven to eight hundred elephants. From forty to sixty thousand people followed the camp, with grain and merchandise. When the vizier set out from his palace at Lucknow, a line was formed with the prince in the centre, mounted on an elephant, with two attendant elephants,—one carrying his state howdah, the other his sporting howdah. A line of elephants was prolonged on each side the prince, and was flanked at each extremity by the cavalry. The immense cavalcade proceeded straight through the country, regardless of the mischief that was a necessary consequence; the poor cultivators running after the vizier, crying aloud for mercy. When any game was started, a continual fire was kept up along the line; and, if a herd of antelopes was discovered, the elephants halted, and the cavalry hemmed them in, that his Highness and his courtiers might leisurely destroy them. Proceeding in this manner by day, and halting in the evening at appointed stations, where every luxury was prepared in sumptuous tents, the army at length approached the Thibet Mountains, where tigers, panthers, leopards, and buffaloes were to be found. An encampment being formed, their sporting was continued for several weeks upon a grand and formidable scale; and, mounted upon their elephants, the prince and his nobles scoured the country in pursuit of the ferocious beasts that destroyed the flocks and herds of the peasantry. The array of despotism was here of some service, for the numbers of carnivorous animals that were killed was generally in proportion to the magnitude of the force employed against them."

The curious uses to which elephants have been put are endless. An English officer, who served in India, says, "I have myself seen the wife of a mahout [for the followers often take their families with them to camp] give a baby in charge of an elephant while she went on some business, and have been highly amused in observing the sagacity and care of the unwieldy nurse. The child, which, like most children, did not like to lie still in one position, would, as soon as left to itself, begin crawling about, in which exercise it would probably get among the legs of the animal, or entangled in the branches of the trees on which he was feeding; when the elephant would, in the most tender manner, disengage his charge, either by lifting it out of the way with his trunk, or by removing the impediments to its free progress. If the child had crawled to such a distance as to verge upon the limits of his range [for the animal was chained by the leg to a peg driven into the ground], he would stretch out his trunk, and lift it back as gently as possible to the spot whence it had started."

M. D'Obsonville observed two elephants engaged in breaking down a wall at the command of the mahouts, who stood by, imploring, ordering, and coaxing by turns. The trunks of these animals were protected by leather shields.

At Barrackpoor, there was an elephant in the early part of this century, noted for its intelligence in working without a mahout. Once loaded with parcels, it would enter the

Ganges, swim across, and then unload itself. Another elephant, who was kept near the fort at Trarancore, was employed to carry out the treasure-boxes of the rajah of Trarancore. It was totally unattended, and marched solemnly into the court-yard of the fort, bearing a box, repeating this until all the boxes were piled up in regular order.

It was reported in the press soon after Lord Dufferin had been appointed viceroy to India, that he had been presented with an elephant paper-cutter, which if true, — and it is not by any means improbable, — would be one of the singular uses to which an elephant was ever put, and perhaps the most expensive. As the story goes, the tusks of a fine young elephant were beautifully carved into the shape of the huge paper-cutters now so fashionable; and the animal itself was taught to take an uncut pamphlet or book in its trunk, and cut the leaves.

The greatest practical value of the elephant is seen in their work as laborers; and in hauling lumber they are especially of great service, their great strength enabling them to haul logs from localities that are ordinarily inaccessible. At Moulmien these huge laborers can often be seen at work in the lumber-yards, and observers say that their power is most advantageously employed where great exertion is required for a short distance in a limited space of time.

In the above-mentioned yards they may be seen carrying huge timbers, sometimes two or three animals engaged at one, exercising the greatest care and exactitude in the work, and obeying the slightest sign of the mahout. In lifting a heavy burden, the plank is edged or helped on to the tusks with the trunk, which is then wound around to steady it, while all the strain comes upon the tusks. (See Plate XIII.)

In hauling, a regular harness is employed, which consists of a leather collar that goes about the neck; or sometimes a girth, a stout rope ninety feet in length that fits behind the shoulders. To either of these the dragging-rope is attached; and if it is strong, and the elephant has not been frightened by frequent breakings, occasioned by the carelessness of drivers, it will make the most extraordinary endeavors and exertions to draw heavy loads, often bending forward so that its forehead almost touches the ground.

When light timber is to be hauled, a rope is fastened to the end of the log, and taken by the elephant between its teeth, and dragged along, the end elevated from the ground.

Elephants are also harnessed to wagons just as horses. Travellers through Bridgeport some years ago were entertained by seeing one of Mr. Barnum's elephants harnessed to a plough, but it is very likely that the broad feet of the animal tramped down the earth about as fast as it was loosened up.

At the elephant establishment at Dacca, two regular elephant carts are used, to which are harnessed these animals, and employed in removing the refuse about the stables.

While the elephant can carry a very heavy burden, it is exceedingly susceptible to gall; almost every elephant in use, where great care is not taken, having a sore back. The natives, not especially humane, are apt to purposely neglect the animal, and allow its back to become sore; as, if the elephant cannot be used, they are relieved from duty. Sharp elephant owners prevent this by putting the attendants on half pay for as many weeks or months as it takes the poor creatures to recover. Elephants can be used in countries where a carriage would be impossible, and can carry a greater load than can be packed on a large wagon; hence they are highly valued in a rocky and rough country. In such a place, a different gear is used from that already described. It consists of a thick, soft-padded cloth that covers the entire back, hanging down half way to the ground. Upon this the saddle fits, consisting of two large pads or sacks, each about two and a half feet broad, and six feet in length, and filled with a mass of dried grass or cocoanut fibre, so that they are about a foot thick. They are connected by cross-pieces, so that they fit one each side of the animals' backbone, the skin of which is thus protected from galling. Upon these pads another large one is placed, and upon this the load is packed; so that the weight rests upon the ribs on each side of the vertebræ, as the weight of a rider on horseback.

The weight that can be loaded on an elephant depends upon the size of the animal. An ordinary elephant can carry half a ton continuously on a level country, but in a hilly district seven hundred-weight is a good load. Female elephants have been known to carry a pile of rice-bags, weighing twenty-four hundred pounds, for a short distance; but the regulation amount allowed by the Bengal commissariat is sixteen hundred and forty pounds, exclusive of attendants, harness, chains, etc., which is estimated at three hundred pounds extra.

The magnificent howdahs, or saddles, used by some of the rajahs are extremely heavy. Thus, one of the silver state howdahs and trappings of his excellency the viceroy weighs a little over half a ton; or, to be more exact,—

	CWT.		LBS.
Howdah	6	1	22
Gold cloth	1	0	14
Punkahs, etc.	0	2	25
Ropes and gear	1	5	15

Elephants are often used, as we use saddle-horses, as steeds by European officers in India; and a light, well-broken elephant has an easy motion quite agreeable. The Meerga caste, or breed, from their long limbs, are generally the fastest; while small calves are often employed, the rider sitting astride as in horseback-riding. A large saddle and stirrup is used; and in rough country, the little fellows are a welcome addition to the travellers' party.

Elephants are very sure-footed at their work, and, when going at full speed, rarely stumble; if they do, they only go upon the knees. Like horses, they will run away at times; and a bolting elephant is much more to be dreaded than a bucking horse.

The Mysore officer in charge of elephants says, "I have felt, on the one or two occasions which I have been on a bolting elephant, as a man might feel if bestriding a runaway locomotive, and hooking the funnel with the crook of his walking-stick to hold it in. It is a very difficult thing," he says, "to cure a confirmed bolter, as the habit has its origin in fear; and the animal is always liable to be startled by unexpected sounds or sights, chiefly the former. It is a rare trick, however; and I have only known two elephants subject to it. One was a fine baggage animal, but almost useless for jungle-work from this trick. I, however, cured him in the following way: I had a stout hoop of iron made with sharp spikes on the inside, to encircle one of his hind-legs. This was kept in its place round the leg by being suspended from the pad by a rope; and it fitted the leg loosely, so as not to inconvenience the elephant except when required to do so. To the ring was attached a chain fifteen feet long, at the other end of which was a pickaxe's head. This grappling apparatus was slung to the pad by a small cord in a slip-knot, handy to the mahout. If the elephant began to run, one pull freed it; and before the anchor had been dragged many yards, it caught in the roots or bushes, and brought the elephant up with such a twinge, that it soon began to think twice before making off."

The howdah is an ornamental covered saddle; though some resemble small houses, and cost their owners vast sums of money. They are used on state occasions, and in tiger-hunting. The motion is hard, and rather unpleasant to the novice. Another saddle is called a chárjámá. It is merely a broad board with cushions upon it, and footboards attached to each side. There is a rail upon each end; and four persons sit upon it, two on each side, back to back, somewhat after the fashion of a jaunting car.

Riding-elephants will travel at about four miles an hour, while some long-legged fellows will make five or more miles in this time. Wounded elephants, as we have seen, sometimes make remarkable time.

Concerning the motion of elephants, Bishop Heber says, —

"At Barrackpoor, for the first time I mounted an elephant, the motion of which I thought far from disagreeable, though very different from that of a horse. As the animal moves both feet on the same side at once, the sensation is like that of being carried on a man's shoulders. A full-grown elephant carries two persons in the howdah, besides the mahout, who sits on his neck, and a servant on the crupper behind. The howdah itself, which Europeans use, is not unlike the body of a small gig, but without a head."

Capt. Williamson says, —

"The gait of an elephant is very peculiar, being similar to

the artificial pace of ambling taught to some horses. It is far from displeasing in a horse, but causes such a motion, when mounted on an elephant, as rarely to be borne for any distance. Indeed, I know nothing more uncomfortable and tedious, I may even say painful, than a long journey in a howdah. It occasions a lassitude not to be described. We must suppose that habit reconciles people to it; as we see the natives travel, for perhaps twenty miles or more in a forenoon, without any apparent uneasiness. The largest elephants are, in general, the most uncomfortable in this respect."

In mounting an elephant, the animal either kneels, or a ladder is used to climb upon its back; while natives descend by means of a rope. Generally a mahout, or professional driver, is employed to guide the elephant. Mr. Crawford states, that in his time this was not always the practice in Ava. He says, —

"After the elephant combats were over, the king prepared to take his departure. His elephant, one of the noblest animals I have ever seen, having the trunk, head, and part of the neck, of a white flesh-color, and in other respects altogether perfect, was brought up close to the shed under which we were sitting; and he mounted it with great agility, placed himself upon the neck of the animal, took the hook in his hand, and seemed to be perfectly at home in this employment. We afterwards saw the heir-apparent, a child of thirteen years of age, guiding his elephant in the same way. This practice is, I believe, peculiar to the Burmans; for, in Western India at least, no person of condition ever condescends to guide his own elephant. There is, at least, some manliness in the custom; and I should not be surprised to find that the neck of the elephant would be found, on experience, the most agreeable and easy seat to the rider."

The Emperor Akbar, in the same manner, rode every kind of elephant, making them obedient to his command.

Timour's elephant team is described by Sir John Mandeville as presenting a remarkable appearance: "A chariot with four wheels, upon which is a fair chamber of sweet-smelling lignum aloes, which is within covered with plates of fine gold, dubbed with precious stones and great pearls, and drawn by four elephants." Jehanghir rode through the streets of his capital on an elephant, followed by "twenty royal elephants for his own ascending, so rich, that in precious stones and furniture they braved the sun."

The famous tree-mound of Kublai Khan was built by the aid of elephants. "Not far from the palace," says an old writer, "on the northern side, and about a bow-shot distance from the surrounding wall, is an artificial mound of earth, the height of which is full an hundred paces, and the circuit at the base about a mile. It is clothed with the most beautiful evergreen-trees: for, whenever his majesty receives information of a handsome tree growing in any place, he causes it to be dug up; however large and heavy it may be, he has it transported by elephants to this mount."

When Timour built his great mosque at Samarcand, he employed ninety-five elephants to draw the stones. In the early days of ship-building in India, these huge animals were engaged to haul the vessels from the stocks; and Verthema, who travelled in India in 1503, gives the following example of their power:—

"I saw an instance of the extraordinary strength of these animals while at Cananore, where some Mahometans endeavored to draw a ship on the land, stern foremost, upon three rollers; on which occasion three elephants, commodiously applied, drew with great force, and, bending their heads down to the ground, brought the ship on the land."

Another writer states that he saw a tree overthrown by an elephant, which twenty-three men had attempted in vain.

In the war of Coromandel, in 1751, the gates of the fort of Ponomaley were attacked by elephants, whose heads had been covered with iron plates for the purpose.

Among the curious uses to which elephants have been put, may be mentioned fishing. A hunter came to a pool in the valley of the Chengree, India, once, with about twenty-five elephants. The natives discovered that it was alive with fish; but there were no boats. No one had a line; and, even if they had, the water was too shallow near shore, and too deep in the centre. The sportsman solved the difficulty by mustering all the elephants without their gear: then providing themselves with spears and baskets, the natives mounted the elephants, and commanded them to wade in. This they quickly did, rather enjoying the sport, and soon, by stirring up the mud, had the finny occupants of the pool flying about in all directions. Very soon the large fish began to come to the surface; and the elephants began to chase them, guided by their mahouts, who struck them with their spears; and, as soon as one was impaled, it was drawn upon the elephant, beheaded, and thrown into the basket. According to the hunter, who invented this curious method of fishing, the elephants exhibited remarkable sagacity in following the game, abstaining, at a hint from the mahout, from blowing under water, as they are apt to do, or splashing; indeed, acting exactly as if they knew that a noise of any kind would retard the progress of the sport. Sometimes several elephants would start after the same fish; and, as the water was four or five feet deep, the scene would become intensely exciting, the men standing on the great animals, and literally using them as boats. Occasionally a man would lose his balance, and tumble over, to rise, gasping, and half-strangled by the muddy water which soon dried, and gave them the appearance of having been white-washed. One elephant stepped into a deep hole, and nearly turned a somerset, tossing the men into the water; and, all in all, it was a very laughable and amusing sight to witness, and withal successful, as seventy pounds of fish were caught from the fleet of elephants.

Even after death, the elephant is of more or less value, exclusive of its ivory. In various countries certain portions, as the head and tongue, are esteemed as articles of food. The bones are used in Ceylon in enriching estates. The hair of the tail is utilized by native goldsmiths in bracelets, and teeth are well known as ivory. The feet are mounted as seats and footstools; and the great ears of the African elephant are harnessed to oxen, and dragged about to convey merchandise of various kinds. Sir Samuel Baker says that he has often used the large, soft ear of the African elephant as a couch after the fatigues of the hunt.

So valuable is the elephant in the East, that the inhabitants of the country wonder how Americans and others carry on the ordinary work of life without them; and, when Abraham Lincoln was president, the King of Siam conceived the idea of relieving the American people by providing them with these animals, which were to be raised just as ostriches are now on the California coast. The facts concerning this offer are extremely interesting, and I am indebted to the correspondent of "The Philadelphia Times" for the following. The communication is now in the keeping of the United States Treasury:—

"The letter is kept in a box of polished light-colored wood, about three inches deep, twelve inches long, and eight inches in width, gilded inside, and securely locked. The envelope for the letter is a bag of cloth of gold, long and narrow. The letter is written upon thick paper, the size of foolscap, with a broad gold border all around it. It is in Siamese; and accompanying it, and tied to it with a silken cord, is what is stated at its head to be a 'true translation' of the letter of the King of Siam. At the top of the first page, in the upper left-hand corner, is a curious little seal, not larger than a quarter of a dollar. Its impression is in gilt, and the device one peculiar to Siam, and unlike any thing else in nature or art.

"The letter begins with the names, title, and possessions of the King of Siam, whose personal letter it is supposed to be. Following this, on the same page, is the following address:—

"'*To His Most Respected Excellent Presidency,*—

"'The President of the United States of America, who, having been chosen by the citizens of the United States as most distinguished, was made president and chief magistrate in the affairs of the nation for an appointed time of office; viz., Buchanan, Esq., who had forwarded an official letter to us from Washington, 10th May, Anno Christi 1859, which was Wednesday, tenth night of waxing moon . . . in the year of Monkey, with a package of books, a hundred and ninety-two volumes in number, which came to hand in the year following. Or to whomsoever the people have elected anew as chief ruler in place of President Buchanan . . . [here some more complimentary titles and allusions are inserted] sendeth friendly greeting.'

"The letter goes on to comment upon the difficulties of sending communications from Siam to the United States, and to explain the indirect course letters took: so the king congratulated himself on having found an excellent opportunity — a sailing vessel of the United-States navy, the 'John Adams,' in command of Capt. Berrien, having come into the chief port of Siam, and its officers desiring to make a friendly visit to the king, and having been received by him — to forward his letter and some complimentary presents — a sword and a photographic likeness of himself — to the President of the United States.

"The king mentioned, that, in reply to questions asked by him of Capt. Berrien, he had learned that there are no elephants on the continent of America; and that so great a curiosity are they, that thousands of people will crowd to see even a large tusk of an elephant when exhibited in some public place, saying it was a wonderful thing: and he had learned that elephants are regarded by Americans as the most remarkable of all the large quadrupeds. He had also been informed that there were no camels on the continent of America: the Americans have sought for and purchased them, some from Europe, some from Arabia; and that now camels propagate their race, and are serviceable and of benefit to the country, and are already numerous in America. From this, one might infer that Capt. Berrien imposed somewhat on the credulity of this graciously inclined monarch.

"Having heard this about the camels, it occurred to the

king, continued the letter, that 'if on the continent of America, there should be several pairs of young male and female elephants turned loose in forests, where there was abundance of water and grass, in any region called by the English the torrid zone, and all were forbidden to molest them, to attempt to raise them would be well; and, if the climate should prove favorable to elephants, we are of opinion, that, after a while, they will increase till there be large herds, as there are on the continent of Asia, until the inhabitants of America will be able to catch them and tame them, and use them as beasts of burden, because, on account of the great strength and size of the elephants, they could be made to carry very heavy loads, and would be of benefit to the country, since they can travel where carriage and other roads have not been made.'

"The king, to illustrate how feasible it is to introduce elephants, and raise them successfully in countries where they had been unknown, cites examples from ancient times of the 'transplanting of elephants' to places where there were none, instancing the island of Ceylon, to which they were first taken four hundred years ago, and have become very plentiful there.

"He then proposed to give a number of young elephants of both sexes to our country if the United States will furnish a vessel for their transportation, supplied with food enough for them during the voyage. He further suggested that a steamer tow the ship on which they travel to America to hasten their arrival, so that the elephants would be received in good condition in their new home. He says very positively, that, as soon as they arrive in America, they must be turned loose in a jungle in the torrid zone.

"The king desires 'the President of the United States, and Congress, who conjointly with him rule the country,' to let him know their views as soon as possible, as to his offer to furnish the elephants, and whether or not they are wanted. He sends with this letter a pair of the largest size of elephants' tusks, 'both from the same animal, to be deposited for public inspection in the United States, that thereby the glory and renown of Siam may be promoted.'

"This letter, as stated at its close, was 'given at our royal audience hall, Anant Samagome, in the Grand Palace,' etc., at Bangkok, Siam, 'on Thursday, the fifth night of the waxing moon, in the lunar month from the commencement of the cold season in the year of Monkey, corresponding to the solar date of 14th February, Anno Christi 1861, which is the eleventh year, and this day is the 3,564th day of our reign.'

"It is scarcely necessary to say that this generous offer of the King of Siam to stock an elephant farm in America, was in due time declined, with thanks, by the authorities at Washington. By the time the letter was received, Abraham Lincoln was President, and Mr. Seward Secretary of State; and it is said, that, when the latter asked Mr. Lincoln what should be done with the elephants if they came, Mr. Lincoln said he did not know, unless 'they were used to stamp out the rebellion.'

"It is on the statute-books, however, that the Emperor of Morocco once presented a lion and two horses to the United States Consul at Tangier, to be sent to the government at Washington; and that it was done, and the matter called to the attention of Congress, whereupon it was

"'*Resolved*, By the Senate and House of Representatives in Congress assembled, That the President of the United States be, and he is hereby, authorized to cause the two horses received as a present by the Consul of the United States at Tangier, from the Emperor of Morocco, to be sold in Washington City, by public auction, on the last Saturday in February, 1835, and to cause the proceeds thereof to be placed in the Treasury of the United States, and that the lion received in like manner, be presented to such suitable institution, person or persons, as the President of the United States may designate.

"'Approved Feb. 13, 1835.'"

CHAPTER XVIII.

IVORY.

ONE of the most valuable, and certainly the most beautiful, of animal products is the substance we call ivory, which composes the upper incisor teeth of elephants. From the very earliest times, it has been esteemed by man, and has gradually grown more valuable as years have gone by, until now the demand is so great that the extermination of the noble animals that produce it is threatened, merely that we may have knife-handles, billiard-balls, piano-keys, and many articles of luxury.

The trade in ivory is of great antiquity; and doubtless, in very early times, there was a far greater demand for it than at present, and elephants were slaughtered in vast numbers. But after this, came a cessation; and the great animals had an opportunity to increase. According to Herodotus, Africa yielded her tributes of elephant teeth to the kings of Persia. The people of Judæa built ivory palaces; and even the galleys of Tyre, according to Pliny, had benches of ivory. In the Odyssey, we read of the luxury of the early Greek princes, —

> "The spoils of elephants the roofs inlay."

The Etruscan attributes of royalty were sceptres and thrones of ivory, and the ancient kings and magistrates of Rome sat upon ivory seats.

It is said, that, in the time of Pliny, the supply of African ivory almost gave out, when, only two centuries earlier, it was so plentiful, that, according to Polybius, the finest tusks were used as door-posts on the confines of Ethiopia, and even for palisades about the fields.

The decay of the ivory trade commenced with the fall of Rome: no longer were the commonest articles made of ivory, and even the Roman ivory tablets (*libri elephantini*) fell into disuse.

This sudden change was not without its effect; and, at the beginning of the seventeenth century, elephant tusks were a drug in the market. According to Battell, the natives had their idols of wood in the midst of their towns, fashioned like a negro: and at the foot thereof was a great heap of elephants' teeth, containing three or four tons of them; these were piled in the earth, and upon them were set the skulls of dead men, which they had slain in the wars, in monument of their victory."

When the Portuguese first established themselves at Angola and Congo, they found that the natives had accumulated vast stores of ivory, which was applied to the same superstitious uses. The Portuguese collected all they could, and shipped the tusks to Europe, reaping a rich harvest, and so depleting the supply, that in the middle of the seventeenth century it was almost exhausted again. In 1840 there were eleven manufactories of ivory goods in Dieppe, France; and nearly every large city to-day has one or more such. The extreme tastes that in the time of Leo X. required ivory beds, are not gratified in the present day; yet there is a constant demand for ivory.

It is extremely difficult to obtain the facts regarding the

PLATE XVI.

ASIATIC ELEPHANT AND TIGER.

Page 199.

importations of ivory in former years. In eleven years, from 1788 to 1798, 18,914 hundred-weight of ivory were imported into Great Britain, or about an annual importation of 192,-579 pounds. In 1827 about 118,000 pounds were imported.

In the sixteenth century the English traded for ivory on the Guinea coast; and a few years ago, even Cape Town was a headquarters for quantities of ivory; but the restricted area of the elephant, results in the tusks being taken to the nearest shipping-places on the coast, nearer Central Africa.

The natives were often grossly cheated. Mr. Burchell saw a party of twenty, — men, women, and children, — who had brought a thousand pounds of ivory to Cape Town, and only received the simplest articles for it. In the interior he met a Hottentot who had bought twenty fine tusks of the Bachapins, at a rate of a sheep for a tusk. These men offered Mr. Burchell two oxen and two tusks (each too heavy for a man to carry) for a gun. The native chiefs of to-day have a better appreciation of the value of ivory, and Europeans cannot hunt for elephants without making them valuable presents.

The present demand for ivory comes principally from England, America, and the European nations; while many tusks, as the huge teeth are called, are sent to China. In 1885, which may be considered an average year, — though the importations differ, and there has been a depression, — 439 tons of ivory were imported into England, for which several million dollars were paid.

By the courtesy of F. Grote & Co. of New York, and Westendorp & Co., London, I am enabled to present a table of extreme interest, showing the imports of ivory into Great Britain for the last forty years. It tells an interesting story of the destruction of the elephant: it is also interesting to note how the averages differ. The average number of tons for the years 1845–49 was 294; 1870–74, 627 tons; and for 1880–84, 514 tons; the imports of 1885 showing a falling off of one hundred tons. The imports by the year are as follows:—

YEAR.	TONS.	YEAR.	TONS.	YEAR.	TONS.	YEAR.	TONS.
1845	325	1856	491	1866	541	1876	567
1846	273	1857	489	1867	489	1877	627
1847	314	1858	624	1868	473	1878	652
1848	232	1859	539	1869	649	1879	444
1849	328	1860	542	1870	667	1880	536
1850	406	1861	589	1871	645	1881	546
1851	302	1862	568	1872	586	1882	425
1852	426	1863	499	1873	630	1883	596
1853	436	1864	538	1874	605	1884	466
1854	457	1865	548	1875	680	1885	439
1855	437						

To produce this enormous amount of ivory, and that imported into other countries, not less than seventy-five thousand elephants a year are destroyed. It has been estimated that fifty-one thousand are killed annually on the western coast of Africa, and probably twenty-five thousand does not cover those slaughtered in other localities. Much of this ivory comes from Africa, about one-fourth being obtained in India. In 1875–77 the yearly product of the latter country was between nine thousand and seventeen thousand pounds; a certain amount of this being cut from the tusks, not necessitating the death of the animal.

All the tuskers which are taken by Sanderson and others, in Asia, have their tusks shortened or cut, the tips being valuable ivory. The end is bound with a brass ring to prevent the tusk from splitting: Jumbo's tusks were cut off in this way. As the tusk is continually growing, the pulp being converted into ivory, the trimming operation can be repeated at certain intervals, generally every eight or ten years.

The finest ivory is that obtained from Equatorial Africa; either the natives bringing it out, or, as we have seen in a former chapter, Europeans penetrating the little-known recesses of the Dark Continent to procure it.

The west-coast ivory, when received, is generally almost black upon the outside, and presents any thing but an attractive appearance. The tusks are received by the wholesale trade, as Westendorp & Co. of London, and Grote & Co. of New York, the leading ivory-firms, wrapped in raw hides, sewed up by raw-hide thongs. These outside wraps are called "Schroons" by the trade. The different ivories have various tints; and an expert can tell at a glance where a tusk, or even a small piece of ivory, came from. The ivory which is shipped at Calcutta has a slight pink hue, and is very fine; while that received from Egyptian ports is brittle and poor. A visit to the ivory-vaults of the Messrs. Grote & Co., New York, would well repay any one interested in the subject of the economic value of animals. Here all kinds of ivory may be seen, and the extent and variety of objects made from it are astonishing. Here we find numbers of rings of ivory which are awaiting shipment back to Bombay, where they will be sold as bangles or bracelets to Hindoo women. Numerous flat ivory slabs are sold to Sheffield, England; and, finally, we may see them returned in the shape of knife-handles.

Some of the largest tusks in the Grote vaults are six inches in diameter at the base; and the tusk at the door of this firm, on 14th Street, used as a business sign, is nearly nine feet in length. This house manufactures almost every article that ivory can be made into; and objects ranging from billiard-balls to flat spatulas, for testing flour, may be seen in their cases. Billiard-balls require the choicest kind of ivory. The best are made here, and sell at five dollars each. I believe the Chinese have alone successfully produced the famous concentric balls of ivory, for which they have been so long and justly famous. Nothing is wasted in the ivory-shop. Even the dust is collected, and sold to the New-York florists, who claim that its results upon roses and other choice flowers are astonishing. It is also used in tempering certain steel tools, and in the manufacture of some acids.

To respond to this great demand, many professional ivory-hunters are constantly in the field. In a single season a small party have obtained twenty thousand pounds of ivory; for which they received twenty thousand dollars at Khartoom, or one dollar per pound. The tusks of elephants differ much in size; and, to show the loss in wear, Holub states that the wear on a pair of African tusks in the animal's life-time may equal six pounds,—the ivory being ground down when the animal uproots trees, and uses them in similar ways.

In the Abyssinian and Taba regions, tusks rarely exceed forty pounds, and average only about twenty-five. In Equatorial Africa they average about forty pounds, and range up to one hundred and fifty.

Gen. De Lima, returning from Mozambique, brought two straight tusks for a cross on the high altar of the cathedral at Goa. One weighed one hundred and eighty pounds, and the other one hundred and seventy. They had the slightest possible curve. "The Friend," a paper published in Ceylon, states that the officers of the ships "Quorrah" and "Alburhok," engaged in the Niger expedition, were shown two tusks by a native king which measured two feet and a half in circumference at the base, were eight feet in length, and weighed two hundred pounds each. According to Broderip, a tusk of three hundred and fifty pounds weight was sold at Amsterdam; but he gives no authority. Tusks often take peculiar shapes. An elephant was seen, in 1844, in the district of Bintenne, near Friars-hood Mountain, one of whose tusks took a complete turn, then resumed its original direction; and in the museum of the College of Physicians and Surgeons, there is a spiral tusk. The most remarkable freak of nature relating to tusks, that I am familiar with, is recorded by Thomas Baines, F. R. G. S., who was with Livingstone on the Zambesi. In various chapters, one, two, three, and four tusked elephants have been referred to; but this giant had nine. Mr. Baines says that it was shot in 1856; and a Mr. Edwards, a partner of Chapman, with whom he travelled, bought six of the tusks. "It had on the right side five, and on the left four, all growing, as usual, out of the upper jaw. The pair occupying the usual place were of about thirty pounds weight each; just behind them projected a pair somewhat larger, pointing downward and backward; between these were situated two others, and before and behind them in the right jaw were two more, but in the left only one, behind all these, being much smaller."

The ivory is always sold by weight; and the buyers are often deceived, as the tusks are liable to contain cavities, or have the pulp loaded with metal by designing traders. The size of the tusk generally determines the price; the larger it is, the more valuable, those below six or seven pounds being held at less than half the price per pound than those much larger. Many tusks are ruined through the ignorance of the natives. They are generally, however, transported with great care, the finest being wrapped in wax, or some similar substance.

Before considering the different kinds of ivory, and the various uses to which it is put, let us glance at its composition. In structure, it is equivalent to dentine, the material of which nearly all teeth are composed, and has an organic base or matrix, which upon examination is seen to be permeated by a vast number of very small and delicate canals, each of about one-fifteenth of an inch in diameter, which seem to commence at the pulp-cavity, presumably the axis, and extend outward to the periphery of the tusk. The little canals are not packed closely together, but are separated by spaces of about their own diameter. To these tubes, the regularity of their disposition and their delicacy, the ivory owes its fineness of grain, and its remarkable elasticity. By examining them, an expert can distinguish elephant ivory from any other; as they have a peculiarity of making a series of decided bends in their course, from the axis to the periphery, which produces a graining in the ivory, unique and peculiar.

Ivory is often confused with bone, but is a very different substance. It is much finer in general structure, much more elastic, and is without the canals that convey blood-vessels through the bones. If a section of a tusk is made some distance from the growing pulp, the centre, or core, will be found to be darker than the rest, and of a different nature. This is the remains of the pulp. The outer portion of the tusk is still different, or composed of a compact layer of cementum that covers or encloses the entire tusk. The intermediate substance is ivory, which shows many circular lines about the central dark spot, calling to mind the growth-marks seen in sections of trees, and due to the fact that in all ivory there are great numbers of very minute spaces known as "interglobular spaces." The localities occupied by these spaces are characterized by a smaller proportion of lime-salts and a greater proportion of organic matter than other portions. Hence this part of the ivory is not so dense as the rest, and is more liable to decomposition: so, in many of the fossil tusks that are found, a sectional view often shows it separated into six or seven distinct rings, the intermediate organic matter having disappeared. It is supposed, that, in living ivory, these interglobular spaces are filled with some organic substance. According to Von Bibra, ivory contains from forty to forty-three per cent of organic matter; while human dentine contains from twenty-four to thirty-four per cent.

From its delicate structure, ivory takes a rich polish; and it is also susceptible of being dyed. The ease with which it is carved, makes it one of the most valuable of all materials for artistic carving.

The ivory used in England and America is mostly from the African elephant; but in Russia much of it comes from the tusks of mammoths, described in chapter fourth. These elephantine monsters existed in great numbers in former days; and in some localities, their tusks are found in great abundance. When the first explorers examined the New Siberian Islands, they found mammoth tusks projecting from the sand in many places; and in others the tundra seemed to be fairly made up of them.

The best localities are at the mouth of the Lena and other Arctic rivers and the Liakhoff and New Siberian Islands.

The mammoth tusks are much more curved than those of existing elephants, and much heavier, weighing as much as three hundred and twenty pounds a pair. Some are preserved as perfectly as if the animal had but recently died, while many more are ruined by the weather; but to-day, even after years of collecting, the supply may be said to not only equal the demand, but to be practically inexhaustible.

As a rule, the mammoth ivory is too dry and brittle for fine work, and is said to turn yellow. Fine tusks bring large prices. One recently offered to the Oxford Museum was valued at five hundred dollars; and about ten years ago, over one thousand were sent to London for sale, weighing from one hundred and forty to one hundred and sixty pounds each. The best of these found a ready market; but, as a rule, mammoth ivory is not esteemed.

Westendorp has investigated this ivory, and finds that about fourteen per cent is good; seventeen per cent could be used in some way; fifty-four was bad; and fifteen per cent utterly useless. He considered about 1*s*. 6*d*. per pound a fair price.

The life of the ivory-hunter of the North is equally as dangerous as that of the South, as the tusks, as a rule, are found only in the most desolate places; yet there is an element of excitement about it far greater than that which is experienced in shooting the African elephant. It is true that the great mammoth is dead; but yet the possibility of finding the carcass of one of these monsters in the flesh, and clothed with hair, has been sufficient incentive to keep many hunters in the field.

In the chapter on the mammoth, some of the most remarkable discoveries have been referred to. The ivory-hunters have for years found vast quantities of tusks at the New Siberian Islands, which lie to the north and east of the Lena delta.

The first mammoth tusk was brought to England by Josias Logan in 1611, and was obtained in the region of the Petchora. It is estimated that about one hundred pairs are yearly offered for sale; and, according to Nordenskiöld, the tusks of at least twenty thousand mammoths have been collected since Siberia was first investigated.

The frozen bodies of the mammoth were originally called mummies; and the first one that is mentioned is in a sketch of the journey of the Russian ambassador, Evert Yssbrants Ides, who, in 1692, journeyed through Siberia to China. A professional ivory-hunter travelled with him, and described the parts of a specimen which he found; and, to show how perfectly it was preserved, the neck was still colored by blood.

This same collector found a pair of tusks which weighed two hundred kilograms. He informed Ides that the heathen Yakuts, Tunguses, and Ostyaks believed that the mammoth lived underground, just as did the Chinese; and that it died only when it came to the surface, and saw or smelled air.

An interesting account of the folk-lore of the natives, relating to this point, will be found in J. B. Müller's work referred to in the bibliography.

In 1839 a complete mammoth was uncovered by a landslide on the shores of a lake near the Yenisej River.

Nordenskiöld says, "Under the guidance of natives, I collected, in 1876, at the confluence of the river Mesenkin with the Yenisej, in 71° 28′ north latitude, some fragments of bones, and pieces of the hide, of a mammoth. The hide was twenty to twenty-five millimetres thick, and nearly tanned by age, which ought not to appear wonderful, when we consider, that, though the mammoth lived in one of the latest periods of the history of our globe, hundreds of thousands, perhaps millions, of years have, however, passed since the animal died, to which these pieces of skin once belonged. It was clear that they had been washed by the neighboring river Mesenkin out of the tundra-bank; but I endeavored, without success, to discover the original locality, which was probably already concealed by river-mud. In the neighborhood was found a very fine cranium of the musk-ox."

African-elephant ivory, which is esteemed above all others, on account of its close grain, and less tendency to turn yellow when exposed, is semi-transparent when first cut, and in this condition is called "green" by the ivory-workers. As it dries, it becomes lighter, and more opaque, owing to the drying out of the water. During this process, the ivory shrinks more or less, as wood does; and in making box-covers, billiard-balls, and in all delicate work, great care is required, the ivory being generally roughly shaped, and placed in a warm room to gradually shrink and dry true. The plates used on piano-keys are dried and shrunk at once by being baked in an oven.

The greatest skill of the worker is, perhaps, shown in the original cutting, as here much waste can be made by ignorance or carelessness. Often the cutter finds cavities in the ivory, and not uncommonly bullets, and parts of various weapons. These have been shot into the tender pith at the base of the tusk, and, in time, become incorporated in the ivory.

A specimen of a tusk in the Odontological Society, London, shows a spear-head embedded in the ivory, completely enclosed by it and secondary dentine, though measuring seven and a half by ten inches. In another instance, the tusk was formed into a cup, while the embedded spear-head was left exposed as a stand. A javelin firmly embedded in ivory is exhibited in the collection of the College of Physicians and Surgeons, London.

Ivory is easily worked; and veneers have been cut, according to Tomes, by a reciprocating saw making a spiral shaving around the tusk forty feet in length, and twelve inches in width.

As ivory grows old, it turns yellow, especially if kept in the dark. It is said that the ancients possessed the secret of softening it. If this is so, it is one of the lost arts, as it cannot be done to-day; though it is rendered more flexible by submitting it to the solvent action of phosphoric acid.

The uses to which ivory is put are innumerable. Formerly it was used in the manufacture of false teeth, and it is used to some extent to-day by native dentists in India. The dust and chips of ivory are all used, and are either boiled down into a gelatine, or calcined into ivory-black.

The confectioners are said to use ivory-dust as a basis for groups, and it is often utilized when a delicate size is required. The calcined ivory affords a fine black pigment called ivory-black, and is also used as fine printing-ink, and in printing etchings and engravings.

All the objects manufactured at Dieppe to-day can, perhaps, trace back many of their methods to Demosthenes, the father of the orator, who was a worker in ivory. He had an extensive manufactory of cabinet-ware, and used great quantities of ivory. He had another manufactory, where ivory knife-handles were made, and was also a wholesale dealer in the commodity.

We are indebted to Messrs. F. Grote & Co. for the following interesting item, which was received too late for insertion in the proper place: —

"The tusk which stands at our door, in 14th Street, New York, was brought from Zanzibar, Africa, being from the species *Elephas Africanus.* Its length, on the outside curve, is eight feet and eleven inches; its length on the inside curve is eight feet and one half inch; its diameter at base is six and one half inches; its weight is one hundred and eighty-four pounds."

This is a notable example, and one which has long excited public interest.

We are also indebted to Messrs. Totans & Schmidt, of Fulton Street, New-York City, for the dimensions of a pair of tusks of an African elephant, which have long graced their show-window. They measure respectively, eight feet and six inches, and eight feet four inches, in length. The larger weighs one hundred and thirty-five pounds, and its circumference is twenty inches and three quarters at base.

CHAPTER XIX.

THE ELEPHANT IN THE ARTS.

THE elephant has figured prominently in the arts from the earliest times. The first artist in ivory was undoubtedly contemporaneous with the mammoth; as upon a piece of mammoth's tusk, taken from a cave in France, there is a rude but quite correct representation of one of these huge animals: and the figure of the elephant seems to have been a favorite with the sculptors of all times. On the island of Elephanta, there are the remains of an ancient statue of an elephant. A fine cutting of an Indian species with young was found upon the walls of Pompeii; and the animal is often seen on the bass-reliefs along the Nile (Plate XXII).

It is upon medals, however, that the elephant figured most prominently, these now valued relics having been struck off in honor of the ancient kings and queens to commemorate their deeds of valor. An interesting medal (Plate XXI., Fig. 1) was struck in honor of Tranquillina, the wife of Gordian; the Romans at this time, in a spirit of poetical exaggeration, choosing the elephant as a symbol of eternity. The legend "Æternitas Aug." is expressive of a wish that the emperor shall live as long as an elephant, which was then believed to be three or four hundred years.

The sagacity of the elephant is often referred to in the

ancient mythology of the Hindoos; and Ganessa, the god of wisdom, is represented in the temples of India with a human body and an elephant's head: curiously enough, several ancient medals show the head of Socrates united with that of an elephant in connection with two other heads. Plate XXI., Fig. 2, is explained by Chifletius as referring to the trial of Socrates; and the two heads are supposed to be those of Anytus and Melitus, his accusers. This, however, has been questioned. A Neapolitan medal (Plate XXI., Fig. 3), supposed to be antique, represents an elephant standing before the tripod of Apollo, upon which the sacrificial fire is burning. Medals are in existence in Europe, showing the pretended religion of the elephant. Such a one was struck by Cardinal Zabrella (Plate XXI., Fig. 4), and shows one of these animals worshipping the moon.

In the "Museum Cuspinianum," edited by Laurentius, there is figured a medal (Plate XXII., Fig. 5) which is supposed to represent Alexander after his conquest in Persia, entering through the gate of a city, or a triumphal arch, in a chariot drawn by four elephants. On the other side of the medal, the head of Alexander is shown, with Neptune on one side of his helmet. Some experts consider this medal as spurious.

Alexander figures on many medals, and a very fine one (Plate XXI., Fig. 6) represents his head covered with an elephant's skin. On the reverse is Minerva, armed with a helmet, shield, and spear; and before her an eagle holding lightning in his talons. Berger supposes it to refer to the defeat of the elephants of Porus.

Quite similar in general appearance to this is a medal (Plate XXI., Fig. 7) supposed to represent Ptolemy Philadelphus. The head of an elephant, or the skin of the head, is used as a head-covering, the tusks extending over the head as in a Roman medallion of Africa (Plate XXII., Fig. 9).

The last record of the elephant in Syria is found upon a coin (Plate XXI., Fig. 8) struck in honor of Antiochus, who was raised to the throne in the two hundred and twenty-fifth year of the era of the Seleucidæ, 87 B.C. The elephant is represented as bearing a torch, according to the custom of the Syrian monarchs, with the horn of plenty behind him. Julius Cæsar had many medals struck off in his honor. One (Plate XXII., Fig. 10) represents his head, the reverse being a triumphal chariot drawn by four elephants, and is supposed by experts to relate to the conquest of Juba and the Mauri in Africa. Another medal, which was struck by the Emperor Trajan (Plate XXI., Fig. 11), in honor of Julius Cæsar, represents an elephant trampling upon a serpent, probably relating to the same event.

The Emperor Augustus was voted by the senate a triumphal arch, a chariot drawn by two elephants, and a statue, for the great deeds he accomplished; all of which is recorded on a medal (Plate XXI., Fig. 12). After the death of Augustus, his statue was conveyed on a chariot by four elephants to the circus, after which the games commenced, this post-funereal honor being also commemorated by a medal. Caligula was also thus honored by the senate; and a medal (Plate XXI., Fig. 13) pictures him sitting upon the chariot, as a god surrounded by stars. Nero and his mother, Agrippina, are represented (Plate XXI., Fig. 14) in a somewhat similar position.

The inventive genius of Severus in suggesting new pleasures was commemorated in a medal (Plate XXI., Fig. 15) which represents numerous animals, including the elephant, about a ship which, loaded with ferocious animals, he sailed on a small lake for the diversion of his favorites.

One of the finest elephant medals extant represents the statue of Pertinax drawn by four elephants in a triumphal chariot after his death (Plate XXII., Fig. 16); and these are but a few that are to be found in collections in various parts of the world, but show that the elephant took an important part in all the deeds of the great men of the time.

The ivory of elephants has been employed in artistic work since very early times. The British Museum has specimens of ivory plaques of rich design taken from Nineveh, which are supposed to date from 900 B.C. The execution in some is very fine; many figures being in high, and some in low, relief, but all showing that the worker was an expert in the art.

"Traces of gilding," says Tomes, "remain on many of them; and they were often, furthermore, enriched by being inlaid with fragments of *lapis lazuli*, or of a colored glass in apparent imitation of this: the edges of the larger heads were generally rendered conspicuous by this means. In one of the panels, the border of the dresses, the thrones on which the figures were seated, the ornaments above the cartouche, and the cymbals upon the cartouche itself, were thus inlaid with color. The largest object is a carved staff, perhaps a sceptre. Amongst the smaller pieces are heads of animals, and entire animals, griffins, human heads, crossed and clasped hands, rings, etc. Like the ivory-carvers of a later period, these early workers seem to have studied the economy of their material. Thus, a beautiful carving in high relief of two griffins, standing upon papyrus flowers, has been worked in the interior segment of a large tusk, the natural curvature of which it follows." Besides these discovered at Nineveh, some other ivories of great antiquity exist; and ivory-workers are mentioned as a distinct class of artificers at the commencement of the Christian era. Many writing-tablets of ivory, with raised rims inside, where wax was spread over their surfaces, have come down to us. These were often made to fold together, and the exterior richly ornamented with carvings. It was the custom for newly appointed consuls under the empire to send these plaques to persons of importance, and the covers sometimes have portrayed upon them the consul in his robes of office.

These ancient relics are invaluable. In the South Kensington Museum, there is exhibited a beautiful ivory plaque of the third century, for which two thousand dollars were paid. It forms one-half of a diptych, and measures eleven and three-quarters by four and three-quarters inches. The other half is in the Hotel Cluny.

Many of the ancient carvings deal with sacred subjects. One of the most beautiful is a Pieta, representing the Virgin holding the dead Christ in her lap, and dates from the fourteenth century. Schliemann, in his excavations on the supposed site of Troy, has found many ivory objects, as pins, buckles, etc.

The most profligate and, it must be confessed, magnificent use of ivory is seen in the attempts of the early Greeks to add to the splendors of their national religion. During the time of Pericles, 445 B.C., there was a demand for fine statues of the gods; and it was reserved for Phidias, the most famous of all the ancient sculptors, to invent the ivory statue,—not the diminutive creations with which we are familiar, but colossal figures formed of an aggregation of small pieces. The Greeks had figures of wood and stone; but finally the public taste seemed to demand something more refined, and the combination of gold and ivory was the result. (See Plate XVII.)

The use of ivory in art-work had preceded this many years. From the time of the Trojan war, they had used ivory arms and furniture; and two hundred years later we hear of Solomon introducing it in Judæa. "Once in three years came the navy of Tarshish, bringing gold and silver, ivory, and apes and peacocks;" and being thus supplied with the elephants' teeth of India, "the king made a great throne of ivory, and overlaid it with the best gold." One hundred years after Solomon, the sacred historian speaks of "the ivory house of King Ahab" as so wonderful, that it is enumerated in Chronicles with all the cities that he built. "The ivory house of Ahab," and "the ivory palaces" of the forty-fifth psalm, no doubt referred to buildings profusely ornamented with ivory.

Phidias, then, must have been familiar with ivory-work, having such illustrious examples in history; but none of his predecessors had attempted the stupendous works which rendered him famous. Unfortunately the creations of this celebrated artist were all destroyed, and we have only the descriptions left.

When Greece fell, her oppressors, the Turks, a race of barbarians, destroyed all the grand works in marble they could find. For two or three hundred years, they pounded up the beautiful statues of the Parthenon to obtain lime to make their miserable hovels; and it is probably to them that is due the destruction of the works of chryselephantine (gold and ivory) statuary that were so celebrated, that almost every ancient writer described them. One was so richly ornamented with gold, that Pericles mentions it as one of the resources for carrying on the Peloponnesian war. The gold was stolen, and carried off by Leochares during the siege of Athens by Demetrius.

The masterpiece of Phidias was the Jupiter of Olympia. "The god," says Pausanias, "made of gold and ivory, is seated upon a throne. On his head is a crown, representing an olive-branch. In his right hand he carries a Victory, also of gold and ivory, holding a wreath, and having a crown upon her head. In the left hand of the god is a sceptre, shining with all sorts of metals. The bird placed upon the summit of the sceptre is an eagle. The sandals of the god are of gold, and his mantle is also golden. The figures of various animals, and of all sorts of flowers, particularly lilies, are painted upon it. The throne is a diversified assemblage of gold, of precious stones, of ivory, and of ebony, in which figures of all kinds are also painted or sculptured."

Curiously enough, this writer does not give the dimensions of the work, an omission that is supplied by Strabo. "Phidias," he says, "had made his Jupiter sitting, and touching almost the summit of the roof of the temple: so that it appeared, that, if the god had risen up, he would have lifted off the roof. The interior of the temple is said to have been sixty feet high, and the statue was about forty-eight feet in height." Equalling if not rivalling Phidias in the estimation of some, was Polycletus, who produced the Juno of Argos. His works were not on so grand a scale as his contemporary Phidias, but excelled them in beauty and execution. Pausanias thus describes his masterpiece: "The statue of Juno is seated on a throne. Her size is extraordinary. She is of gold and ivory. On her head is a crown, whereon are worked the figures of the Hours and Graces. In one hand she holds the sceptre, in the other the fruit of the pomegranate." Maximus Tyrius says, "Polycletus enabled the Argives to contemplate the queen of the gods in all her majesty. She is seated upon a throne of gold, where we admire the whiteness of her breast and arms of ivory."

The Minerva of the Parthenon, a gold and ivory statue, was a marvellous piece of work, and one of the earliest productions of Phidias. There is no known description of it, though frequent allusions to it are found in the works of ancient writers. From Plato, we learn that the gold on the statue predominated over the ivory. "Phidias," he says, "made neither the eyes, nor the face, nor the feet, nor the hands, of his Minerva of gold, but of ivory;" and Plutarch records the fact that Phidias arranged to meet his critics, by so disposing the gold about the statue that it could be taken off and weighed, if his honesty was doubted.

After the death of Alexander, statues of himself and family, in gold and ivory, were placed in the Philippeum of Olympia. The funeral monument of Hephæstion was ornamented with statues of ivory and gold.

The successors of Alexander made lavish use of ivory. Ptolemy Philadelphus, at the time of his triumph in Egypt, was followed by six hundred elephants' tusks borne by slaves; and, according to Quatremère de Quincy, some of the many statues drawn upon the cars in his triumphal march were of gold and ivory.

To show the abundance of ivory at this time, Ptolemy used it to build a portico in his favorite ship, described by Athenæus.

PLATE XVII.

STATUE OF JUPITER.

(Made of Ivory and Gold, by Phidias.)

Pages 217 and 236.

According to Dion Cassius, Cæsar caused a statue of himself to be executed in ivory; and Passiteles, a contemporary of Pompey, executed an ivory statue of Jupiter for the temple built by Metellus. The doors of the Palatium, which Augustus raised after the victory of Actium, were of ivory. A similar statue was decreed to Germanicus by the senate, and the Emperor Titus had an equestrian statue executed in honor of Britannicus.

Colossal statues of ivory continued in favor under the Romans, and Phidias had many followers: thus Adrian had completed the temple of Jupiter at Athens; he erected in it a large statue of gold and ivory.

These grand works fell into disuse when Christianity was established under Constantine, and probably many of these works of art were destroyed at this time. All that remain of the vast numbers of ivory statues is a figure about eight inches in height, and the works referred to on previous pages.

At the present day, ivory sculpture is confined to small figures of various kinds, the most extensive work being done by the Chinese and Japanese artists: the latter delight in the grotesque productions of their art.

According to the Davenport Academy of Sciences, to which I am indebted for permission to use the accompanying engravings, the mastodon figured in the arts of the mound-builders. The pipes shown in Plate XVIII. presumably represent a proboscidian; and many notable archæologists believe that the pipe-makers were familiar with the mastodon, and perpetuated its form in the pipes. According to Mr. Charles E. Putnam, president of the Academy, one of the pipes was found, in 1880, in a mound on the farm of Mr. P. Hass, in Louisa County, Io., the discoverer being the

Rev. A. Blumer, a Lutheran clergyman, who presented the pipe to the Academy. The other pipe was obtained by Rev. J. Goss from a farmer in the same county, who found it while planting corn on his farm some time previous. The famous big elephant mound in Grant County, Wis., is supposed to represent an elephant in profile, the huge, pillar-like legs and the trunk being plainly seen; though it might well have been intended to represent any other animal of like shape.

CHAPTER XX.

ELEPHANTS IN THE AMPHITHEATRE.

AS the elephant was used in the early days to add to the pomp and glory of the Roman conquerors, it is not surprising that they were also employed in the games and sports of the people. It was the custom in the days of old Rome, to match men against the most ferocious animals; and, long before the elephant was known in Italy, brave men met the lion, single-handed, in the arena. When the elephant was introduced, it was evident that the amphitheatre had new possibilities; and forthwith the huge animals became a feature of the barbaric pastimes of the period. It is needless to say that a people given to such diversions, which involved the torture of thousands of living creatures, were grossly debased morally.

Milton has thus described the times and men under Tiberius: —

> "That people, victor once, now vile and base,
> Deservedly made vassal; who, once just,
> Frugal, and mild, and temp'rate, conquered well;
> But governed ill the nations under yoke,
> Peeling their provinces, exhausted all
> By lust and rapine; first ambitious grown
> Of triumph, that insulting vanity;

> Then cruel, by their sports to blood inured
> Of fighting beasts, and men to beasts exposed;
> Luxurious by their wealth, and greedier still,
> And from the daily scene effeminate."

For four hundred years Rome was given over to displays, in which the most brutal passions were aroused, and of which the Spanish bull-fight is the sole modern representative. The great circus where these exhibitions took place was the Colosseum, in which five thousand wild beasts were slaughtered at its dedication by Vespasian; and its skeleton-walls still stand to-day, a monument to the skill and misdirected talent of the people of that time.

The Roman circus was thoroughly a government institution, and a part of the political machinery of the time in this way, that the exhibitions of strange wild beasts was devised by the victorious Roman rulers to show to their constituents and countrymen the wonders of the foreign countries they had conquered.

According to Pliny, Mutius Scævola (102 B.C.) first exhibited a combat of lions at the circus, and C. Scipio Trasica and C. Lentulus were the originators of contests between men and wild beasts.

In these terrific struggles, lions and tigers were let loose in the arena, and fought with human slaves and convicts.

When Pompey dedicated his theatre, he gave the most remarkable exhibition on record. Five hundred lions and eighteen hundred elephants are said to have been pitted against a body of armed men. The huge animals were attacked in every possible way, — sometimes by swords, again by lances. In the second consulate of Pompey (54 B.C.), a herd was matched against a company of Getulian archers;

and, according to Pliny, one of the elephants, enraged by its wounds, rushed upon an archer, and hurled his shield high in air. Another, wounded by a javelin, created a panic among the rest; the great animals rushing against the railing of the circus with such force, that it gave way, and numbers of the spectators were wounded.

As a rule, the elephants were defeated; and the historian Dion adds a description of a wonder no less honorable to the Roman people than to the sagacity of the elephants. "The spectators," he says, "so compassionated the animals, when they saw them raising their trunks to heaven, roaring most piteously, as if imploring the gods to avenge the cruel treachery which had compelled them to come from their native forests, that they demanded that they should be saved." Pliny, relating the same story, states that the populace were so touched by the terror which the elephants exhibited, and so full of admiration at their sagacity, that regardless of the presence of Pompey, and forgetful of his munificence, they rose from their seats, and demanded, with imprecations against the consul, that the combat should be at an end. But habit appears soon to have reconciled the people to the torturing cruelties of the amphitheatre, —

> "Where murder breathed her bloody steam;"

and we have few other recorded instances of their clemency.

The elephant tournaments of Cæsar added greatly to his popularity as dictator. "When Cæsar, the conqueror of the world," says Velleius Paterculus, "returned to the city, he forgave all who had borne arms against him [which passes all human belief], and exhibited ship-fights, and contests of horse and foot, together with elephants." "On this occasion the spectators were well secured by ditches, which surrounded the arena, from the charges of the infuriated beasts, who had annoyed them considerably at the games of Pompey. In these sports of the great dictator, twenty elephants were opposed to five hundred men on foot."

Entertainments of this kind naturally tended to debase and brutalize the people, and the demand for slaughter was ever on the increase. It is said that Claudius rose at daylight to go to the circus, that he might not miss a single pang of the victims, human or brute. During his reign, and that of Nero, a famous sport was to match an elephant against a single fencer, who sometimes attacked the great beast on horseback, and again on foot.

The Colosseum was the natural outcome of the passion for such barbarous sports. The old one did not afford room enough, and Vespasian commenced the new one, which was completed by Titus (A.D. 79); and it still stands, as a monument of a dark era in the history of Rome.

While these exhibitions would seem only a remnant of the most barbarous ages, they have been permitted, even at the present day. In certain parts of India, elephants are now baited to afford entertainment to certain native princes and nobles; and fifty or sixty years ago it was very common.

When Bishop Heber was at the court of Baroda, "The Rajah," he says, "was anxious to know whether I had observed his rhinoceros and his hunting-tigers, and offered to show me a day's sport with the last, or to bait an elephant for me, — a cruel amusement which is here not uncommon. . . . I do not think he understood my motive for declining to be present."

"At the palace of Jyepoor," says the same writer, "we

were shown five or six elephants in training for a fight. Each was separately kept in a small, paved court, with a little litter, but very dirty. They were all what is called 'must;' that is, fed on stimulating substances, to make them furious: and all showed in their eyes, their gaping mouths, and the constant motion of their trunks, signs of fever and restlessness. Their mahouts seemed to approach them with great caution; and, on hearing a step, they turned round as far as their chains would allow, and lashed fiercely with their trunks."

Mr. Crawford states that elephant combats were common in his day; but, as a rule, the animals, directed by mahouts, fought across a stout railing, the method of attack being to butt each other, and cut with the tusks.

Father Tachard, a French Jesuit, witnessed an elephant-fight in Siam, in 1685, before the king. The animals were matched against each other, but were securely tied by the hind-legs, so they could not severely injure each other. They fenced with their tusks, striking such powerful blows that one of the combatants lost its tusks.

Elephant-fights have been a favorite amusement in India from the very earliest times. At Agra, according to the "Ayeen Akbery," the emperor built a large amphitheatre especially for these performances; and Robert Covert, who travelled in Hindostan in 1609, in referring to Agra, tells of elephants fighting before the Mogul, parted with rockets of wild-fire, made round, like hoops, which they thrust in their faces.

The finest account extant of one of these combats is given by Bernier:—

"The festivals generally conclude with an amusement

unknown in Europe, — a combat between two elephants, which takes place in the presence of all the people, on the sandy space near the river; the king, the principal ladies of the court, and the omrahs, viewing the spectacle from different apartments in the fortress.

"A wall of earth is raised three or four French feet wide, and five or six high. The two ponderous beasts meet one another face to face, on opposite sides of the wall, each having a couple of riders, that the place of the man who sits on the shoulders, for the purpose of guiding the elephant with a large iron hook, may immediately be supplied if he should be thrown down. The riders animate the elephants, either by soothing words, or by chiding them as cowards, and urge them on with their heels, until the poor creatures approach the wall, and are brought to the attack. The shock is tremendous; and it appears surprising that they even survive the fearful wounds and blows inflicted with their teeth, their heads, and their trunks. There are frequent pauses during the fight; it is suspended and renewed; and the mud wall being at length thrown down, the stronger or more courageous elephant passes on, attacks his opponent, and, putting him to flight, pursues and fastens upon him so obstinately, that the animals can be separated only by means of cherkys, or fireworks, which are made to explode between them; for they are naturally timid, and have a particular dread of fire, which is the reason why elephants have been used with so very little advantage in armies since the use of fire-arms. The boldest come from Ceylon; but none are employed in war which have not been regularly trained, and accustomed for years to the discharge of muskets close to their heads, and the bursting of crackers between their legs.

PLATE XVIII.

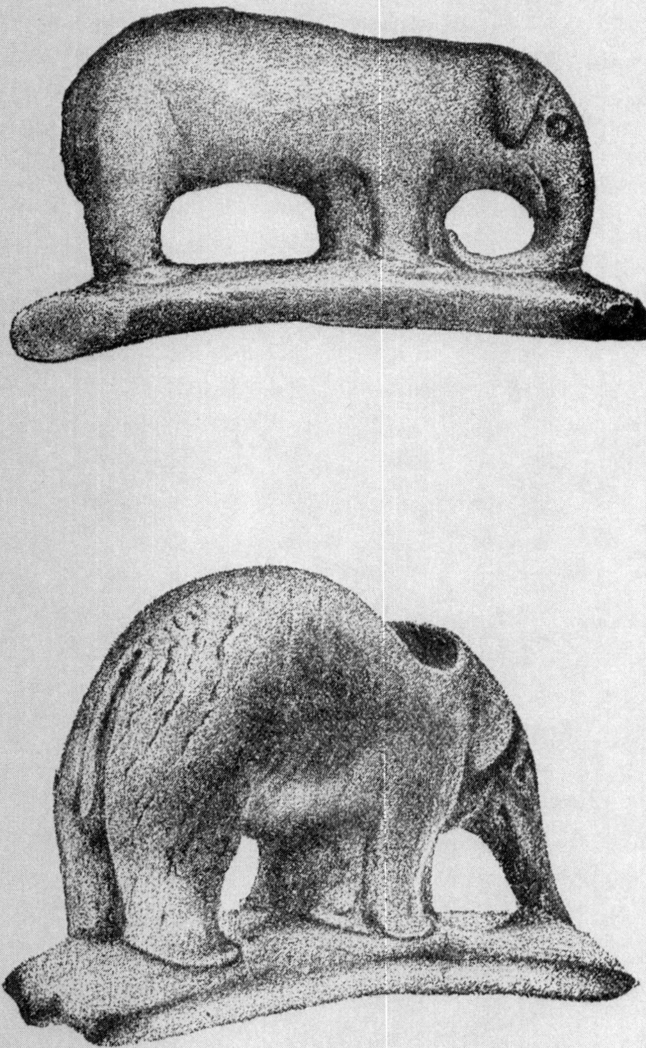

PREHISTORIC STONE PIPES.

Page 239.

"The fight of these noble animals is attended with much cruelty. It frequently happens that some of the riders are trodden under foot, and killed on the spot; the elephant having always cunning enough to feel the importance of dismounting the rider of his adversary, whom he therefore endeavors to strike down with his trunk. So imminent is the danger considered, that, on the day of combat, the unhappy men take the same formal leave of their wives and children as if condemned to death. They are somewhat consoled by the reflection, that, if their lives should be preserved, and the king be pleased with their conduct, not only will their pay be augmented, but a sack of peyssas (equal to fifty francs) will be presented to them the moment they alight from the elephant. They have also the satisfaction of knowing, that, in the event of their death, the pay will be continued to the widows, and that their sons will be appointed to the same situation. The mischief with which this amusement is attended does not always terminate with the death of the rider: it often happens that some of the spectators are knocked down and trampled upon by the elephants, or by the crowd; for the rush is terrible when, to avoid the infuriated combatants, men and horses, in confusion, take to flight. The second time I witnessed this exhibition, I owed my safety entirely to the goodness of my horse and the exertions of my two servants."

In the middle of the seventeenth century, elephant-fighting was a favorite amusement among the princes of the Mogul empire. Almost every day some exhibition was given, devised to afford a display of the greatest cruelty. A single elephant was matched against six horses, which were killed by being clasped about the neck by the elephant, and suffocated, or impaled by their tusks. On other occasions, the elephant was matched against a tiger. Mr. Crawford witnessed such a performance. The tiger was muzzled, and its claws cut, and was finally killed by successive tosses from the tusks of the infuriated elephant, who hurled the helpless animal a distance of thirty feet.

At one of the Mogul entertainments, an English bull-dog was matched against an elephant. The pugnacious animal seized the trunk of the elephant, and clung to it until it was jerked into the air to a great height. But it held on so long, that bull-dogs became great favorites with the Mogul, who had them carried about in palanquins with him, and is said to have fed them himself with silver tongs, made expressly for the purpose. Pliny gives an account of two remarkable dogs, which were presented to Alexander the Great by the King of Albania, one of which vanquished an elephant. Happily, the day for these barbarous contests has gone by, at least in civilized nations.

CHAPTER XXI.

THE ELEPHANT IN PAGEANTRY.

IN all the magnificent ceremonials and pageants of the Orient, the elephant forms a prominent feature: and even to-day we are delighted and amused with the impressive spectacle a herd presents as it marches in the procession of the circus; the dignified bearing of the animals, their measured tread, and large stature, all adding to the grandeur of the scene.

That this was recognized in olden times, is well known; and, whenever a king desired to show his power and riches to the best advantage, the elephant was employed. Bernier has given a vivid description of some of the processions of the East.

"I cannot avoid," he says, "dwelling on this pompous procession of the seraglio. It strongly arrested my attention during the late march, and I feel delight in recalling it to my memory. Stretch imagination to its utmost limits, and you can conceive no exhibition more grand and imposing than when Rochinara Begum (Aurengzebe's sister), mounted on a stupendous Pegu elephant, and seated in a mikdember, blazing with gold and azure, is followed by five or six other elephants, with mik-dembers nearly as resplendent as her own, and filled with ladies attached to her household.

Close to the princess are the chief eunuchs, richly adorned and finely mounted, each with a cane in his hand; and, surrounding her elephant, a troop of female servants from Tartary and Kashmire, fantastically attired, and riding handsome pad-horses. Besides these attendants, are several eunuchs on horseback, accompanied by a multitude of pagys, or lackeys, on foot, with large canes, who advance a great way before the princess, both to the right and to the left, for the purpose of clearing the road, and driving before them every intruder. Immediately behind Rochinara Begum's retinue appears a principal lady of the court, mounted and attended much in the same manner as the princess. This lady is followed by a third; she by a fourth; and so on, until fifteen or sixteen females of quality pass, with a grandeur of appearance, equipage, and retinue, more or less proportionate to their rank, pay, and office. There is something very impressive of state and royalty in the march of these sixty or more elephants; in their solemn and, as it were, measured steps; in the splendor of their mik-dembers, and the brilliant and innumerable followers in attendance. And if I had not regarded this display of magnificence with a sort of philosophical indifference, I should have been apt to be carried away by the similar flights of imagination as inspire most of the Indian poets, when they represent the elephants as carrying so many goddesses, concealed from the vulgar gaze."

For many years after the capture of India by the British, elephants were employed by the princes and nobles; but now their use is prohibited in Calcutta, on account of the many accidents that resulted; and in British India the animal is rarely seen on occasions of ceremony, except at the courts of native princes who still have some authority.

Elephants were employed in the ceremonies of the Juggernaut; five elephants preceding the car containing the idol, "bearing towering flags, dressed in crimson caparisons, and having bells hanging to their caparisons."

At the time when the two sons of Tippoo were received as hostages by Lord Cornwallis, they approached his lordship mounted on a richly ornamented elephant, and seated in a silver howdah.

According to a contemporaneous writer, at the Vizier Ally's wedding, 1795, "The procession was grand beyond conception. It consisted of about twelve hundred elephants, richly caparisoned, drawn up in a regular line, like a regiment of soldiers. About one hundred elephants in the centre had howdahs, or castles, covered with silver: in the midst of these appeared the nabob, mounted on an uncommonly large elephant, within a howdah covered with gold, richly set with precious stones."

The Moguls were particularly fond of parade and display, and daily they had an elephant dress-parade; all their finest elephants being marched before them, harnessed in the most magnificent manner.

The elephant-parades at the court of Aurengzebe have been described by Bernier, and those of the court of Jehanghir by Sir Thomas Rowe. The latter says, "His greatest elephants were brought before him, some of which, being lord elephants, had their chains, bells, and furniture of gold and silver, attended with gilt banners and flags; and eight or ten elephants waiting on him, clothed in gold, silver, and silk. Thus passed about twelve companies, most richly furnished; the first elephant having all the plates on his head and breast set with rubies and emeralds, being a beast of a wonderful stature and beauty. They all bowed down before the king."

The secret of this adulation was not any particular respect to the king, as might be expected from this description. When the elephant passed its royal master, the driver perched upon its neck pricked him so violently with his instrument, that the elephant bent its knee, raised its trunk, and roared lustily with pain.

All kings and potentates could not afford to keep up such an expensive establishment; and many were the tricks that were resorted to, to make a few elephants afford a great display. When Mr. Bell, the famous traveller, visited Pekin, he was entertained by the officials with what was intended to be a magnificent display of elephants. "After dinner," he says, "we saw the huge elephants, richly caparisoned in gold and silver stuffs. Each had a driver. We stood about an hour admiring these sagacious animals, who, passing before us at equal distances, returned again behind the stables, and so on, round and round, till there seemed to be no end to the procession. The plot, however, was discovered by the features and dress of the riders: the chief keeper told us there were only sixty of them."

An Eastern account of the embassy from Shah Rohk, son of Tamerlane, to the emperor of China, describes the grand feast in China on New-Year's Day, A.D. 1420. "The elephants were adorned with a magnificence not to be expressed, with silver seats and standards, and armed men upon their backs. Fifty of them carried the musicians: these were preceded or followed by fifty thousand, in profound silence and order." Undoubtedly the same mystification was adopted with the ambassadors as in the case of Mr. Bell, only it was more successful.

In Rome, Julius Cæsar and his successors employed the elephant to draw them in gorgeous chariots. When Cæsar celebrated his victories in Gaul, elephants were used to carry torches to illuminate the processions, which generally took place after dark. In celebrating his African triumphs, the captured spoils were borne upon chariots of ivory; and when Pompey returned from his victories in Africa, he was borne in a chariot that was drawn by four elephants of the largest size, to the very gates of Rome.

Gibbon thus describes the triumph of Aurelian (A.D. 274):—

"The pomp was opened by twenty elephants, four royal tigers, and above two hundred of the most curious animals from every climate of the north, the east, and the south. They were followed by one thousand six hundred gladiators, devoted to the cruel amusement of the amphitheatre. The triumphal car of Aurelian on this memorable occasion (it had formerly been used by a Gothic king) was drawn either by four stags or by four elephants."

The most remarkable display of elephants in modern times, is undoubtedly that made in honor of the visit of the Prince of Wales to India. At Kandy, Ceylon, he witnessed the wonderful festival of Perahara, in which long processions of these noble animals passed in review, caparisoned in the most costly manner, bearing howdahs that defy description. One of the latter, which was presented to him at Jyepore, was of silver, and a work of art in all its parts. At Agra, the prince, mounted upon a huge elephant, covered with costly trappings, passed in between a double line of elephants, bearing the native princes and men of rank, probably the most imposing spectacle of his visit. At the rehearsal of the Perahara at Kandy, the prince fed the great elephants with sugar-cane, and with his suite, and numbers of ladies and gentlemen, reviewed the host of giants. (See Plate XX.)

At Lahore his Royal Highness was greeted with salutations from long lines of gayly bedecked elephants, which, with crowds of natives, extended for a great distance along the drive: and finally, at Colombo, two huge pachyderms were stationed, face to face, upon opposite sides of the road, bearing upon their backs various ornamentations and placards of welcome; and, when the prince appeared, the huge animals raised their trunks aloft, and joined them over the road, bearing aloft a crown. Under this living arch, the austere company of guests and guards passed. (See Plate XIX.)

Many of the conquests and ceremonies of the early days are commemorated on medals, described in Chap. XX.; and fine bass-reliefs are in existence, telling the story of the wonderful deeds in which the elephant took no minor part.

PLATE XIX

THE ROYAL VISIT TO INDIA.

CHAPTER XXII.

WAR ELEPHANTS OF MODERN ASIA.

DURING the recent war between England and Burmah, which resulted in the overthrow of King Theebaw, the elephant was frequently mentioned in despatches as being a valuable auxiliary to the troops when on the march; and that these noble animals constitute an important feature of many military posts in India, is, perhaps, not generally known. Such, however, is the case; and the service they perform when it is necessary to transport troops, is invaluable. The elephant is not only attached to divisions as a baggage-carrier, but is utilized in actual service, elephant-batteries being organized for field-work. The Bengal, Bombay, and Madras artillery establishments each comprise an armament of two eighteen-pounder S. B. guns, one eight-inch iron howitzer, two eight-inch mortars, and two bronze mortars of five and a half inch calibre, with seven gun-carriages and platforms, and twenty-two ammunition-wagons drawn by bullocks. Nine elephants and two hundred and ninety bullocks were required for the battery, with ten riding mahouts, and one hundred and fifty native drivers.

The appearance of an elephant-battery in the field is very striking, and certainly the huge animals offer a good target to the artillery of the opposing force. Each elephant has a large pad, or saddle, strapped upon it, upon which rests the ammunition-box, or other article, as the case may be. Upon the neck of each elephant sits the mahout; while behind the ammunition-chest is stationed a soldier, who serves out the shot to the man detailed to carry it. It is said that the animals soon become accustomed to the noise of firing, and do not mind it in the least.

In the last Burmese war, the variety of uses to which these intelligent animals could be put, was shown on many occasions. After Theebaw had been overthrown, the country of Upper Burmah was overrun with gangs of robbers, called *dacoits*, blood-thirsty miscreants who pillaged the villages of peaceful natives, and even threatened Mandalay. To suppress them, the armed steam-launches "Pegu" and "Patrol" were sent up the river Sittang; and, in the chase, the "Patrol" ran aground on a shoal. There were literally no appliances for hauling her off, until some one happened to think of the elephant: forthwith, a large tusker was harnessed to the launch, and, urged by its mahout and the men of the other launch near by, the huge animal plunged into the river, and drew the heavy boat into deeper water.

Elephant-batteries have been used by the British Government in various parts of the East. In the third command of the Royal Artillery, the elephants transport the guns; and, on their return from the Lughman-valley expedition, they carried the battery in perfect safety across the dangerous and rapid Cabul River, where, a few months previous, a number of soldiers had lost their lives. When about to march, the gun, limber, and eight ammunition-boxes are hoisted upon the backs of the elephants in six minutes, fourteen gunners being required to perform the service. In some of the batteries, camels are employed to bear the ammunition. Often, when guns and carriages become caught in rocks or mud, the elephant is used to rescue them. Count de Warren mentions an instance that occurred in his brigade in the Coorg war in India. He says, "Having reached a point where the bed of the torrent fell in cascades, it became a question as to the mode of raising the guns up the almost vertical declivity of a granite rock, the surface of which the waters had worn and polished. The oxen which drew the cannon gave up the attempt after one or two efforts, and lay down, as they always do in desperate cases. I was then determined to send for some elephants of the convoy. Two of the most docile were stripped of their loads, and led by their guides to the place where the cannons were left. It was indicated to them, by voice and gesture, what was expected from their courage; and the confidence thus shown in them was not misplaced. One of the colossal beasts, placing himself behind the gun, applied the base of his trunk to it, and, pushing it before him, whilst the cannoneers guided it, sent it up the rocky chasm."

An instance is recorded during the march to Lucknow in 1858, that illustrates the nerve of the elephant under fire, and shows how perfect is their obedience to the mahout. Gen. Outram, desiring to annoy the enemy's flank, ordered the elephant-battery into line. The guns were soon dismounted; and, as soon as firing commenced, one of the elephants, Kudabar-Moll, was stationed by his mahout, or driver, behind the piece, and in a short time was almost alone, the artillery-men being shot down by the musketry of the enemy. Soon the man that served the shot fell, leaving three men to fire the piece. This they did for a while;

the elephant, acting under instructions of his mahout, handing them cartridges from the wagon. As the last shot was loaded, and before it could be fired, two men were killed, and one badly wounded; yet he held up the match to the elephant, who, at his driver's command, touched it to the vent, and fired the gun, the act being witnessed by a company of infantry that came to the rescue, and ultimately put to flight the opposing force.

In telling this story, it is very tempting to leave the mahout out of the question, which was once done, giving the elephant the entire credit; but it is quite enough that the animal should obey so implicitly under such trying circumstances.

Elephants have been known, innocently of course, to turn the tide of battle; and a story is told in Lahore, India, of a noble old animal who was the standard-bearer in an Indian battle, carrying on his broad back the royal ensign which was the rallying-point of the Poonah host. For some time the huge animal bore the standard in the midst of the fray. Suddenly the enemy made a vigorous charge; and the mahout at the same moment commanding him to halt, the old elephant stood firm, while the opposing force came on. The mahout dropped dead from his back; the men about were routed, turned, and fled; and in a short time the elephant was almost surrounded by the enemy. A moment more, he would have been captured, when a mighty shout rose from the retreating forces. They saw the standard still firm on the elephant's back; and, refusing to believe they were beaten, with a victorious cry they charged the enemy with such valor that they were swept down like chaff; and the elephant, who still stood like a rock amid the dead and dying, was once more within its own lines, the true victor. The mahout's last command had been obeyed, and the animal remained like a statue until some one took the dead driver's place.

In the last centuries, elephants were used much more than at present, and an army camp was an extraordinary sight; curiously enough, the attendants and camp-followers often amounting to ten times the actual fighting-men. When the Marquis Cornwallis took the field in the war with Tippoo, the followers were estimated at one million souls. The number of elephants, compared to the bullocks, horses, and camels, was insignificant; but the rule was fifty elephants to every eight thousand soldiers: and, to give an idea of these astonishing campaigns, I introduce an account by an officer who took part in this one, Lieut. Shipp.

"My post of baggage-master being a situation which is, I believe, peculiar to India, it may not be improper to state its duties. He is a staff-officer, and, when not employed in his particular department, is attached to the suite of the commander of the division as much as the commissary-general, quartermaster-general, or any other staff-officer of the division. On the line of march, he is held entirely responsible that neither men nor baggage precede the column of march, and that they are on their proper flank, which is regulated by the general orders of the day. If the reader recollect what I before stated, that he may safely calculate ten followers in a Bengal army to every fighting-man; and when he is informed, that, according to the calculations made in our camp, including the several native contingencies we had with us, our followers were not less in number than eighty thousand men, women, and children; some thirty thousand following the army for what they could pick up, by fair means or otherwise,—my situation cannot be supposed to have been a sinecure. It was truly one of great labor and activity. I had twenty men belonging to a corps of local horse. These men were provided with long whips, and placed at my disposal. To attempt to talk the numberless camp-followers into obedience was quite out of the question, and, therefore, these whips were for the purpose of lashing them into something like discipline. To the great number of human beings I have spoken of, must be added fifty elephants, six hundred camels, five thousand bullocks, five thousand horses, one thousand ponies, two hundred goats, the same number of sheep, fifty ruts, one hundred palanquins, one hundred dogs, and one hundred hackeries, or carts."

The elephant in a heavily wooded country is greatly appreciated in time of war; as their huge bodies can crush through the underbrush, trample down the reeds, and make a good road, over which the gun-carriages and teams can be hauled. A writer on an early Burmese war says, "The road lay partly through a thick jungle; but with the aid of three elephants, a passage was forced." When a bog is met, or roads have been overflowed, making ordinary passage almost impossible, the elephants, under direction of their mahouts, place their heads (the base of the trunk) against the teams, and push them along, or take ropes attached to the gun-carriages between their teeth, and haul them out of the mire.

Capt. Williamson lays much stress upon the importance of the work performed by these animals. "Many of our most arduous military operations have been greatly indebted for their success to the sagacity, patience, and exertion of elephants. Exclusive of their utility in carrying baggage and stores, considerable aid is frequently supplied by the judgment they display, bordering very closely on reason. When cannon require to be extricated from sloughs, the elephant, placing his forehead to the muzzle, — which, when limbered, is the head of the piece, — with an energy scarcely to be conceived, will urge it through a bog, from which hundreds of oxen or horses could not drag it. At other times, lapping his trunk round the cannon, he will lift, while the cattle and men pull forward. The native princes attach an elephant to each cannon, to aid its progress in emergencies. For this purpose, the animal is furnished with a thick leather pad, covering the forehead, to prevent its being injured. It has sometimes happened, that in narrow roads or causeways, or on banks, the soil has given way under heavy cannon; when an elephant, being applied to the falling side, has not only prevented the piece from upsetting, but even aided it forward to a state of security."

Small howitzers, that can be placed upon the elephant's back, were not the only guns the animals had to carry. Aurengzebe had cannon in his army which required twenty yoke of oxen, besides elephants, who pushed at the wheels, and hauled.

The patience and fidelity of the elephant when on the march are proverbial, and they can nearly always be depended upon. In the steep passes, or ghauts, of India, the work is often of the most laborious description. An eye-witness thus describes a scene where their pluck and sagacity were put most thoroughly to the test: —

"There was a small ravine branching off from the bed of

a dry river, in which our encampment lay, and its entrance looked like the dreary access to some deep cavern. We entered this little gaping cavern, leaving the principal part of our force for the protection of our standing tents and baggage. We were equipped as lightly as possible. Two six-pounders were conveyed on elephants; and our march seemed to lie through the bed of this ravine, which was rocky, and watered by a crystal current, that rippled along its flinty bed. We did not proceed at the rate of more than one or two yards an hour, — ascending and descending every twenty paces; at one time deep sunk in some dark excavation, and shortly afterwards perched upon the summit of a rock, the falling of the numerous cataracts drowning the noise made by our approach. . . . Our march now became more and more tardy, and the ascents and descents more difficult and intricate. In some places, rocks of gigantic size hung some hundred feet overhead. These sudden and tremendous hills and dales indicated that we could not have far to go; for the last hill was scarcely accessible. . . . We halted a considerable time, — till broad daylight, when we could see, from where I stood, the soldiers in advance of us, ascending by means of projecting rocks and boughs. We were halted in a kind of basin, surrounded by high hills. In the course of a couple of hours, the whole of the Eighty-seventh Regiment, with our gallant general and suite, ascended this difficult ghaut. From this eminence we could see a great distance; and on every hill we could discern signals, which were communicated from post to post. . . . What will not good examples effect on the minds of soldiers? Our general walked every yard of this critical march, encouraging his men. The question now was, how to get the guns up, and the powder and shot; but those who are accustomed to wars in India, are not often at a loss for expedients. Having got all the men up, except the rear-guard, the pioneers went to work with their pickaxes, some making a road, and others felling trees. As we were but two regiments, the general's primary object was to place our little force to the best advantage. This accomplished, the guns were our next object. Having cut a good deal of the most prominent part of the hill away, and lain trees on the ascent as a footing for the elephants, these animals were made to approach it, which the first did with some reluctance and fear. He looked up, shook his head, and, when forced by his driver, roared piteously. There can be no question, in my opinion, that this sagacious animal was competent instinctively to judge of the practicability of the artificial flight of steps thus constructed; for, the moment some little alterations had been made, he seemed willing to approach. He then commenced his examination and scrutiny, by pressing with his trunk the trees that had been thrown across; and after this he put his fore-leg on, with great caution, raising the fore-part of his body so as to throw its weight on the tree. This done, he seemed satisfied as to its stability. The next step for him to ascend by, was a projecting rock, which we could not remove. Here the same sagacious examinations took place, the elephant keeping his flat side close to the side of the bank, and leaning against it. The next step was against a tree; but this, on the first pressure of his trunk, he did not like. Here his driver made use of the most endearing epithets, such as 'wonderful, my life,' 'my wife;' but all these endearing appellations, of which elephants are so fond, would not induce him to try again. Force was at length resorted to; and the elephant roared terrifically, but would not move. Something was then removed; he seemed satisfied, as before: and he in time ascended that stupendous ghaut. On his reaching the top, his delight was visible in a most eminent degree: he caressed his keepers, and threw the dirt about in a most playful manner. Another elephant, a much younger animal, was now to follow. He had watched the ascent of the other with the most intense interest, making motions all the while, as though he was assisting him by shouldering him up the acclivity, — such gestures as I have seen some men make when spectators of gymnastic exercises. When he saw his comrade up, he evinced his pleasure by giving a salute something like the sound of a trumpet. When called upon to take his turn, however, he seemed much alarmed, and would not act at all without force. When he was two steps up, he slipped, but recovered himself by digging his toes in the earth. With the exception of this little accident, he ascended exceedingly well. When this elephant was near the top, the other, who had already performed his task, extended his trunk to the assistance of his brother in distress, round which the younger animal intwined his, and thus reached the summit of the ghaut in safety. Having both accomplished their task, their greeting was as cordial as if they had been long separated from each other, and had just escaped from some perilous achievement. They mutually embraced each other, and stood face to face for a considerable time, as if whispering congratulations. Their driver then made them salaam to the general, who ordered them five rupees each for sweetmeats. On this reward of their merit being ordered, they immediately returned thanks by another salaam."

The British forces in India during a war rarely put elephants into the field for active service, the animals being too conspicuous, and too valuable to risk. But with the Burmese, this was different; they were prodigal of their elephants. During a Burmese war, a garrison of infantry and cavalry marched out with seventeen war elephants, fully caparisoned, and bearing a number of armed men. They advanced upon a fort amid a murderous fire, which killed the men upon them, and their mahouts; but in no case did an elephant lose its head. They stood the fire steadily until their mahouts were shot; and then, feeling themselves unrestrained, they slowly and calmly walked back to their fort, their bravery and courage being greatly admired by the opposing force.

In the last half-century, in any revolt, or where Indian native troops have been brought against the English, elephants have been rarely used; experience showing that their slow movements render them unfit for valuable or active service in the field.

Perhaps the last time they were seen in their former grandeur was in the war of Coromandel, when the British were fighting the native chiefs. The latter came out on some occasions equipped like the old Mogul emperors, to be described later on. The nabob of Arcot and his famous rival, Chundasaheb, both came upon the field on elephants; and had not a French bullet put an end to the former, a duel by these potentates would have been witnessed. As soon as the nabob caught sight of his rival's elephant, bedecked with its owner's standard, he became furious, and offered his mahout a valuable reward if he would make his elephant overthrow that of his enemy, who was the author of his defeat.

The mahout was urging the elephant on, when a bullet struck the nabob in the heart, and he fell from the howdah. Soon after this tragic event, Nazir-jing, a son of the Mogul, entered the Carnatic with a most imposing force, — a battalion of thirteen hundred elephants, three hundred thousand soldiers, and eight hundred pieces of cannon. He, too, was shot from his elephant.

An elephant duel was observed in the field between Murzafa-jing, the Soubah of the Carnatic, and the nabob of Canoul. The elephants of the rivals were urged toward each other by the mahouts; and Murzafa-jing raised his sword to strike, when his adversary thrust his javelin, which pierced his forehead, killing him on the spot. At the same instant, at least a thousand bullets were fired at the nabob, who also fell, mortally wounded, from his elephant.

The introduction of fire-arms into warfare was the cause of the withdrawal of the elephant from active field-work. The great creature was too prominent a target, and the men upon its back were the most conspicuous objects in the field. It was a long time, however, before the natives would give up this animal, so strong was custom. From its back, the old generals directed their warriors and the movements of the battle; and, when the elephant left the field, it was usually a sign that a retreat had been ordered, and rout generally followed.

In the battle in which Aurengzebe gained the victory over Dara, he ordered his elephant's legs to be chained, so that he could not retreat. Bernier tells this story as follows: —

"Calil-ullah had suffered some indignity at the hands of Dara, and he considered the hour arrived when he might gratify the resentment which had never ceased to rankle in his bosom. His abstinence from all share in the battle did not, however, produce the mischief intended, Dara having proved victorious without the co-operation of the right wing. The traitor, therefore, had recourse to another expedient. He quitted his division, followed by a few persons; and riding with speed towards Dara, precisely at the same moment when that prince was hastening to assist in the downfall of Morud-Bakche, he exclaimed, while yet at some distance, 'Mohbarek bad! Hazaret! Salamet! Elhamd-ul-ellah! May you be happy! May your Majesty enjoy health, and reign in safety! The victory is your own! But let me ask, why are you still mounted on this lofty elephant? Have you not been sufficiently exposed to danger? If one of the numberless arrows or balls, which have pierced your canopy, had touched your person, who can imagine the dreadful situation to which we should be reduced? In Heaven's name, descend quickly, and mount your horse: nothing now remains but to pursue the fugitives with vigor. I entreat your Majesty, permit them not to escape.'

"Had Dara considered the consequences of quitting the back of his elephant, on which he had displayed so much valor, and served as a rallying-point of the army, he would have become master of the empire; but the credulous prince, duped by the artful obsequiousness of Calil-ullah, listened to his advice as though it had been sincere. He descended from the elephant, and mounted his horse; but a quarter of an hour had not elapsed, when, suspecting the imposture, he inquired impatiently for Calil-ullah. The villain was not, however, within his reach; he inveighed vehemently against that officer, and threatened him with death; but Dara's rage was now impotent, and his menace incapable of being executed. The troops having missed their prince, a rumor quickly spread that he was killed, and the army betrayed; a universal panic seized them; every man thought only of his own safety, and how to escape from the resentment of Aurengzebe. In a few minutes the army seemed disbanded, and (strange and sudden reverse!) the conqueror became the vanquished. Aurengzebe remained for a quarter of an hour steadily on his elephant, and was rewarded with the crown of Hindostan. Dara left his own elephant a few minutes too soon, and was hurled from the pinnacle of glory to be numbered among the most miserable of princes."

The younger brother of Dara, the famous Sultan Sujah, lost his empire in an almost identical manner, or owing to the elephant being a rallying-point. A French engineer raised the siege of Daman by an ingenious device. They had a large supply of fireworks, principally rockets; and, sallying forth, they fired them in among Aurengzebe's elephants, causing them to turn on their own troops, creating the greatest confusion and an ultimate rout.

In the old Mogul empire, the armor of elephants called to mind that used in the age of chivalry. The elephants of Akbar wore plates of massive iron upon their foreheads; while the king of Ternassery, who was famous for his enormous elephants, all being selected, like the Swiss Guard, for their great size, had his animals covered completely with armor made of beef-hides, which were fastened beneath the stomach with heavy chains. The "Ayeen Akbery" (a native work) "is more minute. 'Five plates of iron, each one cubit long and four fingers broad, are joined together by rings, and fastened round the ears of the elephant by four chains, each an ell in length; and betwixt these another chain passes over the head, and is fastened in the *kellawah;* and across it are four iron spikes, with *katasses* and iron knobs. There are other chains, with iron spikes and knobs, hung under the throat and over the breast, and others fastened to the trunk: these are for ornament, and to frighten horses. *Pakher* is a kind of steel armor that covers the body of the elephant: there are other pieces of it for the head and proboscis. *Gejjhemp* is a covering made of three folds, and is laid over the *pakher.*' Dow adds, that 'a sword is bound to their trunk, and daggers are fastened to their tusks.' But the mighty power of the animal in crushing the ranks of an enemy was principally relied upon. The armor and the swords were to add to the dismay which an immense troop of elephants were of themselves calculated to produce. The emperor of Akbar well knew their power in scattering masses of terrified men. On one occasion, when he stormed the fort of Chitar, the garrison retired to the temples. 'Akbar, perceiving he must lose a great number of his troops in case of a close attack, ordered a distant fire to be kept up upon the desperate Rajaputs, till he had introduced three hundred elephants of war, which he immediately ordered to advance to tread them to death. The scene now became too shocking to be described. Brave men, rendered more valiant by despair, crowded around the elephants, seized them even by the tusks, and inflicted upon them unavailing wounds. The terrible animals trod the Indians like grasshoppers under their feet, or, winding them in their powerful trunks, tossed them aloft into the air, or dashed them against the walls and pavements. Of the garrison, which consisted of eight thousand soldiers and of forty thousand inhabitants, thirty thousand were slain, and most of the rest taken prisoners.'

In the rapid marches of this victorious prince, the elephants suffered greatly. Purchas, speaking of his progress from Kashmire in 1597, says, 'This country he left when summer was past, and returned to Lahore, losing many elephants and horses in the way, both by famine, then oppressing the country, and the difficulty of the passages; the elephants sometimes, in the ascent of the hills, helping themselves with their trunks, leaning and staying themselves, being burthened, thereon, as on a staff.'"

The terror which elephants produced on foot-soldiers was well appreciated three centuries ago, and victory was generally gained by the side that possessed the greatest number of these animals. The fear of elephants was the greatest difficulty the famous adventurer Timour had to deal with when on his victorious march through Persia, Siberia, and Russia. His men replied to his war-speeches, "We may subdue Hind; yet it hath many ramparts, rivers, wildernesses, and forests; soldiers clad in armor; and the elephants, the destroyers of men."

When the army arrived upon the plains in front of Delhi, he had to take the most extraordinary precautions to prevent this morbid fear from resulting in a rout. An enormous ditch was built around the camp, to prevent an inroad of invading elephants. Buffaloes were tied together by the neck, and arranged about the ramparts, and their horns bedecked with rushes, while men were stationed to set them on fire at the first approach of the terrible elephants. What would have been the effect of this conflagration on the unfortunate bullocks, imagination can picture. The opposing force to Timour in this battle (A.D. 1399) was the Sultan Mamood, and the remarkable armament of his elephants

PLATE XX.

THE ROYAL VISIT TO INDIA.

THE PRINCE OF WALES AT AGRA.

By permission Illustrated London News. *Page 253.*

was certainly enough to strike terror to the boldest heart. His army consisted of ten thousand horse, forty thousand foot-soldiers, and elephants. The latter were arrayed in armor, and mounted with bastions filled with men armed with crossbows. Their tusks were elongated with poisoned daggers; and on scaffolds hung to the sides stood armed men, bearing fire and melted pitch and iron-pointed rockets to hurl and throw at the enemy. As this army marched forward, the men upon their backs beating kettledrums, cymbals, bells, and trumpets, the brave followers of Timour fell back, utterly demoralized, before the appalling sight; and the commander himself fell upon his knees in prayer, — a characteristic one: "As my vast conquests have caused the destruction of a great number of God's creatures, I have resolved to atone for the crimes of my past life by exterminating the infidels of China." In some way the Delhi elephants threw their own left wing into disorder. Timour's horsemen rushed forward; and the elephants, demoralized at their sabre-cuts, fled in great confusion, while the sharp weapons aimed at their trunks left many upon the field. As the great animals fled, Timour's men saw that the elephants were not invincible, and, rushing to the front, completed the disastrous rout. Timour's grandson, a boy of fifteen, made himself conspicuous by attacking and wounding an elephant, overthrowing its riders, and driving the huge animal into his grandfather's camp. The day following the battle of Delhi, Timour sat upon the throne of the Indian monarch, and a procession of twelve rhinoceroses and one hundred and twenty captive elephants were paraded before him; and afterwards sent as presents to the Persian provinces; while the unfortunate people were slaughtered by his soldiers.

Elephants were not always demoralized in these wars; and in another battle this same conqueror had the front of his army protected by a line of elephants, their towers filled with archers and Greek fire-flingers. At the word of command they started forward, their drivers ordering them to coil their trunks so that the sabres of the Mamelukes could not reach them.

The Syrians fled before them, and were crushed under foot; others were hurled forty or fifty feet into the air; the defeat being complete, and chiefly due to the elephants.

Timour's curious experiment of adopting elephants in warfare, after he had witnessed their demoralization, was not without precedent, as Kublai Khan and Alexander did the same. Marco Polo gives a clear idea of the way elephants were used in battle: —

"It happened, that, in the year 1272, the Grand Khan sent an army into the countries of Vochang and Karazan, for their protection and defence against any attack that foreigners might attempt to make. . . . When the King of Mien and Bangala in India, who was powerful in the number of his subjects, in extent of territory, and in wealth, heard that an army of Tartars had arrived at Vochang, he took the resolution of advancing immediately to attack it, in order that by its destruction the Grand Khan should be deterred from again attempting to station a force upon the borders of his dominions. For this purpose he assembled a very large army, including a multitude of elephants (an animal with which his country abounds), upon whose backs were placed battlements, or castles, of wood, capable of containing the number of from twelve to sixteen in each. With these, and a numerous army of horse and foot, he took the road to Vochang, where the Grand Khan's army lay, and, encamping at no great distance from it, intended to give his troops a few days of rest. The King of Mien, learning that the Tartars had descended into the plain, immediately put his army in motion, took up his ground at the distance of about a mile from the enemy, and made a disposition of his force, placing the elephants in the front, and the cavalry and infantry in two extended wings in their rear, but leaving between them a considerable interval. Here he took his own station, and proceeded to animate his men, and encouraging them to fight valiantly, assuring them of victory, as well from the superiority of their numbers, being four to one, as from their formidable body of armed elephants, whose shock the enemy, who had never before been engaged with such combatants, could by no means resist. Then, giving orders for sounding a prodigious number of warlike instruments, he advanced boldly with his whole army towards that of the Tartars, which remained firm, making no movement, but suffering them to approach their intrenchments. They then rushed out with great spirit and the utmost eagerness to engage; but it was soon found that the Tartar horses, unused to the sight of such huge animals, with their castles, were terrified, and, wheeling about, endeavored to fly, nor could their riders by any exertions restrain them; whilst the king, with the whole of his forces, was every moment gaining ground. As soon as the prudent commander perceived this unexpected disorder, without losing his presence of mind, he instantly adopted the measure of ordering his men to dismount, and their horses to be taken into the wood, where they were fastened to the trees. Being dismounted, the men, without loss of time, advanced on foot towards the line of elephants, and commenced a brisk discharge of arrows: whilst, on the other side, those who were stationed in the castles, and the rest of the king's army, shot volleys in return, with great activity; but their arrows did not make the same impression as those of the Tartars, whose bows were drawn with a stronger arm. So incessant were the discharges of the latter, and all their weapons (according to the instructions of their commander) being directed against the elephants, these were soon covered with arrows, and, suddenly giving way, fell back upon their own people in the rear, who were thereby thrown into confusion. It soon became impossible for their drivers to manage them, either by force or address. Smarting under the pain of their wounds, and terrified by the shouting of the assailants, they were no longer governable, but, without guidance or control, ran about in all directions, until at length, impelled by rage and fear, they rushed into a part of the wood not occupied by the Tartars. The consequence of this was, that, from the closeness of the branches of large trees, they broke, with loud crashes, the battlements, or castles, that were upon their backs, and involved in the destruction those who sat upon them. Upon seeing the rout of the elephants, the Tartars acquired fresh courage; and filing off by detachments, with perfect order and regularity, they remounted their horses, and joined their several divisions, when a sanguinary and dreadful combat was renewed. The battle ended in a complete victory."

Perhaps the most remarkable displays of elephants were those of Kublai Khan. In an old cut before me, he is shown as he appeared on his elephants, after he had conquered his unfortunate relative, Nazam, and smothered him between two carpets. He is represented in a large wooden castle, which rests upon four large tuskers, whose bodies, according to Dow, were protected with coverings of thick leather hardened by fire, over which were housings of cloth of gold. The castle contained many crossbow men and archers; and on the top of it was hoisted the imperial standard, adorned with representations of the sun and moon.

In his invasions into Hindostan, in the eleventh century, Mamood of Ghizni employed a magnificent army of thirteen hundred elephants. Dow thus describes his battle with the King of Kaslegar: —

"Mamood, perceiving the enemy's progress, leaped from his horse, and, kissing the ground, invoked the aid of the Almighty. He instantly mounted an elephant-of-war, encouraged his troops, and made a violent assault upon Elieh. The elephant, seizing the standard-bearer of the enemy, folded round him his trunk, and tossed him aloft into the sky. He then pressed forward like a mountain removed from its place by an earthquake, and trod the enemy like locusts under his feet. When Mamood invested Callinger, the rajah of that city sued for peace, and offered him three thousand elephants and other presents. The Indian prince probably considered that his enemy might be unacquainted with the habits of the animal; and he, therefore, ventured upon an experiment, not very likely to conciliate the rough hero of Turquestan. The king (Mamood) agreed to the terms proposed; and the raja, to try the bravery of the sultan's troops, intoxicated the elephants with certain drugs, and let them loose, without riders, in the camp. Mamood, seeing the animals advancing, perceived the trick, by the wildness of their motions, and immediately ordered a party of his best horse to seize, kill, and drive them from the camp. Some of the Turks, emulous to display their bravery in the presence of their king and of both armies, mounted the greatest part of the elephants, and drove the rest into an adjacent wood, where they were soon reduced to obedience."

In the Book of Maccabees, there is an interesting passage describing the armor of elephants, and their use in the wars of Asia after the conquest of India:—

"To the end they might provoke the elephants to fight, they shewed them the blood of grapes and mulberries. Moreover, they divided the beasts among the armies, and for every elephant they appointed a thousand men, armed with coats of mail, and with helmets of brass on their heads; and beside this, for every beast were ordered five hundred horsemen of the best. These were ready at every occasion: wheresoever the beast was, and whithersoever the beast went, they went also, neither departed they from him. And upon the beasts were there strong towers of wood, which covered every one of them, and were girt fast unto them with devices: there were also upon every one thirty-two strong men, that fought upon him, beside the Indian that ruled him."

These are but a few selections from many, showing the importance of the elephant in comparatively modern times. And when we remember what an imposing appearance twenty elephants, the largest number ever seen in America together, make, we can imagine the scene when over a thousand of these huge beasts were arranged in line, each clad in armor, and bearing armed warriors.

CHAPTER XXIII.

WAR ELEPHANTS OF ALEXANDER THE GREAT AND HIS SUCCESSORS.

THE earliest mention of war elephants is made by Ctesias, where he describes Cyrus as making war against King Amoræus, who placed a large number of elephants in ambush, putting the horses of Cyrus to flight. Ælian quotes Ctesias as saying that the king of the Indians went to war with an army of ten thousand elephants, which was undoubtedly an exaggeration.

In olden times, elephants seemed to be a necessity, and would-be conquerors were often put to some remarkable straits to procure them. Perhaps the most amusing substitution was that adopted by Queen Semiramis, who made mock elephants out of hides, and put camels within them, with what laughable results Diodorus Siculus shall tell us. The story is so quaint, and replete with curious situations, that I give it complete in the language of the old historian:—

"Semiramis, having settled her affairs in Egypt and Ethiopia, returned with her army into Asia to Bactria; and now having a great army, and enjoying a long peace, she had a longing desire to perform some notable exploit by her arms. Hearing, therefore, that the Indians were the greatest nation in the whole world, and had the largest and richest tract of land of all others, she resolved to make war upon them.

"Stabrobates was at that time king, who had innumerable forces, and many elephants, bravely accoutred, and fitted to strike terror into the hearts of his enemies. For India, for the pleasantness of the country, excelled all others; being watered in every place with many rivers, so that the land yielded every year a double crop; and by that means was so rich, and so abounded with plenty of all things necessary for the sustenance of man's life, that it supplied the inhabitants continually with such things as made them excessively rich, insomuch that it was never known that there was ever any famine amongst them, the climate being so happy and favorable; and upon that account, likewise, there is an incredible number of elephants, which for courage, and strength of body, far excel those in Africa. Moreover, this country abounds in gold, silver, brass, iron, and precious stones of all sorts, both for profit and pleasure. All of which being noised abroad, so stirred up the spirit of Semiramis, that (though she had no provocation given her) yet she was resolved upon the war against the Indians. But knowing that she had need of great forces, she sent despatches to all the provinces, with command to the governors to list the choicest young men they could find; ordering the proportion of soldiers every province and country should send forth, according to the largeness of it; and commanded that all should furnish themselves with new armor and arms, and all appear in three years' time at a general rendezvous in Bactria, bravely armed and accoutred in all points. And having sent for shipwrights out of Phœnicia, Syria, Cyprus, and other places bordering upon the seacoasts, she prepared timber for them fit for the purpose, and ordered them to build vessels, that might be taken asunder, and conveyed from place to place whenever she pleased. For the river Indus bordering upon that kingdom, being the greatest in those parts, she stood in need of many river-boats to pass it, in order to repress the Indians. But being there was no timber near that river, she was necessitated to convey the boats thither by land from Bactria. She further considered, that she was much inferior to the Indians in elephants (which were absolutely necessary for her to make use of): she therefore contrived to have beasts that should resemble them, hoping by this means to strike a terror into the Indians, who believed that there were no elephants in any place but in India. To this end, she provided three hundred thousand black oxen, and distributed the flesh amongst a company of ordinary mechanics, and such fellows as she had to play the cobblers for her, and ordered them, by stitching the skins together, and stuffing them with straw, to imitate the shape of an elephant; and in every one of them she put a man to govern them, and a camel to carry them, so that at a distance they appeared to all that saw them, as if they were really such beasts.

"They that were employed in this work, wrought at it night and day, in a place which was walled round for the purpose, and guards set at every gate, that none might be admitted either to go in or out, to the end that none might see what they were doing, lest it should be noised abroad, and come to the ears of the Indians.

"Having therefore provided shipping and elephants in the space of two years, in the third she rendezvoused all her forces in Bactria. Her army consisted (as Ctesias says) of three millions of foot, two hundred thousand horse, a hundred thousand chariots, and a hundred thousand men, mounted upon camels, with swords four cubits long. The boats that might be taken asunder, were two thousand; which the camels carried by land as they did the mock-elephants, as we have before declared. The soldiers made their horses familiar with these feigned beasts, by bringing them often to them, lest they should be terrified at the sight of them; which Perseus imitated many ages after, when he was to fight with the Romans, who had elephants in their army out of Africa. However, this contrivance proved to be of no advantage, either to him or her, as will appear in issue herein a little after related.

"When Stabrobates, the Indian king, heard of these great armies, and the mighty preparations made against him, he did all he could to excel Semiramis in every thing. And first, he built of great canes four thousand river-boats, for abundance of these canes grow in India about the rivers; and ferns, so thick as a man can scarce fathom; and vessels made of these reeds (they say) are exceeding useful, because they will never rot or be worm-eaten.

"He was very diligent, likewise, in preparing of arms, and going from place to place throughout all India, and so raised a far greater army than that of Semiramis. To his former number of elephants he added more, which he took by hunting, and furnished them all with every thing that might make them look terrible in the face of their enemies; so that, by their multitude and the completeness of their armor in all points, it seemed above the strength and power of man to bear up against the violent shock of these creatures.

PLATE XXI.

15
12
3
1
11
6
8
13
2
14
4
7
LAETITIA
TEMPORVM
AETERNITAS AVG
S C
CAESAR
EYTYXICTOY

"Having, therefore, made all these preparations, he sent ambassadors to Semiramis (as she was on her march towards him), to complain and upbraid her for beginning a war without any provocation or injury offered her; and by his private letters, taxed her with a dissolute course of life; and vowed (calling the gods to witness), that, if he conquered her, he would nail her to the cross. When she read the letter, she smiled, and said the Indian should presently have a trial of her valor by her actions. When she came up with her army to the river Indus, she found the enemy's fleet drawn up in a line of battle; whereupon she forthwith drew up her own, and, having manned it with the stoutest soldiers, joined battle, yet so ordering the matter as to have her land-forces ready upon the shore, to be assisting as there should be occasion. After a long and sharp fight, with marks of valor on both sides, Semiramis was at length victorious, and sunk a thousand of the enemy's vessels, and took a great number of prisoners. Puffed up with this success, she took in the cities and islands that lay in the river, and carried away an hundred thousand captives. After this, the Indian king drew off his army (as if he fled for fear), but in truth to decoy his enemies to pass the river. Semiramis, therefore (seeing all things fall out according to her wish), laid a broad bridge of boats (at a vast charge) over the river, and thereby passed over all her forces, leaving only threescore thousand to guard the bridge, and with the rest of her army pursued the Indians. She placed the mock-elephants in the front, that the enemy's scouts might presently inform the king what multitudes of elephants she had in her army: and she was not deceived in her hopes; for when the spies gave an account to the Indians what a great multitude of these creatures were advancing towards them, they were all in amaze, inquiring among themselves, whence the Assyrians should be supplied with such a vast number of elephants: but the cheat could not long be concealed; for some of Semiramis's soldiers, being laid by the heels for their carelessness upon the guard (through fear of further punishment), made their escape, and fled to the enemy, and undeceived them as to the elephants; upon which the Indian king was mightily encouraged, and caused notice of the delusion to be spread through the whole army, and then, forthwith, marched with all force against the Assyrians; Semiramis, on the other hand, doing the like. When they approached near one to another, Stabrobates, the Indian king, placed his horse and chariots in the vanguard, at a good distance before the main body of his army. The queen, having placed her mock-elephants at the like distance from her main body, valiantly received her enemy's charge: but the Indian horse were most strangely terrified; for in regard, the phantasms at a distance seemed to be real elephants, the horses of the Indians (being inured to these creatures) pressed boldly and undauntedly forward; but when they came near, and saw another sort of beast than usual, and the smell and every thing else almost being strange and new to them, they broke in with great terror and confusion, one upon another, so that they cast some of their riders headlong to the ground, and ran away with others (as the lot happened) into the midst of their enemies; whereupon Semiramis, readily making use of her advantage, with a body of choice men, fell in upon them, and routed them, forcing them back to their main body: and though Stabrobates was something astonished at this unexpected defeat, yet he brought up his foot against the enemy, with his elephants in the front; he himself was in the right wing, mounted upon a stately elephant, and made a fierce charge upon the queen herself, who happened then to be opposite to him in the left. And though the mock-elephants in Semiramis's army did the like, yet they stood the violent shock of the other but a little while: for the Indian beasts, being both exceeding strong and stout, easily bore down and destroyed all that opposed them, so that there was a great slaughter; for some they trampled under foot, others they rent in pieces with their teeth, and tossed up others with their trunks into the air. The ground, therefore, being covered with heaps of dead carcasses, and nothing but death and destruction to be seen on every hand, so that all were full of horror and amazement, none durst keep their order or ranks any longer. Upon which the whole Assyrian army fled outright: and the Indian king encountered with Semiramis, and first wounded her with an arrow in the arm, and afterwards with a dart (in wheeling about) in the shoulder; whereupon the queen (her wounds not being mortal) fled, and by the swiftness of her horse (which far exceeded the other that pursued her), she got off."

Curiously enough, in early times the camel was used in Persia, instead of the elephant, to carry burdens. The name of the elephant is not found in the Hebrew language; but the Grecian and Roman poets made frequent mention of it one hundred years before the time of Alexander, so that he must have known something of the strange animal when he contemplated his Indian invasion. He first met them in the flesh, according to Arrian, in the battle of Arbela, where he defeated the king of Persia, who had a few in his army, which Alexander captured. Soon after this he was presented with a number which had been brought from India by Darius, and later the victorious army of the great soldier captured a number on the banks of the Indus. It is known that Alexander was familiar with the advantages to be derived from elephants, but whether he added them immediately to his army is not known. One military writer, Polyænus, states that he did, and that a fine battalion of elephants was placed upon the left wing of the Macedonian army. But, on the other hand, Alexander said, according to Quintus Curtius, "I have so despised those animals, that, when I had them at my command, I did not employ them." Alexander is pictured on a medal, a cut of which was published in the "Museum Cuspinianum," edited by Laurentius Legatus, as riding in a chariot drawn by elephants when entering Babylon.

When Alexander passed the Indus, he met the army of King Porus with a large force of elephants. "There," writes Quintus Curtius, "stood those huge bulks of overgrown bodies, the elephants; which, being on purpose provoked, filled the air with a horrible noise." "The river had to be passed with boats; and the great danger to be apprehended was, that the horses of the Greeks, upon perceiving the elephants, would be seized with fear, and leap into the water. For several days the Macedonians and the Indians lay encamped on the opposite banks of the river, the one effecting to attempt the passage by stratagem, the other constantly resisting the attempt with the terror of the elephants. Porus, however, relaxing in his watchfulness, and being deceived by a division of a part of the army of Alexander, the great body of the Macedonians were safely conveyed across. But the Indian king was resolved not to yield up his dominions without a struggle. "He drew up his army in order of battle," says Arrian, upon "a plain where the soil was not incommodious by reason of the slippery clay, but firm and sandy, and every way fit wheeling his chariots round upon. First, he placed the elephants in the front, at the distance of one hundred feet from each other, to cover the whole body of foot, and at the same time to strike a terror into Alexander's horse; for he imagined that none, either horse or foot, would be so hardy as to endeavor to penetrate through the spaces between the elephants. The horsemen, he thought, could not, because their horses would be terrified at the sight; and the foot would not dare, because the armed soldiers would be ready to gall them on each hand, and the elephants to trample them under their feet. The foot possessed the next rank. They were not, indeed, placed in the same order with the elephants, but so small a way behind that they seemed to fill up the interstices. At the extremities of each wing he placed elephants bearing huge wooden towers, wherein were armed men. The foot were defended on each hand by the horse, and the horse by the chariots, which were placed before them."

"With the caution which is the best characteristic of a skilful general, Alexander resolved to avoid a direct attack upon the main body of the elephants. Perhaps the alarm which his soldiers are described to have felt at 'those beasts, which, being disposed amongst the men in front, at a distance bore the appearance of towers,' might have somewhat influenced this determination. The elephant which carried Porus himself, a man of extraordinary stature, was greatly superior to all the rest in height. Alexander is described as rejoicing in the splendid appearance of the enemy which he trusted to subdue. 'At last I have met with a danger suitable to the greatness of my soul.' The long pikes of the Macedonian phalanx, the rapid movements of the cavalry, and the cloud of arrows poured in by the light-armed Thracians, soon spread a panic amongst the Indians. But the elephants for a long time sustained the assaults of their impetuous enemies. They trampled the infantry under their feet; and 'the most dismal thing of all was when these animals took up the armed soldiers with their trunks, and delivered them up to their governors on their backs.' The day was far spent, and still the fight was doubtful, till at length the Macedonians directed all their power against the sagacious beasts that threatened to baffle the skill and bravery of the most disciplined troops of the earth. The Greeks chopped their legs with axes; and cut off their trunks with a crooked weapon resembling a scythe. While the infantry of Alexander thus encountered the principal strength of the Indians, his cavalry closed round them in overwhelming masses. 'And the beasts now being pent up in a narrow space, and violently enraged, did no less mischief to their own men than the enemy; and as they tossed and moved about, multitudes were trampled to death; besides, the horse being confined among the elephants, a huge slaughter ensued, for many of the governors of the beasts being slain by the archers, and the elephants themselves, partly enraged with their wounds, and partly for want of riders, no longer kept any certain station in the battle, but running forwards, as if madness had seized them, they pushed down, slew, and trampled under foot friends and foes without distinction; only, the Macedonians, having the advantage of a more free and open space, gave way, and made room for the furious beasts to rush through their ranks, but slew them whenever they attempted to return. But the beasts at last, quite wearied out with wounds and toil, were no longer able to push with their usual force, but only made a hideous noise, and, moving their fore-feet heavily, passed out of the battle.'

"Although his forces were scattered all around him, the courage of the Indian king remained unconquerable. Exposed 'as a mark at which every one levelled,' he had received nine wounds, before and behind; but he still continued to hurl his javelins at the enemy, till they might be said 'to drop from his faint arm, rather than be delivered.' The governor of Porus's elephant at last put the beast to flight, and Alexander himself slowly followed him upon a wounded horse. At length Porus, exhausted by his wounds, slid down from the back of the elephant; and the Indian guide, thinking the king desired to alight, commanded the animal to kneel down. The whole of the elephants were accustomed to imitate the movements of that upon which the king rode; and in like manner they instantly knelt down, and thus became a prey to the conquerors. Their habitual obedience to their masters involved their common ruin."

An interesting medal is known to antiquarians, which is supposed to commemorate this victory of Alexander over Porus. On one side is shown the head of Alexander, covered with an elephant's head-skin, and on the other a representation of Minerva, armed with a helmet, shield, and spear, and before her an eagle holding lightning in its talons. Whether Alexander used the elephants he captured, or not, is not known; but he preserved them, and created a new office,—the *elephantarch*, or governor of the elephants, whose business it was to take entire charge of them. At the death of

Alexander, great numbers of elephants were owned by the Macedonians; and his successors, who had, perhaps, more faith in them for purposes of war, often used them in many of the sanguinary engagements of their time.

Many of the elephants of King Porus were afterwards employed by Eumenes; and, in his fiercely contested battle with Antigonus, elephants were used on both sides. In the attack made upon the city of Megapolis by Polysperchon, the latter employed sixty-five elephants which were considered invincible; but the foot-soldiers of the other army stole out, and built ditches in front of them, placing upright spears and spikes in them, and covering all with grass and leaves. When the elephants and the army charged, the great animals fell into the traps, and during the confusion the entire force was routed.

In those times the expense of keeping elephants was enormous, and oftentimes the animals suffered greatly. At the siege of Pydua, in Macedonia, the elephants were obliged to eat sawdust; and many died, or, as Diodorus Siculus says, "pined away for want of food." In the histories of the wars that were waged between the generals of Alexander and Ptolemy, elephants are often mentioned, and were evidently relied upon more than any branch of the service. Diodorus Siculus says, when Perdiccas marched to the Nile, and assaulted the fort called the "Camel's Wall," he "boldly led up his army close to the fort, and forthwith the targeteers with their ladders mounted the wall; and those that rode upon elephants threw down the fortifications, and demolished the bulwarks. Whereupon Ptolemy, with those of his own guard about him, to encourage the rest of his officers and friends manfully to behave themselves, catched hold of a sarissa, and mounted the bulwark; and so, being on the higher ground, struck out the eyes of the foremost elephant, and wounded the Indian that sat upon him; and as for those that scaled the walls, he hurled them down, dreadfully cut and wounded, into the river. After his example, Ptolemy's friends valiantly exerted themselves; and, by killing the Indian that governed the next elephant, the beast became unserviceable." When Ptolemy and Seleucus attacked Demetrius at Gaza, their first care was to protect their army from the shock of the elephants of their enemy; and for this purpose they prepared "an iron palisado, sharp-pointed with iron, and fastened together with chains." That this precaution was not taken in vain, the same author shows in the following: "And now, when the fight between the horse had been a long time doubtful, the elephants, forced on by the Indians, made so terrible an onset that it appeared impossible for any force to have stood against them. But when they came up to the palisado, the darters and archers sorely galled both the beasts and their riders; and being still forced on, and whipt by the Indians, some of them stuck upon the sharp points of the palisado, with which, besides the multitude of the darts and arrows that galled them, they were in such pain and torment that they caused a horrible tumult and confusion: for these creatures, in plain and level places, bear down all before them; but in those which are rough and craggy, they are of no use or service, because of the tenderness of their feet. Ptolemy, therefore, wisely foreseeing of what advantage this palisado would be, by that means frustrated the rage and fury of the beasts. At length, most of the Indians that rode them being killed, all the elephants were taken, upon which the greatest part of Demetrius's horse were in such a consternation that they forthwith fled."

Where elephants created so much confusion and demoralization, it was but natural that the great generals should invent mechanical devices to rout them in turn, and create disorder; and we read that Ptolemy was often successful. Yet he fully appreciated the value of the elephants; and, after meeting them in several engagements, he determined to possess an elephant army of his own. The enemy obtained their elephants from India; and, although the African elephants were not considered so well fitted for war purposes, he decided to secure his recruits from the Dark Continent. He immediately issued an edict prohibiting their slaughter, and ordered that they be captured alive. Exactly where these great creatures were obtained would be interesting to know, but Ptolemy's historians do not tell us. Ptolemy III. has left an inscription called adulis, found in the travels of Cosmas, a traveller of the sixth century, to the effect that the elephants were obtained from Ethiopia, and the country of the Troglodytes.

The famous battle of Raphia, between Ptolemy Philopator, the fourth of the dynasty, and Antiochus the Great, in which numbers of elephants were employed, is thus described by Polybius: "The signal was sounded to engage; and the elephants, approaching first, began the combat. Among those that belonged to Ptolemy, there were some that advanced boldly against their adversaries. It was then pleasing to behold the soldiers engaged in close combat from the towers, and pushing against each other with their spears. But the beasts themselves afforded a far nobler spectacle, as they rushed together, front to front, with the greatest force and

PLATE XXII.

5

9

5

18

17

16

10

10

ANCIENT ELEPHANT MEDALLIONS.

fury. For this is the manner in which they fight. Twisting their trunks together, they strive, each of them with his utmost force, to maintain his own ground, and to move his adversary from his place; and when the strongest of them has at last pushed aside the trunk of the other, and forced him to turn his flank, he then pierces him with his tusks in the same manner as bulls in fighting wound each other with their horns. But the greater part of the beasts that belonged to Ptolemy declined the combat. For this usually happens to the elephants of Afric, which are unable to support either the smell or cry of the Indian elephants. Or rather, perhaps, they are struck with terror at the view of their enormous size and strength; since even before they approach near together, they frequently turn their backs, and fly. And this it was which at this time happened. As soon, therefore, as these animals, being thus disordered by their fears, had fallen against the ranks of their own army, and forced the royal guards to break the line, Antiochus, seizing the occasion, and advancing round on the outside of the elephants, charged the cavalry, which was commanded by Polycrates, in the extremity of the left wing of Ptolemy. At the same time, also, the Grecian mercenaries, who stood within the elephants, near the phalanx, advanced with fury against the peltastæ, and routed them with little difficulty, because their ranks, likewise, were already broken by the elephants. Thus the whole left wing of the army of Ptolemy was defeated, and forced to fly."

One hundred and fifty years after this, a successor of Antiochus employed elephants in battles against the Jews; and nearly all the monarchs who succeeded Alexander employed them in war. They were used in Syria; and Seleucus Nicator valued them so highly, that, according to Strabo, he gave Sandrocottus an entire province on the Indus for five hundred of the animals. They were stabled at Apamea, in Syria; so that elephants commanded a high price, even in these early times. Two centuries later, when Syria and various Eastern countries became tributary to Rome, the war elephant fell into disuse; and one of the last references to it in Syria is found on a coin struck in honor of Antiochus, surnamed Epiphanes Dionysius, who succeeded to the throne in the two hundred and twenty-fifth era of the Seleucidæ (87 B.C.). It represents an elephant bearing a torch, after the custom of Syrian monarchs; a horn of plenty being shown behind it. (See Plates XXI., XXII.)

CHAPTER XXIV.

WAR ELEPHANTS OF THE ROMANS AND CARTHAGINIANS.

THE war elephant was a feature of the armies of the Orient many years before it was known in Italy. We have seen that the huge animal was especially effective in spreading terror among the opposing hosts, from its gigantic size and peculiar form: and nations that had never heard of, nor seen, an elephant, were so demoralized at the sight, that they often fled without giving battle; their horses and other animals, equally alarmed, completing the rout and confusion. The Romans were no exception to this; and, with all their valor and courage, they quailed before the astonishing array of monsters — for so they considered them — that King Pyrrhus of Epirus brought upon the field in the reign of Heraclear (280 B.C.). His elephant detachment was a small one, being composed of twenty animals, which bore upon their backs tall wooden towers filled with armed bowmen. The Romans soon rallied, however; but their defeat, according to Florus, was directly due to the terror inspired by the elephants. When Fabricus went to Epirus to negotiate with Pyrrhus for an exchange of prisoners, the latter endeavored to bribe him, and then to frighten him, by producing one of the largest of his elephants. But the old Roman replied on leaving, "Neither your gold yesterday, nor your beast to-day, has made any impression upon me."

Four years later the Romans had become perfectly familiar with elephant warfare; and Curius Dentalus organized his men especially to demoralize the elephants, ordering them to attack the animals with burning torches in one hand, and sharp swords in the other. This plan was successful, and was aided by an unforeseen accident. An elephant calf accompanied its mother upon the field of battle; and, becoming wounded early in the fight, its roars so enraged its mother, and demoralized the others, that they charged, and threw the troops of Pyrrhus into complete disorder. They were finally captured by the Romans, and four led in triumph to Rome, — the first ever taken there.

To show what vague notions of the elephant the Romans had, they called the great creatures Lucanian oxen; and, according to Pliny, the Roman writers, in general, gave them this name, probably because they first saw them in Lucania.

King Pyrrhus was extremely unfortunate in the management of his elephants. At the siege of Argos, when his men had battered in the gates of the town, the mahouts lost control of the beasts in the excitement, and they attempted to rush through the low gates; but the tall towers struck them, and forced them back in great disorder, and many of their own soldiers and masters were trampled under foot, and killed. In describing this event, Plutarch relates that one of the elephants exhibited remarkable courage and affection for its rider; keeping a large number of enemies at bay when its master was dismounted, finally taking him in its trunk, and removing him to a place of safety. The animal doubtless received some instruction from its master.

The old writers were fond of accrediting to the elephant many more virtues, courage, generosity, and self-sacrifice, than they seem to possess to-day; and, undoubtedly, they often gave the animals credit for spontaneous actions, when they were really obeying a command of their mahout, or driver. I have referred particularly to this and the opinions of Sanderson in the chapter devoted to the intelligence of the elephant. Plutarch and Ælian both record the story of an elephant of Porus that drew darts from its master's body. Such may have been the case; but I think, if true, it was at the direct order of Porus, and not actuated by compassion, as the old authors would have us believe.

It was fortunate that the Romans had acquired some experience with Asiatic elephants, as, soon after, they became involved in a series of wars in which the enemy employed large numbers of African elephants. Their familiarity with the Asiatic elephants did not always avail them. In the first Punic war, Regulus, the Roman consul, the Buonaparte of his time, captured a division of eighteen elephants in the battle of Adis; but on another occasion, Xantippus, the Lacedemonian, the general of the Carthaginian troops, used his elephant batteries, as we may call them, so judiciously, and with such marked skill, that the Romans were utterly routed. The elephants, under direction of their enraged riders, and infuriated themselves by their wounds, charged into the fleeing Romans, trampling them under foot, tossing them high in air, and goring them with their tusks; committing such frightful carnage, that for a long time the Romans dreaded to meet them.

The Carthaginians not only fought with elephants on their own soil, but they carried them into Sicily. At the siege of

Panormus (Palermo), they employed one hundred and forty African elephants in a solid phalanx, a most impressive sight, and moved upon the city. But the Romans fired at them with darts from the city-walls, and turned the huge animals upon their own men. Then taking advantage of the confusion, Metellus, the Roman consul, who was in command, led his troops upon the Carthaginians, and utterly routed them, and captured one hundred or more of their finest war elephants.

Such a victory offered a rare opportunity to Metellus to exhibit his prowess and the spoils to his countrymen: so he commanded that an immense raft be built, composed of empty barrels covered with planks, and in turn packed with earth; and upon this the elephants were floated over the straits to Rhegium (Reggio). For some time the Romans kept the noble creatures on exhibition, and treated them with great indignity, driving them about the circus with blunted spears; all of which was undoubtedly done to convince the people that the elephant was not the terrible beast he had been pictured, and to erase from the public mind the terror they had inspired when Regulus was defeated. Again, it was the custom to parade captive kings before the populace in chains, and treat them with great indignity; and the elephants probably came under this head. When the Roman citizens were surfeited with the display, it occurred to the state that a herd of animals that could devour seventy-two thousand pounds of green food in twenty-four hours was a great luxury; and in a moment of economy, according to Verrius, who is cited by Pliny, the unfortunate captives were killed.

That the Romans overcame their fear of elephants did not

prevent the Carthaginians from retaining them as an important branch of the service. Hannibal carried them into Spain; and after the capture of Saguntum (218 B.C.), we hear of him sending to Africa for a new supply.

In the second Punic war, which commenced about this time, Hannibal began operations on Roman soil with an army of fifteen thousand men, and, according to Appian and Eutropius, thirty-seven elephants. He crossed the Pyrenees, and the Rhone at Orange. Livy, Silius Italicus, and Polybius, all describe some of the events of this campaign; but that of the latter is the most comprehensive and valuable, giving, evidently, a correct account of the management of war elephants at this time. The Greek historian says, —

"Hannibal, having posted his cavalry as a reserve on the side towards the sea, commanded the infantry to begin their march, while himself waited to receive the elephants, and the men that were left with them on the other side of the river. The passage of the elephants was performed in the following manner: When they had made a sufficient number of floats, they joined two together, and fastened them strongly to the ground, upon the bank of the river. The breadth of both together was about fifty feet. To the extremity of these they fixed two more, which were extended over into the water; and to prevent the whole from being loosened and carried down the river by the rapidity of the current, they secured the side that was turned against the stream, by strong cables, fastened to the trees along the bank. Having in this manner finished a kind of bridge, which was extended to the length of about two hundred feet, they then added to it two other floats of a much larger size, which were very firmly joined together, but were fastened in so slight a manner to the rest, that they might at any time be separated from them with little difficulty. A great number of floats were fixed to these last floats, by the help of which, the boats that were designed to tow them over might hold them firm against the violence of the stream, and carry them in safety with the elephants to the other side. They then spread a quantity of earth over all the floats, that their color and appearance might, as nearly as was possible, resemble the ground on shore. The elephants were usually very tractable upon land, and easy to be governed by their conductors, but were at all times under the greatest apprehensions whenever they approached the water. Upon this occasion, therefore, they took two female elephants, and led them first along the floats; the rest readily followed; but no sooner were they arrived upon the farthest floats, than, the ropes being cut which bound them to the rest, they were immediately towed away by the boats towards the other side. The elephants were seized with extreme dread, and moved from side to side in great fury and disorder. But when they saw that they were every way surrounded by the water, their very fears at last constrained them to remain quiet in their place. In this manner, two other floats being from time to time prepared and fitted to the rest, the greater part of the elephants were carried safely over. There were some, indeed, that were so much disordered by their fears, that they threw themselves into the river in the midst of their passage. This accident was fatal to the conductors, who perished in the stream: but the beasts themselves, exerting all their strength, and raising their large trunks above the surface of the river, were by that means enabled not only to breathe freely, but to discharge the waters also, as fast as they received them; and having, by long struggling, surmounted likewise the rapidity of the stream, they at last all gained the opposite bank in safety."

Hannibal's march along the bank of the Isère, in his approach to the famous pass of the Little St. Bernard, was attended by many dangers. The natives mounted the sides of the high passes, and hurled huge rocks and bowlders down upon the elephants and men. But everywhere the strange beasts produced the greatest terror; and, as they approached the Alps, forces that had gathered to oppose them fled at the sight of them. The march was accomplished in fifteen days, at an enormous loss, the passes being strewn with men and beasts.

> "Great was the tumult there,
> Deafening the din, when, in barbaric pomp,
> The Carthaginian, on his march to Rome,
> Entered their fastnesses. Trampling the snows,
> The war-horse reared, and the towered elephant
> Upturned his trunk into the murky sky,
> Then tumbled headlong, swallowed up and lost,
> He and his rider."
>
> ROGERS'S *Italy*.

Many elephants were lost in the mountain passes, but enough were saved to make a formidable appearance in the battles of Ticinus and Trebia. How so many were taken over, considering the nature of the Alpine passes, is somewhat astonishing; and it is stated by Livy, that in some places the elephants of Macedon were delayed while special bridges were constructed for them to cross. Hannibal, on the other hand, pushed through with the energy that characterized all his movements; and the passage of his army and elephants through the Alps is one of the most remarkable feats in military history, ancient or modern.

Ancient history contains interesting accounts of the battles in which the elephant took part. Livy says that the Gauls, who were the allies of the Romans, fled before them. According to Appian, the Roman horse were alarmed at the sight and smell of the strange animals; and Silius Italicus gives the elephant of Hannibal full credit for all his victories. The poet of the Punic war thus, in characteristic language, describes a fight between an elephant and a Roman soldier: —

"For as
The towered elephants attempt to pass,
Into the flood with violence they fell
(As when a rock, torn from its native hill
By tempests, falls into the angry main);
And Trebia, afraid to entertain
Such monstrous bodies, flies before their beast,
Or shrinks beneath them, with their weight oppressed.
But as adversity man's courage tries,
And fearless valor doth to honor rise
Through danger, stout Fibrenus doth disclaim
A death ignoble, or that wanted fame;
And cries, 'My fate shall be observed, nor shall
Fortune beneath these waters hide my fall.
I'll try if earth doth any living bear
Which the Ansonian sword and Tyrrhen spear
Cannot subdue and kill.' With that, he pressed
His lance into the right eye of the beast,
That, with blind rage, the penetrating blow
Pursued; and tossing up his mangled brow,
Besmeared with reeking blood, with horrid cries
Turns round, and from his fallen master flies;
Then with their darts and frequent arrows all
Invade him, and now dare to hope his fall.

> His immense shoulders and his sides appear
> One wound entire; his dusky back doth bear
> Innumerable shafts, that, like a wood,
> Still waving as he moved, upon him stood;
> Till, in so long a fight, their weapons all
> Consumed, he fell, death hasting through his fall."
>
> *Silius Italicus*, by THOMAS ROSS.

After the battle of Trebia, the elephants were marched with the army, over the Apennines; and Livy tells us that seven starved to death; later, in passing the Arno, which was a raging torrent, numbers of men, elephants, and horses were swept away, the only elephant left being the one the great general himself rode.

Previous to this, in crossing the Po, Hannibal had arranged his elephants in a long line across the shallow river, to break the force of the stream by a living dam. Perdiccas did the same, in an unfortunate attempt to cross the Nile near Memphis; but the waters of the Arno were too swift, and, notwithstanding the fact that elephants are fine swimmers, they were carried away and drowned. Hannibal was not cast down by his misfortune, and immediately sent for a new supply of elephants from Carthage. At the battle of Cannæ (216 B.C.), the Roman forces attacked the elephants with torches, and succeeded in firing the towers upon their backs. This terrible scene is thus described by Silius Italicus:—

> "The yet prevailing Roman, to withstand
> The fury of these monsters, gives command
> That burning torches, wheresoe'er they go,
> Should be opposed, and sulph'rous flames to throw
> Into their towers. This, with all speed, obeyed,
> The elephants they suddenly invade;

Whose smoking backs with flames collected shined,
That, driven on by the tempestuous wind,
Through their high bulwarks fire devouring spread.
As when on Rhodope or Pindus' head
A shepherd scatters fire, and through the groves
And woods, like an hot plague, it raging moves,
The leafy rocks are fired, and all the hills,
Leaping, now here, now there, bright Vulcan fills.
But when the burning sulphur once begun
To parch their skins, th' unruly monsters run
Like mad, and drive the cohorts from their stand:
Neither durst any undertake at hand
To fight them; but their darts and javelins throw
At distance· burning, they impatient grow,
And, through the heat of their vast bodies, here
And there, the flames increasing bear;
Till, by the smooth adjoining stream, at last
Deceived, themselves into it they headlong cast,
And with them all their flames, that still appear
'Bove the tall banks, till, both together, there
In the deep channel of the flood expire."

Silius Italicus, by THOMAS ROSS.

It would seem that Hannibal was sometimes actuated by motives similar to those of our Indians of the West, who, in former days, sometimes offered to release prisoners of war, if they would defeat a number of warriors in a struggle. After the battle just referred to, he offered some Roman prisoners their liberty if they could conquer the elephants. One of the Romans accepted the offer, and actually killed the elephant single-handed. But Hannibal broke his word, perhaps fearing, that, if such an instance was circulated among the Roman soldiers, they would lose their fear of the animals; so he had the courageous Roman murdered.

When the Carthaginians were before Capua, they had a strong force of elephants, and we read of their obtaining re-enforcements from Carthage as early as 215 B.C.; so that this city must have been a central depot of elephant supplies.

The management of war elephants in Spain was mostly conducted by Asdrubal, who was in command of the Carthaginian forces in the absence of his brother. According to Livy, he was defeated in the famous fight between the two Scipios at Tortosa, but managed to save his elephants. In other battles, large numbers of these animals were killed and left upon the field.

The effect of a panic among the war elephants was greatly dreaded by the generals who owned them; and Asdrubal provided his drivers with a knife and mallet, with instructions, if the elephant became unmanageable, to drive the knife between the junction of the head and spine. In the battle of Metaurus, this expedient was also employed. The Romans attacked them with such ferocity, that the elephants turned, and began trampling their own troops; and, in obedience to their instructions, the drivers slaughtered six while in their headlong flight, falling with them to the ground. This, however, did not prevent the utter rout of the forces; and, in a frenzy of rage, Asdrubal threw himself single-handed at a battalion of the enemy, and fell, opposed by thousands.

It is evident that in these days the range of the African elephant extended farther to the north; and that they were much more abundant, is shown by some passages in the old works. Thus, when Scipio was about to invade Africa, the Carthaginians made great preparations to prevent his advance; and, according to Appian, a large number of elephants were taken in a short time, and trained for war. This could not have been done if they had to be sought at a great distance. They may have been found in Barbary, which would explain the ease with which re-enforcements were made in all these wars.

When Scipio invaded Africa, Mago, the brother of Hannibal, proceeded against Italy with a new and magnificent army; and the vast array of elephants he drew up before the Roman cavalry on the field of Insubria, is said to have been almost unequalled in the annals of ancient warfare. Notwithstanding this, the Romans were successful. Scipio was followed into Africa by Hannibal; and the two warriors, both equally famous, met on the field of Zama. Hannibal had eighty elephants in line, a formidable array; but Scipio, aware that his horses were useless, sent them to the rear, and ordered his archers to direct their arrows at the trunks of the elephants of the enemy. So vigorous was the assault, that the elephants, panic-stricken, turned, and in a moment were rushing wildly to the rear; their trumpeting, and the cries of the dead and dying trampled under foot, producing an indescribable scene. The entire right wing of the Carthaginian general was broken, and, utterly routed, he retreated to Adrumetum; the action of his own elephants bringing to a close the second Punic war (201 B.C.). A treaty of peace was now arranged; and with due respect for the elephant, as an engine of war, the Romans bound the unfortunate Carthaginians to deliver up all their war elephants, and never tame others for military service. The elephants captured by Scipio were forwarded to Rome; and in his triumphal procession to the Capitol, they followed the sacrificial victims.

Curiously enough, for a period of eighty years after the Romans became familiar with the advantages of the elephant as a valuable adjunct to the service, they did not employ them. The warriors, however, were specially drilled in elephant warfare; and many devices were invented by the skilful generals to discomfit the huge animals. The great object was to turn the elephants upon their own masters, as we have seen; and to this end, the men were directed to fire their darts and arrows at the trunk of the elephant, which was known to be the most sensitive point. Chariots were constructed to bear men who carried enormously long spears. The horses were clothed in mail, and trained to charge at the elephants at full speed; and, as they passed, the spearmen would prod them in the trunk, and endeavor to demoralize them. This branch of the service was, necessarily, one of great danger, and the courageous lancers often lost their lives; horses, chariots, and men, all being crushed to death by the infuriated animals.

Another corps of elephant-men were armed with a peculiar armor, covered with long, sharp spikes, so that the elephant would not attempt to seize them with its trunk. Other soldiers were armed with slings, with which they threw stones at the driver of the elephant, it being their sole business to dismount him; while instruments that could propel their own darts were employed against the body of the elephant. Besides these offensive movements, the troops were drilled in the manner of receiving an elephant's charge. They executed manœuvres in falling back as the animal came on, and in closing in to surround him. Such were a few of the methods employed against the elephant, which serve to show its importance in ancient warfare.

Rome was finally forced to use the elephant herself; and in the first action of the Macedonian war, they formed no inconspicuous corps of the Roman army.

In the third year of the war, according to Polybius, Titus Quintius Flaminius used them with signal advantage against the Macedonian king. In the second Macedonian war, thirty years later, Q. Martius Philippus employed them against Perseus, the last king of Macedon. The latter, unlike his predecessor, who conquered India, had neglected to provide himself with a corps of elephants; and his horses were utterly demoralized by the animals possessed by his enemy. Finding that elephants were necessary to success, he conceived the idea of manufacturing some bogus ones, after the fashion of Semiramis, quoted in a previous chapter, and had a number of wooden elephants made, in the interior of which was concealed a man, who blew upon a trumpet which led into the wooden throat, when the charge was ordered; hoping in this way to imitate living elephants. But the ruse did not succeed; and, after a war of four years, the Macedonians came under the Roman yoke.

In some of these wars, it often happened that the African elephant was marched against its Asiatic ally. This was the case in the battle of Magnesia, when the Roman arms were turned against Antiochus, king of Syria; and, according to the old writers, the African elephants of Scipio were much inferior in size and strength to the Indian ones of Antiochus. The reverse, at least regarding size, is true to-day; and the same was probably true then, African male elephants being at least a foot taller than their Asiatic cousins.

When Scipio found that his elephants were inferior, he placed them in his rear as a reserve; but they were routed, only fifteen escaping: while fifteen thousand men were slain. The Romans utterly defeated them, and insisted upon the same terms which we have seen the Carthaginians made,—Antiochus agreeing to deliver all his war elephants to Rome, and to train no more. If both parties had kept their word, the elephant would have fallen into disuse as a war-factor.

The Romans exacted a similar bond from Jugurtha (111 B.C.); killing large numbers, and continuing the war until the Numidian king consented, and delivered his elephants to Metellus (108 B.C.).

Julius Cæsar probably considered that elephants retarded active movements, and did not have a large corps of them; though a certain number were kept, presumably to re-assure the soldiers, in case the enemy should be supplied with an elephant corps. In his battle with Scipio in Africa, he was confronted with thirty of these animals, having towers of archers; but he sent his elephants to the rear, and succeeded in defeating his enemy.

Some idea of the manner in which elephants fought in battle is given by Cæsar:—

"A wounded elephant, furious with rage, attacked an unarmed follower of the troops, and, kneeling upon him, crushed the life out of his body. A veteran of the fifth legion rushed forward to attack the beast, who was roaring, and lashing with his proboscis. The elephant immediately forsook his victim, and, catching up the soldier in his trunk, whirled him in the air. But the intrepid warrior did not lose his presence of mind: he wounded the elephant in his sensitive proboscis, till, exhausted with pain, he dropped the soldier, and fled in terror to his companions."

The elephant was probably not used to any extent in war

by the Romans, after the establishment of the imperial government. In A.D. 193, we read that Rome was filled with horses and elephants, ready for use in the proposed war between Didius Julianus and Septimius Severus. In the famous battle between Alexander Severus and Artaxerxes (A.D. 230), three hundred elephants were taken from the Persians, and a number marched to Rome in solemn state. The introduction of new appliances of war, and the successful attempts in routing bodies of elephants, probably did much to render them unpopular, for a time at least, among the Roman conquerors.

CHAPTER XXV.

PROBOSCIDIAN FICTIONS.

IN the history of nearly all animals, there will be found associated some curious fiction.

In Burmah and Siam, the white elephant is supposed, by some, to be the abode of a transmigratory Buddha; and in India, certain elephants with a single right tusk are reverenced. In China, the tusks of the mammoth are used in medicine; and in some of the old works, the mammoth itself is described as a huge rat, which lives under the ground in burrows, formed by the tusks, or teeth. The origin of this fable lies in the fact, that, as mammoths were always found beneath the surface, it was assumed, that, when alive, they lived there. Early anatomists stated that the elephant's head was a storehouse for the water which it blew out of its trunk.

It was formerly believed that elephants shed their tusks, as do deer their horns. Ælian says that they drop them once in ten years, which, all things considered, is quite often enough. Pliny repeats the story, but adds some private information of his own, to the effect that they always hid their tusks underground.

This curious error has found its way into many comparatively modern works: thus, Sir William Jardine states, in the naturalist's library, that "the tusks are shed about the twelfth or the tenth year."

Many strange beliefs were entertained regarding the elephant of Ceylon. Travellers of the sixteenth and seventeenth centuries, as Pyrard, Bernier, and Phillipe, stated that this elephant was the superior of all others in India, both physically and mentally; and Tavernier is supposed to be authority for the statement, that, if a Ceylon elephant be introduced among others, the latter will instinctively do him homage by touching the ground with their trunks.

Phile records the fact that elephants have two hearts. He argued that this was so, because the animal showed extremes of temperament, — one heart controlling the beast when good-humored and docile, and the other when it exhibited the characteristics of the rogue.

The older naturalists had few opportunities for making careful anatomical examinations of the elephant, and, naturally, fell into many errors; one of which was, that elephants from sixteen to twenty feet high were not uncommon. Major Denman observed some in Africa which he "guessed" were sixteen feet high; though he afterwards measured one that had been killed, which was twelve feet six inches at the back. Works were published in the last century, which gave the height of the animal as from twelve to fifteen feet; and Sir John Hill, M.D., in his "Natural History of Animals," 1752, states that elephants were said to measure, when full grown, twenty feet at the shoulder.

It is needless to say that this was a gross exaggeration. Reference has been made, in a previous chapter, to the size of elephants; and it will be found that a twelve-foot animal is an extreme rarity. The skeleton that is preserved in the

St. Petersburg museum, which is said to stand sixteen feet and a half high, is the tallest known, being a foot taller than the skeleton of the fossil elephant which was discovered at Jubbalpore. It is doubtful if the European mammoth or the American form, *Elephas Americanus*, — a tooth of which is shown in Plate I., — attained this height. One of the largest elephant skeletons to be seen in this country belongs to the Chicago Medical College, and represents an elephant shot in a gorge of the Himalaya Mountains, about a thousand miles from Calcutta, in 1865. Its dimensions are as follows: —

	FT.	IN.
From top of shoulder to bottom of fore-foot	11	2
From top of head to root of tail	12	
Length of trunk, from root to tip	7	
Circumference of fore-arm	6	3
Circumference of fore-foot	3	3

The following are measurements of a large African male elephant, made by Thomas Baines, F.R.G.S., which show the average dimensions of an animal of the largest size: —

	FT.	IN.
Half the girth of the body	8	9
Half the girth behind the shoulder	7	9
Half the girth before the hind-leg	7	11
Length of tail, exclusive of hairy tuft	4	
From insertion of tail to top of forehead	9	11
Top of forehead to insertion of trunk	3	
Length of trunk	6	8
Total length of animal	20	10
From front of ear to back	3	9
From top to bottom of ear	5	3
Half breadth from eye to eye	1	9
Length of eye		3
From fore-foot to centre of spine	11	6

	FT.	IN.
Actual height at shoulder	10	9
Height at middle of the back	12	
Hind-foot to spine	9	3
Actual height	8	9
Projection of tusk beyond upper lip	2	
Girth of tusk	1	
Breadth of fore-foot	1	6
Length of fore-foot	1	9
Breadth of hind-foot	1	
Length of hind-foot	2	

Some extremely interesting measurements have been made of the skeleton of the elephant Jumbo, by Professor Ward of Rochester, who compares them, in a pamphlet, with a skeleton of the *Mastodon giganteus*, discovered at Orange County, N.Y. It is too lengthy and technical to be introduced in this connection. The measurements already given are sufficient to show that the elephants of over eleven or twelve feet are extremely rare, while those of eighteen and twenty belong to the world of fiction.

The absence of joints was a feature of the elephant, according to some of the old writers. Sir Thomas Browne, in his "Pseudodoxia Epidemica," says, "It hath no joynts;" and "being unable to lye down, it lieth against a tree, which the hunters observing doe saw almost asunder, whereon the beast relying, by the fall of the tree falls also downe itselfe, and is able to rise no more." Sir Thomas thinks that "the hint and ground of this opinion might be the grosse and somewhat cylindrical composure of the legs of the elephant, and the equality and less perceptible disposure of the joynts, especially in the forelegs of the animal, they appearing, when he standeth, like pillars of flesh."

The honor of discovering jointless animals belongs properly to Pliny, who described the *machlis*, a Scandinavian animal without joints. Cæsar, in describing the wild animals of the Hercynian forests, mentions the alce, "in color and configuration approaching the goat, but surpassing it in size, its head destitute of horns, and its limbs of joints." It is evident that Aristotle had some doubt as to whether elephants possessed joints in their knees; and Ælian, writing two hundred years later, perpetuated the error, expressing his surprise that the elephants in Rome could dance, when they had no joints. This fiction was taken up by the poets of the time, and is found in many old writings. Phile, a contemporary of Dante, addressed a poem on the elephant to the Emperor Andross II., in which he expressed the same belief; and Solinus introduced it into his fable "Polyhistor." Though the error was corrected in the year 802, it was revived by Matthew Paris in the thirteenth century, who made a drawing of the elephant presented to King Henry III. by the King of France, in 1255. The animal was represented without joints.

Shakspeare was a victim to the popular belief, and says in "Troilus and Cressida,"—

> "The elephant hath joints, but none for courtesy.
> His legs are for necessity, not for flexure."

Donne, in his "Progress of a Soul," sang of nature's great masterpiece, an elephant,—

> "The only harmless great thing.
> Yet nature hath given him no knee to bend.
> Himself he up-props, on himself relies;
> Still sleeping stands."

I have previously referred to the fact that the mammoth was considered by the Chinese to be an underground, rat-like creature; and in many countries the bones of fossil elephants have been considered those of giants.

In the time of James II., Lord Cherbury was appointed by the king to investigate some bones which had been unearthed near Gloucester; and there was much discussion about them. Many considered them to be the remains of a giant, but scientific men proved them to be those of an elephant.

In the reign of Louis XIII., the scientific world was greatly excited over the remains of an alleged giant, which were dug up in Dauphiné; and so divided was public opinion, that the doctors took sides against one another, some claiming that they were the bones of the giant Tentobrochus. One doctor, named Mazurier, exhibited the remains in Paris, and stated in a pamphlet that they were found in a sepulchre thirty feet long, on the upper stone of which was written *Tentobrochus rex*, the name of the king of Cimbri, who fought against Marius.

In 1577 a gigantic skeleton of an elephant was unearthed in Lucerne; and Professor Felix Pläten of Basle made an examination, by order of the council, and concluded that it was the skeleton of a man nineteen feet in height. The natives of Lucerne were exceedingly proud of this. Goliath was only eleven feet tall; and the giant Gabbarus of Pliny, who lived in the time of Claudius, was about ten feet; but these were pygmies compared to this ancestor of the people of Lucerne, and they determined to commemorate his memory in a fitting manner, namely, in employing a representation to support the arms of the city. The design was made by Professor Pläten; and some of the original bones are still to be seen in the museum of the Jesuit college in Lucerne.

As late as 1645, the skeleton of an elephant found at Crems in Austria was considered a giant; though Dr. Behrens argued that such could not be the case, as "the tallest man we know of was Og of Basan, whose bed is said, in Deuteronomy, chap. iii., to have been eighteen feet long: now, allowing the bed to be but one foot longer than the man, he was seventeen feet high.

Even in the last century, the doctors of Germany prescribed as an absorbent, astringent, and sudorific, the "Ebur fossile," or "Unicornu fossile," which was merely the tusk of an elephant.

In the present days, few believers in these old fables can be found: the stories of the milk and hoop snakes, the nautilus and its sails, and other pleasant fictions, seem to have superseded them.

Shakspeare judges this class perhaps not unfairly in "The Tempest," when he says, —

> "When they will not give a doit to relieve a lame beggar, they will lay out ten to see a dead Indian."

BIBLIOGRAPHY,

Comprising a List of the Published Works relating to the Elephant.

NOTE.—We regret that the material composing this Bibliography has come to us in such an imperfect state, some of the titles being too largely abridged. It is hoped, however, that it may prove useful to some who are desirous to read more on this interesting subject; and, also, it may remain suggestive of more complete work in the future.

A.D.

433. The Mahawanso.

1650. Hist. des Eléphans. S. de Priezæ, Paris.

1673. Billing's Voyages, p. 112.

1682. An Anatomical Account of the Elephant burnt at Dublin. Allen Moulins.

1692. Noord en oost Tartagrye. Witsen, vol. ii.

1707. Dreyjärige Reise nack. E. Ysobrants Ides, China, etc., Frankfort.

1710. Anatomy and Osteology, Philos. Trans., vol. xxvii. P. Blair.

1715. Elephantographia. Petrus ab Hartenfels.

1715. Remarques Anatomiques sur un Eléphant ouvert au St. George. Suply.

1718. On the Organ of Hearing in the Elephant, Philos. Trans., vol. xxx.

1720. Leben und Gewohnheiten der Ostiaken unter dem Polo Artico wohnende. J. B. Muller, Berlin.

1723-33. Essays by Stukeley.

1730. Das nord und ostliche Theil von Europa und Asia. Strahlenberg, Stockholm.

1734. Mémoires de l'Académie Royale des Sciences, tome iii. part iii. C. Perrault.

1734. Locupletissimi rerum Nat. Thesauri, etc. (Fœtus of Elephant). Amsterdam.

1737. The Behemoth, Philos. Trans.

1737. Handbook, Kluger's. Philos. Trans., Breyne.

1758. Mémoires pour servir à l'Histoire Naturelle, des Animaux, vol. ii., Amsterdam.

1764. Buffon, Hist. Nat., Daubenton.

1766. Opuscoli di vario Argomento. Serrao, Naples.

1774. Kort Berigt van de Ontleding eens Jongen Elephants. Camper.
1780. Timour's Institute. Dr. White.
1783. Beschreibung und Abbildung eines neugebornen Elephanten. Zimmermann.
1798. The Musical Capacity of the Elephant. In "Décade Philosophique." Paris.
1799. Wars and Sports of the Moguls, Philos. Trans.
1799. Observations on the Different Species of Asiatic Elephants, and their Mode of Dentition. John Corse.
1799. Some Observations on the Structure of the Teeth of Elephants, Philos. Trans., vol. xxxiv. Ev. Home.
1802. Descrip. Anat. d'un Eléph. (male). A. G. Camper.
1803. Hist. Nat. des deux Eléph., male et femelle, du Museum, Paris. Houel.
1806. Shaw's Zoölogy, London.
1812. De Skeleto Mammonteo Sibirico, Mém. de l'Acad. de St. Pétersbourg. T. V. Tilesius.
1823. Indische Bibliothek. A. W. Schlegel.
1834. Recherches sur les Ossements Fossiles, Paris, 4th ed. tome i. Cuvier et Lourillard.
1839. Anat. Comp. du Système du Nerv. Paris, Leuret et Gratiolet.
1839. Die Übereste vorweltlicher Riesenthiere, etc., Berlin.
1840-44. Odontography. Owen.
1841. A Practical Treatise on the Diseases of the Elephant. Gilchrist.
1841. Treatise on the Treatment of Elephants in Health and in Disease. Slymm.
1843. Asiatic Journal.
1843. Hist. Mil. des Eléph. Revue des deux Mondes.
1844. The Elephant, Knight's Series.
1846-47. Fauna antiqua Sivalonis. Falconer and Cautley.
1847. Reminiscences of Sport in India, Proceedings of Academy of Natural Sciences, Philadelphia. Burton.
1847. On the Anatomy of the Elephant. Robert Harrison. Proceedings of the Irish Academy, vol. iii.-iv.
1847. Beitrage zur Anatomie des Elephanten und der übrigen Pachydermen. C. Mayer.
1852. Description of the Skeleton of Mastodon giganteus. Dr. J. C. Warren.
1855. Narrative of an Embassy to Ava. Capt. Yule.
1856. Vulpian and Phillippaux, Annal. Sci. Nat. Zoö., vol. v.
1856. Notes sur le cœur, le foie, et les poumons d'un Eléphant (Femelle). Vulpian and Phillippaux.
1856. Ivory Teeth of Commerce. Owen in Journal of Society of Arts.
1857. Description of Fœtal Membranes and Placenta of Elephantus Indicus, etc. Owen.

1859. Reminiscences of Sport in India, Proc. Acad. Nat. Sci., Phila. Burton.
1859. Sur la Dentition des Proboscidiens, etc. Lartel. Bulletin de la Soc. Géologie de France, ser. ii. vol. xvi.
1861. Essays and Observations, Hunter edition, by Owen, vol. ii.
1862-67. Animaux Fossiles et Géologie de l'Antique. A. Gaudry.
1865. Mammoth and Elephant. H. Falconer.
1868. Palæontological Memoirs. C. Murchison.
1868. The Hairy Mammoth, American Naturalist, vol. ii.
1868. Palæontological Memoirs, vol. ii. Falconer.
1868. Notes on the Myology of the Elephant, Edinburgh.
1868. On the Malayan Elephant. By Young Shikary. Oriental Sporting Magazine, vol. i.
1868. Comparative Anatomy of Vertebrates. Owen.
1869. Quarterly Journal of Microscopical Science.
1871. Annals of Scientific Discovery, 1871, p. 239.
1871-74. Obs. in Human and Comparative Anatomy. Watson. Journal of Anat. and Physiol.
1873. The Elephant. Lieut. Ouchterlony. An Essay, in The Veterinarian.
1873. Highlands of Central India. Forsyth, in Veterinarian.
1873. Contributions to Extinct Vertebrate Fauna of the Western Territories, U.S. Leidy.
1874. Ostéographie des Eléphans. De Blainville.
1874-75. Mammoth in Fiska Vet. Soc. Förhande. Witsen. 2d ed.
1875. On the Management of the Elephant, and Other Papers on Similar Subjects. Col. Hawkes, in Veterinarian.
1876. Lectures on Comparative Anatomy of the Placenta, Edinburgh. W. Turner.
1878. An article in The Medical Examiner, by J. H. Steel.
1878. Compendium der Helminthologie. Dr. Von Linston.
1879. Range of the Mammoth. Boyd Dawken's Quarterly.
1879. Monograph of British Fossil Elephants, part ii. Lieut. Adams.
1880. The Elephant in Freedom and in Captivity. Journal of the United Service Institute of India, vol. ix., No. 44, July.
1880. Journal of the Philadelphia Academy of Sciences.
1880. The Mammoth in Siberia, Geological Magazine. Howath.
1880. Proboscidea Sivalik und Nasbada, Mem. Geolog. Survey of India. R. Lydecker.
1881. Phenocodus, American Naturalist, December, 1881.
1882. A Notable Elephant. Scientific American, April 15.
1882. Sanderson on Elephant Equipment. In G. O., 23d August, 1882, 4,503, Madras.
1882. Indian Pipes. Barber. (Supposed Prehistoric Elephant Forms in Stone.)

1882. Field, naturalist column, April, 1882.
1882. Indian Commissariat, Code, 1882.
1882. Palæontographical Beitrage zur Nat. der Vorzeit. Herausgegeben Dunker und Zittel.
1884. The Asiatic Elephant in Captivity, Scientific American, May 24, 1884.
1884. Der Zoologische Garten. Frankfort, D. F. C. Noll.
1885. Elephant Pipes: Report of the Davenport Academy of Sciences.
Royal Engineers' and Royal Artillery Manuals for Field Service.
Government Indian Records.
Oriental Field Sports. Williamson.
Notes in Quarterly Journal of Veterinary Science in India.
Asiatic Researches, Journal of the Asiatic Society in Bengal, Philos. Trans.
Wild Sports of India. Shakspeare.
Parasites. Cobbold.
Siam: Its Kingdom and People. Browning.
De Anim., lib. iv. 9. Aristotle.
Natural History. Pliny.
Cæsar, De Bello Gall.
Ancient World. Ansted.
Siam. Pallegoix.
Constitution of the An. Creation, etc. Holland.
Osteology of Man. Flower.
Archæological Album. Wright.
Rose's Southern Africa.
Fossil Remains of Big Bone Lick. Cooper.
Ælian de Animalibus, lib. ii. chap. xi. Genser's Translation.
Mastodon, Geological Transactions, vol. ii. 2d series.
Mémoires sur les Ossements Fossiles d'Eléphant trouvés en Belge.
South Africa. Chapman.
Okarunda River. Andersson.
Thirteen Years among Wild Beasts of India. Sanderson.
Zoölogy of South Africa. Andrew Smith. Tennent's works.
Fossil Elephants and Archæology of Maltese Islands. A. S. Adams.
Principles of Geology. Lyell.
Cassell's Natural History, vol. ii.
Dental Anatomy. C. S. Tomes.
Natural History of America. Hill.
Wolf's Life and Adventures.
Denman's Travels.
Vulgar Errors, book iii. chap. i.
India, and Tiger Hunting. Barras.
American Naturalist, vol. v. pp. 606, 607.
Natural History of New York, vol. iv.

A Second Visit to United States. Lyell. Vol. i. p. 349.
Rambles in Mexico. Latrobe. Vol. i. p. 145.
American Antiquities. Bradford. Page 276.
Prehistoric Races of U. S. Foster. Page 370.
Mexico and Yucatan. De Waldeck.
Amán. Epist., lib. i. cap. 25.
Pausanias, lib. —, cap. 25.
The Nature of Animals. Ælian.
Le Brun's Voyage to Ceylon.
Zoölogical Recreations. Broderip.
Note-Book of a Naturalist. Broderip.
Calcutta. Sterndale.
South Africa. Baldwin.
Large and Small Game of Bengal. J. H. Baldwin.
Elephant Haunts. Falconer.
Sport in British Burmah. Pollock.
Lions and Elephants. Andersson.
Ceylon. Campbell.
Epoch of the Mammoth. Southall.
The Placenta and Generative Apparatus of the Elephant, Proceedings of Phil. Acad. of Nat. Sciences, 2d series, vol. viii., illustrated.
Ossements Fossiles. Cuvier.
British Fossil Mammals. Owen.
The Mammoth, Voyage of the Vega Nordenskiöld.
Ceylon. Sir Emerson Tennent.
Oriental Memoirs. Forbes.
Les Six Voyages de J. B. Tavernier.
Râmâyana. Carey and Marsham.
Asiatic Journal. G. Fairchild.
Sketches of South Africa. Pringle.
Difference between the Human and Elephant's Tympanum. Sir Everard Home.
Discoveries in Africa. Le Vaillant.
Bosman's Guinea.
Asiatic Transactions, vol. 3.
Asiatic Resources. Welford.
Natural History of the Human Species. Smith.
Natural History of the Elephant. Rennie.
Cuvier. Sur les Révolutions de la Surface du Globe.
War Sports. Rankins.
Oration of Demosthenes against Ophobus.
Indian Field Sports. Johnson. Chap. ix.
Dampier's Voyages, vol. ii. p. 68.

Narrative of the Burmese War, p. 170.
Twelve Years' Hunting Adventures. Williamson.
China Illustrated. Kircher. Chap. iv.
Embassy to the Coast of Ava. Crawford.
Travels by Albert de Mandelsloes.
Comparative Anatomy. Home.
Histoire de l'art. Winkleman.
Vegetius, lib. iii. c. 24.
Catalogue of Hunterian Museum, Royal College Surgeons, London.
Holzassffel. Turning, and Mechanical Manipulation.
South Kensington Handbook on Ivories.
Marco Polo. Col. Yule.
First Footsteps in Eastern Africa. Burton.
Layard's Nineveh and its Remains.
Ilios. Schliemann.
Oriental Memoirs. Forbes.
Les Eléphants à la Guerre, Revue des deux Mondes, 1874.
Mémoires pour servir à l'Histoire Naturelle des Animaux, tome ii. p. 503.
Physical Curiosæ, p. 1024.
The Large Game of South Africa. Drummond.
Twenty-first Annual Report of State of New York Museum of Natural History. Hall.
Memoirs of Baber. Blumenbach. Lawrence and Coulson's translation.
Leçons d'Anatomie comparée, tome v.
Every-day Book. Home. Vol. ii. p. 322.
Hindostan. Dow.
Narrative of the Burmese War, p. 170.
Tennent's Indian Recreations.
Shipp's Memoirs.
Bell's Travels.
Struy's Travels.
Mill's British India, book vi. chap. iv.
Abhandlungen der geologischen Reichsanstalt, vol. ii.
Mammifères Tertiaries. Gaudry. Mélanges Biologiques, tome v., St. Petersburg, pp. 645, 740.
The Kilima Njaro Expedition. H. H. Johnson, Scribner and Welford.
Autopsy of an Elephant. A. J. Howe, M.D. Scientific American supplement, No. 186.
Birth of an Elephant (illustrated). G. E. Lussendorff, M.D. Scientific American supplement, No. 343.
Composition of Elephant's Milk. Doremus. Scientific American supplement, No. 288 (illustrated).
Nita Karoli. Eginhard.

Survey of Bhagulpore. Buchanan.
Historical Relation of Ceylon. Knox.
Hunter's Life in Africa. Gordon Cumming.
Elephant Shooting in Ceylon. Major Macready.
The Rifle and the Hound in Ceylon. Baker.
Indian Sporting Review.
The Hastisilpe: A Singhalese Work on the Elephant.
Expositio de Elephante. Phile.
Histoire Militaire des Eléphans. Armandi.
Naturalist's Library, vol. ix., Pachyderms. Sir William Jardine.
Coup-d'œil général sur les Possessions Néelandaiser dans l'Inde Archipélagique. Temminck.
Travels in Mogul Empire. Bernier.
Works of Travel by Pringle, Knox, Shipp, Marco Polo.
Anatomy of the Indian Elephant. Miall and Greenwood. 1878.
Desc. Anatom. d'un Eléphant, Male. Camper.
Gori. Industrial Arts.
Bishop Hakewill's Apology.
The following are from catalogue of Dr. A. E. Foote, of Philadelphia, Penn.: —

No. 37130. Elephas Texicanus. Blake.
No. 37140. Fossil Bones of Mastodon and Elephant, from Benton County, Mo. Dr. Chaloner.
No. 37150. Great American Mastodon.
No. 37160. Entire Head and Other Bones of Mastodon. Homer and Hays.
No. 37210. Fossil Elephant's Teeth of North America, and Mastodon Remains in Ohio. Kilpart.
No. 37220. Discovery of the Great American Mammoth, and its Anatomical Character. J. Ware.
No. 37560. Geological Position of Remains of Elephant and Mastodon in North America.
No. 37630. Big Bone Lick and its Fossil Remains. W. Cooper.
No. 37820. Mammoth from New Jersey. T. P. Stewart.
No. 37820. Fossil Remains of Mastodon, Ontario County, N.Y.
No. 37820. Fossil Tooth of Elephant from Lake Erie shore, and Mastodon from Delaware and Hudson Canal.
No. 31860. Extinct Elephant and Other Animal Remains, Waterford County, Ireland. E. Brenan.
No. 42790. Memoir upon Living and Fossil Elephants. Cuvier.

INDEX.